F O R E W O F

Hi, and welcome to the fourth volume in our American Rock   )nd in
our Midwest sequence. The last volume dealt with Chicago and Illinois. This volume deals
with three of the States which surround Illinois:- Indiana, Iowa and Missouri. It's smaller
than any of our previous volumes simply because to have fitted any of the next batch of
States we've prepared into it would have made it too large. This volume covers the period
from approximately 1960 until the end of 1993. We have endeavoured to include all of the
mainstream rock, pop, jazz-rock, garage, psychedelic, country-rock, folk-rock, punk, new
wave, heavy metal and hardcore artists who came from these three states. Once again we have
generally excluded soul, reggae, hip-hop, rap, house, disco and jazz artists, as these
extend beyond our areas of interest and expertise. Like the previous volume, this one is
illustrated and contains singles discographies for many of the entries.

As ever, we have arranged our book alphabetically. This was by no means a simple task as
there are many ways of tackling such a project. We have doubtless been guilty of
inconsistencies but, as far as possible have observed the following rules:-

1   'The' has been ignored as the first word of a band's name.

2   Individual artists have been alphabetised under surnames, eg. Michael Jackson appears
     in the 'Js'.

3   Where an artist gives his/her real name to a band then it has been alphabetised under
     the artist's surname, eg. Kenny Lee And The Royals. Where the band's name is fictitious
     it has been alphabetised under the first letter of the first word (excepting 'the'),
     eg. Steve Kowalski.

4   Bands whose names are literally numbers or symbols, eg. 23 Lies (Iowa section), preceed
     the alphabetised entries. In other words they are at the beginning of the State
     section.

A tabulated explanation of how to use this book appears at the end of this foreword.

We are, of course, well aware that many entries are incomplete (often ridiculously so), and
that there are omissions. Doubtless, too, there are errors. We have tried to ensure that
the book is as accurate as possible, but much of the data it contains is difficult to
verify. We would, therefore, love to hear from anyone who is able to supply information
that is missing from our book, correct errors in it or make suggestions for its improvement.
If you can do any of these things please contact us care of:-

                    Borderline Productions
                    P. O. Box 93
                    Telford TF1 1UE
                    England.

Please enclose a stamped addressed envelope or an international reply coupon if you wish
to ensure a reply, and please be patient! Reminders are included periodically throughout
the text.

Hugh MacLean and Vernon Joynson, February 1994.

CREDITS

As ever a host of people have offered advice, support and enthusiastic help in the preparation of this volume and other projects. A full list would be too numerous to mention but we would especially like to thank the following:-

BUSINESS/SUPPORT
Paul Barrett   :   Long time friend and supporter
John Caswell   :   Tax Consultant extraordinaire
Iain G. C. MacLean :   New business guru, mail order, etc.
Moira A. Foulds   :   Typing Wizard
Gavin S. Foulds   :   Computer Whiz Kid
Peter Hughes   :   Friend and supporter

DATA SUPPLIERS
Max Waller
Philippe Collignon
Tim Holden
Greg Shaw
Jeff Jarema
John Kass   :   of Susstones Records
Neal Skok
Mark Lawford   :   of KIOZ-KGMG, San Diego
Fred Masotti
Alan Wright
Tim Gassen
Ron Simpson
Laurent Bigot
Ace Brewer
Alec Palao
Jim Huie

(a) <u>NAME OF ARTIST:</u>   Presumably self-explanatory!

(b) <u>ALBUMS</u>
Where more than one, albums are listed (and numbered for textual reference) in order of release. Line entries are as follows:-

1(A) eg.   Let's Have A Party   (USA 102) 1964
                                          U.S. Label + Catalogue No. & Year of Release

Line-up
on album
(Where
Known)

2(B)   Campus Party   (Riviera 701) 1965

(c) <u>SINGLES</u>
Where we have details full (or sometimes partial) discographies are provided. Singles are listed in order of release.

(d) <u>PERSONNEL</u>   Name   Instrument Different Line-Up   Cross-reference System
                                                                   Previous   Next
                                                                   Band/   Band/
                                                                   Project   Project

	Name	Instrument	Different Line-Up	Previous Band/Project	Next Band/Project
	MEMBER 1	bs,gtr,voc	B	"	"
	MEMBER 2	bs	A	"	"
	MEMBER 3	gtr,voc	AB	"	"
	MEMBER 4	KB	AB	"	"
	MEMBER 5	voc,dr	A	"	"
	MEMBER 6	hns	AB	"	"
	MEMBER 7	dr,perc	B	"	"

(e) <u>ASSORTED DATA ABOUT THE GROUP</u>
In the text, the name(s) of other artists who are included elsewhere in this volume also appear in heavy print to facilitate easy cross-reference. The names of songs, albums, 45s, EPs, Soundtracks and films appear in inverted commas.

NBs 1 Where albums are known to be compilations they are identified as such and often listed separately.

2 Occasionally European label and catalogue data is included beneath the album discographies as are reissue details.

3 Double albums are identified by 'dbl' after the name and triple albums by 'triple'.

4 The following instrumental abbreviations have been used:-

voc	=	vocals	cla	=	clarinet
gtr	=	guitar	psg	=	pedal steel guitar
ld.gtr	=	lead guitar	ww	=	woodwind
sl.gtr	=	slide guitar	vibes	=	vibes
dr	=	drums	v	=	violin
KB	=	keyboards	hns	=	horns
perc	=	percussion	elec	=	electronics
tpt	=	trumpet	o	=	organ
bs	=	bass guitar	f	=	fiddle

syn	=	synthesiser	fl	=	flute
trb	=	trombone	p	=	piano
ma	=	mandolin	hca	=	harmonica
ba	=	banjo	sax	=	saxophone

5   We have ignored, except where specifically stated, bootlegs from discographies.

6   Where we do not know years of release, record labels or catalogue numbers, we have left a blank. If you can help complete the blanks please contact us at the address on page 1.

INTRODUCTION

Many of you buying this volume will have purchased the first book in this series, 'California, The Golden State', which is now back in print again. The introduction to that book charted the evolution of rock music in America and is well worth a read before turning to this section.

Our previous volume dealt with the music scene in Illinois and Chicago. Here we look at the music scene of three of the states that surround Illinois - Indiana, Iowa and Missouri. We can't point to any characteristics that are peculiar to these three states (as opposed to any others) so we'll deal with each in turn.

Indiana, the Hoosier State, had its fair share of teen bands during the late fifties and early sixties - mostly playing rockabilly and rock 'n' roll. Bands like **The Blue Angels, The Dawnbeats,** and **Keetie and The Kats**. The early sixties saw the emergence of frat rock bands. One of the best examples is South Bend's **Rivieras** who went on to nationwide success.

Then came The Beatles and Merseybeat ... and with the British invasion a whole new era of bands emerged. Indeed it was more than just another musical style ... with their hair styles, fashions and opinions these bands heralded a new youth culture. All over America teenagers were starting rock 'n' roll bands which were initially influenced by the British invasion sound, which was itself influenced by American rock 'n' roll. Most of these bands comprised average teenagers who could only manage a few chords on a guitar. The better ones played at local fraternity parties, dances, shopping centres ... anywhere they could really ... the cream of the crop played at bigger venues ... the lucky ones managed to cut a record. Often this came as the prize for winning a local 'Battle Of The Bands' competition, though sometimes bands mustered together enough cash to have a record pressed themselves. Most of these received local airplay and some consequently became local hits. Occasionally these were picked up by major labels (always on the search for new talent) for national distribution. A few became national hits, even million-sellers. (The Rivieras' 'California Sun' is a typical example of this process).

The term 'garage' band was coined to depict both this musical phenomenon and, more often than not, their rehearsal space. The music these bands played was very varied but in its purest form was a crudely-recorded, raw, primal three-chord sound, thrashed out on Vox guitars and cheesy Farfisa organs laced with lots of fuzz and snarling vocals. The lyrics dealt with the problems of teenage life - social restrictions and unco-operative parents and girlfriends. When these naive teenage bands started to experiment with psychedelic drugs (from late 1966 onwards) the chords became more discordant, the basic rock 'n' roll rhythms were broken down and the lyrics started to deal with people's dreams or even their nightmares ... hence the phenomenon now known as 'garage psych'.

Indiana, like most other states, had its share of 'garage' bands. Indianapolis (or Naptown as it is sometimes known) had several talented bands in the mid-sixties, such as **The Boys Next Door, The Idle Few** and **Sir Winston And The Commons**. Top 'Naptown' clubs in this era included the Flame Club, the House Of Sounds, Party Time, Pink Panther, The Speckled Axe and The Tiger-A-Go-Go. There was even a local magazine, 'Teen Tempo', which gave local bands much needed publicity. Goshen, too, boasted some pretty hot garage bands ... with **The Dukes** arguably the 'boss band' in town, closely followed by **The Backdoor Men**. When these two became a little less active, **Mere Image** took over as 'top dogs' in town. Other notable garage bands (to mention but a few) were **The Tikis** (from Syracuse), **The Olivers** (precise homeground unknown), **The Endd** (La Porte), **The Cirkit** (Michigan City), **The Teen Tones** (South Bend), **The XL's** (Terre Haute), **The Ferris Wheel** and **Shooting Stars** (both from Winchester). Until recently Indiana had been overlooked as a significant location of sixties garage bands but the 1992 compilation, 'Hoosier Hotshots' (Epilogue EP1 001) has helped to rectify this and contains tracks by almost all of the aforementioned. In the sleevenotes Ron Simpson, who was also the editor of the garage fanzine, 'Hoosier Hysteria', writes:-

> 'If one had to generalize - and sometimes this is unfair as well as inaccurate - the Northern part of the state was more punk-oriented. Perhaps this was due to the bands' rebellious attitudes against the local lifestyle itself, i.e. the coal mines and steel mills portrayed ominous things to come for kids after high school. The central region was a bit more pop-oriented with the usual garage sounds ever-present. 'Course, don't tell this to the Olivers or Joys Of Life as they could play Punk with anyone. The South leans toward the folk/garage mix, but again the XL's weren't exactly the Kingston Trio!'

Indiana's proximity to Chicago inevitably meant that bands migrated to Chicago to record and then stayed there. So some of the bands we included in our Chicago volume - bands like **Mason Proffit, Lord And The Flies** and **Oscar And The Majestics** were originally from Indiana.

Indiana's greatest claim to musical fame, though, must be that its northern mining town, Gary, was birthplace and childhood home to the phenominally successful Jackson family. You can read about all their exploits in this volume.

The aftermath of the psychedelic era, arguably the birth, or at least the puberty of modern rock, brought the arena rock/pomp/metal edged outfits aiming squarely at the major labels and big money. The Midwest as a whole produced more than its fair share of these bands but Indiana produced few that made it and none that became platinum artists. Roadmaster probably came closest to success in that field. In the early seventies the punk explosion rocked the U.K. and the tidal wave soon reached America. Once more, anybody could rock; talent was not especially vital. All you needed was the enthusiasm, the equipment and some inner rage. Indiana produced a great number of punk bands or bands heavily influenced by punk fashions and attitudes. These included MX80, The Zero Boys, Sloppy Seconds, The Lazy Cowgirls and The Gizmos. Some of these bands relocated to California to achieve at least local success.

Indiana's farming areas have produced country singers over the years and inevitably some country-rockers, too, the latest being the highly successful Steve Wariner, one of the stars in the 'new-country' firmament. Blue-collar rock is represented by a string of singer/songwriters, the most prominent of whom are Henry Lee Summer, John Hiatt and the multi-talented John Cougar Mellencamp, the latter being the most successful artist to emerge from the State with the obvious exceptions of the various Jackson family members.

Iowa's sixties scene was rather fragmented and there's no single thread that pulls it all together. In the Northwest of the state the music scene was based around the IGL Recording Studios. Located in Milford the studio was the brainchild of Cliff Plagman, Roger Blunt and John Senn (leader of Dee Jay And The Runaways, who were from Spirit Lake). It opened officialy in March 1965, although prior to this Dee Jay And The Runaways had recorded a test record, 'Jenny Jenny/Boney Maronie' (IGL 100), of which just 100 copies were pressed ensuring that the disk is now hopelessly rare. The most successful release by the studio was Dee Jay And The Runaways' follow-up single in 1966, 'Peter Rabbit/Three Steps To Heaven' (IGL 103), which was later leased to Chicago-based Smash Records for national distribution. It climbed to No.45 in the National Charts. Over 250 45s were released on IGL and the related Sonic label between 1965-1980, as well as over 50 albums, though only three were rock. See Tom Tourville's excellent illustrated discography,' The I.G.L./Sonic Recording Story' for details of all relevant releases. The state's top ballroom in this era was The Roof Garden - all the State's top bands played there, as well as many of The Midwest's and the nation's top acts ... a flavour of what it must have been like was captured on the 1967 compilation, 'Roof Garden Jamboree' (IGL 103), which is now hopelessly rare - perhaps someone will reissue it soon.

Another of the State's music centres in the sixties was Des Moines ... this was home turf for groups like Cle-Shays, The Heritage, The Houserockers, Plastic Mushroom, The Prophets, The Sheffields, Silver Laughter, The Spartans and The Wild Cherries. On the poppier side it was base to Tommy Tucker whose groups in this era included The Esquires, Federal Reserve and Salt River. Des Moines was also a centre for country artists like Jack Barlow and Rene Waters, pop acts like The Ray Fabus Four and R & B acts like The Blendtones, The Martinels and Jimmy McHugh And The Extensions, who are really beyond the scope of this book.

The State's third music centre in the sixties was based around the Fredlo Studios in Eastern Iowa. The best-known band to sixties' collectors from this region were The Daybreakers (from Muscatine), who produced the classic 'Psychedelic Siren' 45 and who later regrouped as Rox and Crusin'. Check out 'The History Of Eastern Iowa Rock, Volume One: The Daybreakers' (Unlimited Productions RRRLP-0002) to hear both sides of their sole single as well as various demos and live performances. Then progress on to 'Dirty Water - The History Of Eastern Iowa Rock, Volume Two' (Unlimited Productions RRRLP 003) to hear some of the region's other hot acts like The Contents Are, Corruption Inc., Depot Rains, Fire And Ice, Junction, Rog And The Escorts, Uncle And The Anteaters, The Untouchables and The XL's. We can't leave Iowa's garage scene without mention of The Gonn (from Keokuk), whose 'Blackout Of Gretely' was for many collectors the State's best garage recording. The band have been brought to a wider audience by virtue of their inclusion as Volume 9 in Greg Shaw's 'Rough Diamonds: The History Of Garage Band Music' (Voxx VXS 200.029). Check this out to learn more about them. Finally we should mention Tom Tourville's Iowa discography, 'Iowa Rocked! The 1960s', which did some good pioneering work in this field.

Like Indiana, Iowa (the Hawkeye State) had a lean time as the garage era died away. The rolling hills produced folkies like Freeman And Lange and Bonnie Koloc. The punk boom of the mid-seventies had little immediate impact on a rural state like Iowa but by the mid-eighties the state was producing a string of good alternative rock bands and gaining a solid reputation for its local talent. The metal band Lynn Allen (from Davenport) led the way but many were to follow. In the main, these bands came from Iowa City. Bands such as The Dangtrippers, Full Fathom Five, Horny Genius, Sonic Disruption and Stickdog started tongues wagging and Des Moines contributed the excellent Hollowmen. Happily, relatively few of these moved to other states so there remains a nucleus which could lead to an exciting decade ahead.

Missouri's two main music centres in the sixties were St. Louis and Kansas City (which straddles the borders of Missouri and Kansas). St. Louis-based garage bands included Cole And The Embers, Exposure, Happy Return and Xtreems, but St. Louis' most successful sixties export was the pop-rock act Bob Kuban And The In-men. Kansas City was home to bands like Chesmann Square and

The Classmen. Of course, most towns had their garage bands. Springfield had The Esquires, Moberly was home to Plato And The Philosophers; Sounds Ltd. operated out of St. Joseph and from somewhere in Central Missouri came The Kyks. As yet no one has seen fit to put out any compilations containing just Missouri bands ... so what are you waiting for you local garage collectors!

In the seventies two of the State's most successful bands were the highly innovative Pavlov's Dog (from St. Louis) and the country-rock outfit Ozark Mountain Daredevils (from Springfield). Other success stories included the duo of Brewer and Shipley and metal styled rockers Mama's Pride, Head East and Granmax. We've also included Ike And Tina Turner along with details of their solo careers in this volume. Although they both spent much time in California and worked in several other American cities, they first met in St. Louis and did much of their work there. Unlike the other states covered in this volume, Missouri spawned hosts of punk styled bands in the late seventies and continued to do so throughout the eighties. These included the likes of the influential Drunks With Guns from St. Louis, Untamed Youth, Strangulated Beatoffs, and Ultraman. Furthermore, the adult oriented rock of bands like Starcastle, Shooting Star and more recently, The Rainmakers continued to do well. The local metal scene is small compared to Illinois but big enough to produce bands of the quality of Anacrusis. All in all, Missouri must be a key Midwestern state in the music stakes and seems set to stay that way through the nineties. So read on ...

I N D I A N A

Nicknamed the Hoosier State, Indiana covers an area of 36,291 square miles to the east of Illinois. It became the 19th State to achieve Statehood on 11 December 1816, and the State flower is the peony. The story goes that in pioneer days when a traveller rode by a log cabin, he would see an occupant peer out of the door and call a congenial, 'Who's there?'. To the passerby, unaccustomed to the Indiana twang, it sounded something like 'Hoosier?'. So this is one version of how Indianians came to be known as Hoosiers. A more likely explanation is that it refers to Samuel Hoosier, a major contractor whose company toiled on the Ohio Falls Canal project in 1826. Hoosier preferred to hire labourers from the Indiana side of the river. They became known as Hoosier's men, and later just as Hoosiers.

The State Capital, Indianapolis (home of the Indie 500 motor race) enjoys a central location in the fertile central farm belt. Anderson (about 30 miles to the North-East) and Terre Haute (in the West near the Illinois border) are both important industrial centres. South Bend, in the North, houses the University of Notre Dame and a 400-year-old Council Oak which sheltered the French explorer, La Salle, in May 1681, as he met with Indian chiefs. Evanston, down in the Southwest, is home to the Mesker Zoo, one of the most up-to-date in America, and Fort Wayne, in the Northeast saw the nation's first night baseball game and manufactured the world's first gasoline pumps. Gary, up on the banks of Lake Michigan (and birthplace of the Jackson family), is known for its fiery steel mills.

The sand dunes beside Lake Michigan in the North of the State are attractive to vacationers. Much of the State consists of farms and small towns set among rolling green hills where people lead a relatively quiet lifestyle. Indeed there are many Amish communities in Indiana who still lead lives taken from the pages of history books. In the hilly southern section rail fences run alongside twisting roads over the famous covered bridges and the wood smoke still rises up from cabins built over 100 years ago.

There are historic towns in Indiana - Wabash, which was the first town in the world to be wholly lit by electricity, and Anderson, which still has a gas-lit district on West 8th Street. The State also boasts a complete frontier fort in Fort Wayne where all the residents still dress and speak in the styles of 1816. In the Southwest lies river country - towns and cities built on river trade, with mansions overlooking the river from high bluffs. Here you will find Vernon, the farthest point North reached by the Confederate army during the Civil War when the area was an important part of the underground railway for escaping slaves.

So that's the State, read on to find out about its music artists.

I N D I A N A

THE ACCENTS

Albums
1(A)	Full Spectrum	(Forward	)	196?
2(A)	Next Bus South	(Forward	)	19??
3(A)	Two Sides Of The Accents	(Forward	)	19??
4(A)	Yesterday, Today And A Touch Of Tomorrow	(RCA LSP1 4251)		1970

Personnel		Ex	To
DICK DONAHUE	A	THE CLASSMEN	
RON RUSSELL	A		
VINCE SANDERS	A		

A popular '60s trio on the Indianapolis nightclub scene.

ACID GREEN

Cassette
1	Feed The Need	( )	1992

An outrageous Indianapolis thrash metal band likened to Gwar. (1) was preceded by a 45, 'As The World Turns' on Rusty Cow Records in 1991.

ACID INDIGESTION

An Indianapolis-based hardcore band who circulated a demo around local labels in 1992.

CHRIS ALLEN AND THE GOODTIMERS

Personnel incl:	Ex	To
CHRIS ALLEN	See also CHRIS ALLEN AND HIS LADS	

A mid-'60s garage band who released one 45, 'My Imagination/Sorry 'Bout That' (New World no No.).

CHRIS ALLEN AND HIS LADS

Personnel incl:	Ex	To
CHRIS ALLEN	See also CHRIS ALLEN AND THE GOODTIMERS	

Based in North Indiana this mid-'60s garage band's sole release was one 45, 'A Heartbreak Tonight/I'll Step Aside' (Beayer 4691).

AMOEBAS IN CHAOS

Album
1( )	On To May Day	(Hardly Music HMLP 1)	1982

Personnel		Ex	To
RICK WILKERSON	syn		
LYNN SHIPLEY	voc		
BRUCE DEMAREE	dr		
RICH LAMPHEAR	bs		

Indiana produced a number of curious new wave bands at the turn of the decade in 1981/2, most of which (including Amoebas In Chaos) appeared on the 1981 Gulcher Records compilation album 'Red Snerts' (Gulcher 102). (1) followed in February 1982.

ANDROPOV'S ASSASINS

Based in Columbus. Only known output was a cut on 'The Columbus Compilation' issued in 1983 on Gravel Voice Records.

ANTENNA SWAY

Albums
1( ) You Are Here   (Mammoth 0030) 1992
2( ) Hideout   (Mammoth   ) 1992

Personnel		Ex	To
JOHN STROHM	gtr,sitar,voc	of BLAKE BABIES	
FREDA LOVE	dr	of BLAKE BABIES	
VESS RUHTENBERG	gtr,voc	J.O.T.	
JACOB SMITH	bs,voc	STEVE KOWALSKI	

Began as an offshoot of **Blake Babies** but emerged an as organised unit and have stayed the course. Strohm/Love have worked variously under the names **Sway**, **Cake**, and Shine.

THE AQUANAUTS

Personnel	Ex	To
STEVE HARDING		
TOM HARDING		
LEE MORRELL		
WALLY MURPHY		
DAN BOTNICH		

An Indianapolis surf band who released a couple of 45s on Safari Records in the early '60s.

ARSON GARDEN

Albums
1   Undertowers   (Community 3   ) 1990
2   Wisteria   (Vertebrae ASKD 66013) 1991

EP
1( ) Drink A Drink Of You   (Vertebrae   ) 1993

A delightfully-named band based in Bloomington. Apart from the above they can be heard on a compilation, 'Uncharted' on March Records in 1992.

THE ASCOTS

Hailed from Vincennes in Southwestern Indiana where they were a frequent teen club attraction between 1964 and August 1966 when they quit because their lead guitarist and drummer went off to college. They recorded 'So Good' for Frat Records which has since resurfaced on 'Back From The Grave, Vol.6' (Crypt CR-007) 1985 and the 'Straight From The Garage Punk Classics (EP), Vol.2' (Garageband EP 2) in 1986. 'So Good' is a raw recording with a rockabilly-style guitar.

THE ASIAN TOURISTS

Personnel incl:		Ex	To
MARK HANCOCK	gtr		
BILL HAMILY	bs		

A hardcore band who can be heard on the Sonic Iguana compilation, 'Children Of The Corn' issued in 1990.

ASTRAL ZOMBIES

Hardcore punkers who evolved in early 1990 into **The Kursed.**

ASTROSURF

<u>Album</u>
1   Ride The Amber Waves   (Ribbon Rail   ) 1981

No other details available.

AZTEX

Gary was their hometown and they started out in 1963 as The Valuables covering Beatles and Everly Brothers songs. By the following year they had got more into the harsher songs of The Kingsmen, Stones and Kinks. In late 1966 they recruited the lead singer/guitarist from another popular Gary band The Squires and recorded a 45, 'I Said Move/The Little Streets In My Town', which was issued on Staff Records in May 1967. Just 100 copies were pressed for friends and family. 'Back From The Grave, Vol.4' (Crypt CR-004) 1986 features 'I Said Move', which was a pretty powerful rocker for its day. 'The Little Streets In My Town', another uptempo number with jangly folk-punk guitar and tambourine, has resurfaced on 'Back From The Grave, Vol.5' (Crypt CR-005) 1985.

B. F. TRIKE

<u>Album</u>
1(A) B. F. Trike   (Rockadelic   ) 198?

<u>Personnel</u>			<u>Ex</u>	<u>To</u>
ALAN JONES	bs,voc	A	HICKORY WIND	
MIKE McGUYER	gtr,voc	A	HICKORY WIND	
BOBBY STREHL	dr	A	HICKORY WIND	

Formed in Evansville in 1969 out of the ashes of **Hickory Wind.** They recorded a live album for RCA Records in Nashville in January 1971, but RCA decided not to sign them up and the album never got released until Rockadelic Records of Dallas, Texas, recently unearthed the tapes and put them out on vinyl. All ten cuts were originals, although 'Time And Changes' had been written and performed originally when the trio were members of **Hickory Wind.**

BACKDOOR MEN

<u>Personnel incl:</u>		<u>Ex</u>	<u>To</u>
STEVE KREIDER	voc,hca		
DEAN TAGGART	dr		
FRED HOSTETTER	ld.gtr		KAREN LAWRENCE + PINZ

This Elkhart-based band issued one 45, 'Evil/Corinna' on the Fujimo label in 1969.

THE MARDEN BAKER QUINTET

<u>Personnel</u>				
MARDEN BAKER	sax	A		
LARRY GOSHEN	dr	A	THE SOUNDS OF THE CROWNS	THE FIVE CHECKS
JACK SCOTT		A		THE CRACKERJACKS
BILL STEWART		A	JERRY LEE WILLIAMS AND THE CROWNS	THE EPICS
GARY THAXTON		A	JERRY LEE WILLIAMS AND THE CROWNS	THE EPICS

A popular early '60s jazz rock attraction of the Indianapolis nightclub circuit. Stewart and Thaxton had earlier played in Jerry Lee Williams And The Crowns, a late '50s outfit which pre-dated the time span of this book. The same was true of The Sounds Of

The Crowns. Goshen's prior band. Baker was one of the top jazz saxophonists in Indiana and **Goshen** played drums for several bands over the years and later became a rock journalist.

BASOOTIES

Gary was home to this garage band whose sole release was one 45, 'I'm So Proud/You Didn't Try To Call Me' (Muffin 001) in the mid-'60s.

THE BEAUTIFUL AUTHENTIC ZOO GODS

<u>EP</u>
1( ) The Beautiful Authentic Zoo Gods   (   ) 1991

A new band from Indianapolis. No other data available except that (1) is a 6-tracker.

BELT

A 1990 band based in New Paris who have issued a three-track 45 on their own Belt Records. The label of the record boasts only a band name and an address - no titles etc. Poor copy **Big Black** in parts and good guitars throughout but hampered by poor production.

BITTERSWEET BRIDGE

A mid-'60s garage band who put out one 45, 'Simon/ ? ' (Bridge 6513) on their own label.

BLACK AND BLUES

A mid-'60s garage band whose sole vinyl offering was, 'Come To Me/Bye Bye Baby' (United Artists 50245). Both sides can also be heard on 'The Finest Hour Of US 60's Punk' (Eva 12039).

BLACKSTONE

This garage band came out of Mishawaka and put out one 45, 'On The Prowl/One More Time' (Blackstone Productions 191) in the mid-'60s.

BLAKE BABIES

<u>Albums</u>
1	Nicely Nicely		(Chewbud	) 1988
2	Earwig		(Mammoth MR 00016)	1989
3	Slow Learner	(mini)	(Utility	) 1989
4	Sunburn		(Mammoth MR 00022)	1990
5	Rosy Jack World	(mini)	(Mammoth MR 00025)	1991
6	Greatest Hits		(Mammoth	) 1993

<u>Personnel incl:</u>			<u>Ex</u>	<u>To</u>
JULIANNA HATFIELD	voc,bs	AB		solo/LEMONHEADS
EVAN DANDO	gtr	A		
LEMONHEADS				
JOHN STROHM	gtr	AB	LEMONHEADS	
FREDA BONER	dr	A		
ANTHONY DE LUCA	dr	B		
MICHAEL LEAHY	gtr	B	DUMPTRUCK	See TACKLEBOX

A band from Bloomington who gained a hot reputation especially during 1989 but have so far failed to click. Status uncertain but links with Boston-based Lemonheads were strong. The fragmentation accelerated with Hatfield working solo and also with Dando in Fruit Child Large. Strohm and Boner also worked with Antenna Sway. (B) toured the UK in 1991. By 1993 Hatfield was working with her own band The Julianna Hatfield Three.

BLATHERSKITE

A hardcore punk band who issued a 1993 split 45 with Natural Cause on Rhetoric Records.

BLUCK

Cassettes
1	It Tasted Better Going Down	( )	1988
2	Blucked Up	( )	1989

Hardcore from Indianapolis.

THE BLUE ANGELS

Personnel		Ex	To
BILL COMPTON	AB		
BUD OSBORNE	A		
KEITH SCHULTZ	AB		
DENIE SMERDEL	AB		
GREG GALBRAITH	B		session work

This instrumental quartet formed in Indianapolis in the summer of 1960. Various members came and went, with Osborne and Smerdel remaining as the heart of the band. In September 1963 Osborne left for college and Galbraith joined as a replacement. They disbanded in 1964 and Galbraith later became a well known Nashville studio musician.

THE BLUE ANGELS

The Singles
Shake A Tail Feather/Dance With Me Lynda	(Cap 077) 196?
Lonesome River Of Tears/Yea You Miss Ann	(Carnaval 1001) 196?

A mid-'60s Gary-based garage band.

BLUES INC.

A garage band whose sole platter was 'Tell Me Girl/Get Off My Back' (Phalanx 1025) in the mid-'60s.

BORBETOMAGUS

Albums
1	Fish That Sparkling Bubble	(Agaric)	198?
2	Snuff Jazz	(Twisted Village)	1991
3	Industrial Strength	(Leo)	1992

Cassettes
1	Live At Inroads	(Cause & Effect)	1985
2	Live In Allentown	(Lowlife)	1991

Personnel		Ex	To
DONALD MILLER	gtr	SICKDICK	
DON DIETRICH	s	SICKDICK	
JIM SAUTER			BAREFOOT IN THE HEAD

Curious fare from Indianapolis. (1) is actually a split project, one side being by the Swiss band, Crack.

THE BOSCO HEPCATS

Personnel		Ex	To
THE BONE	bs		
JOHNSON FAIRBANKS	dr		
TOMMY CRATER	gtr		

A trio formed in the late '70s in Hammond which is on the Northwest border of the state and is viruatlly part of the Chicago complex. No known output.

THE BOYS NEXT DOOR

The Singles
Why Be Proud/Suddenly She Was Gone	(Soma 1439)	1965
There Is No Great Sin/I Could See Me Dancing With You	(Cameo 394)	1966
The Wildest Christmas/Christmas Kiss	(Bad 1301)	1966

Personnel	Ex	To
JIM ADAMS	THE FOUR WHEELS	
SKEET BUSHOR	THE FOUR WHEELS	
STEVE DRYBREAD	THE FOUR WHEELS	
JIM KOSS	THE FOUR WHEELS	
STEVE LESTER	THE FOUR WHEELS	

This Indianapolis group, which evolved out of **The Four Wheels**, operated between 1965-67.

BRAMBLE GRIT

Personnel		Ex	To
BRAD	gtr		
WILL	dr		
TODD	bs		
STEVE	voc		
MATT	gtr		

An average rock combo. The band can be heard on the 'Black Brittle Frizbee' compilation (Hit City HCR 0001) issued in 1988.

B. S. BOWLERS

Cassette
1 Doin' It R'Way	(	)	1990

Hardcore rantings.

THE BY COUNTS

Personnel	Ex	To
MEL JAMES		THE CLASSMEN
RICHIE MARTIN		
ROBBIE McVEY		
JIM THEROS		

An instrumental quartet who were a popular nightclub attraction in Indianapolis in 1963.

D. L. BYRON

Album
1   This Day And Age   (Arista AL 4258) 1980

A name used for the release of this **John Hiatt** album. All other solo output was under the name **Hiatt**.

CAMBRIDGE 5

The Singles
Heads I Win/Floatin'   (USA 850) 196?
I Hate To Laugh Alone/Keep On Running   (USA 875) 196?

A mid-'60s garage band from Mishawaka.

THE CAUSE

A relatively new band from Dyer in the far Northwest of Indiana in the Chicago/Hammond complex. They issued a 45 on Your Future Records in 1990.

THE CAVALIERS

Personnel	Ex	To
LARRY ALLEN		
MIKE SHANE		

A harmony/comedy duo from Indianapolis in the early '60s.

CHANCES 'R'

Personnel		Ex	To
ALLEN KIRSCH	KB		
STEVE FOSSEN	ld.gtr		HEART
RON RUTJES	dr		
CHRIS SKILLMAN	voc		
LARRY STREUBER	bs		

A garage band who operated out of Chesterton and put out one 45, 'I'll Have You Crying/Winds And Sea' (Quill 105) in the mid-'60s. We've also seen this band linked to the Chicago scene. Fossen went on to the Army which evolved into Whiteheart and then collapsed. After a spell in Hokus Pokus Fossen joined a reformed Whiteheart which rapidy became Heart based in Seattle.

CHESSMEN

A garage band who released one 45, 'You Can't Catch Me/Mr. X' (Phalanx 1018) in the mid-'60s. The 'A' side later featured on 'Highs In The Mid-Sixties. Vol.19. Michigan, Part 3' (AIP 10028) 1985, although the band were originally from Indiana.

THE CHOSEN FEW

Albums
1(A) The Chosen Few   (RCA LSP 4242) 1969

The Singles
Foolin' Around With Me/We Walk Together   (Denim 1080) 196?
It Just Don't Rhyme/Lucille   (Denim 1082) 196?
Pink Clouds And Lemonade/Stop In The Name Of Love   (Denim 1092) 196?
Maybe The Rain Will Fall/Deeper In   (Talun 1710) 196?
Maybe The Rain Will Fall/Deeper In   (RCA 74-0217) 1969

I'll Never Change You/Talk with Me   (RCA 74-0254) 1969

Personnel			Ex	To
CARL STORIE	voc	A		LIMOUSINE
DAVE BENNETT	gtr	A		LIMOUSINE
DAVE BARNES	dr	A		LIMOUSINE
JOHN CASCELLA	KB	A		LIMOUSINE
JACK HAMILTON	bs			

A rather obscure late '60s outfit who later changed their name to Limousine and then to Faith Band in 1973. Although (1) was recorded in Chicago, the band were from Muncie, Indiana originally. John Cascella later worked for a local Indianapolis recording studio mostly making commercials and film scores. He also toured with John Cougar Mellencamp and played on his 'Scarecrow' album but died on 14th November 1992 of a heart attack whilst driving his car.

CIRCLES

An Evansville-based garage band whose sole vinyl excursion was one 45, 'Walk Softly/Tell A Lie' (Knight 1001) in the mid-'60s.

THE CIRKIT

Personnel			Ex	To
SCOTT GLEMSIECKE	o	A		
DAVE GOLDMAN	bs	A		
ROD HANSEN	voc	A		
BRUCE HAINEY	gtr	A		
JIM SHINDELL	ld.gtr	A		
MIKE RICHARDS	dr	A		

Based in Michigan City between 1966-68. They recorded one 45, 'Yesterday We Laughed/I Was Wrong' (Unicorn 34941) in 1967, at Universal Studios in Chicago. The 'A' side, in particular, featured some fine grungy reverb guitar work and both sides can be heard on the 'Hoosier Hotshots' (Epilogue EP1-001) 1992 compilation.

THE CLASSMEN

Personnel	Ex	To
JIM BRUHN		also in SWINGIN' LADS
DICK DONAHUE	THE DAWNBEATS	THE ACCENTS
DAVE ELLMAN		ELLMAN-JAMES DUO
MEL JAMES	THE BY COUNTS	ELLMAN-JAMES DUO

A '60s vocal group from Indianapolis. They didn't make it onto vinyl.

CLAYTONS

A Fort Wayne-based garage band whose sole vinyl offering was one 45, 'Need Mine Too/Puttin' Me On' ("M" 50-662) in the mid-'60s. 'Puttin' Me On' got a further airing on 'Boulders, Vol.5' (Moxie MLP 08) 1983.

CLEAR SIGHT

Personnel incl:		Ex	To
RYAN			
MIKE	dr	also in STRIKE THREE	

A hardcore band from 1990.

CORNUCOPIA OF DEATH

A hardcore punk band who can be heard on the 'Children Of The Corn' compilation on Sonic Iguana Records which was released in 1990.

CORVETTES

Released an instrumental, 'Shaftin' on Duncan (401) in the mid-'60s.

COUNTER ATTACK

Personnel			Ex	To
RUSS KLIMCZAK	voc	A		
JOHN MALUFKA	gtr	A		
MARK O'CONNOR	dr	A		
ALEX EULOGA	gtr	A		
BRIAN ROSIN	bs	A		

A heavy metal band from Hammond who are gaining a reputation via some good quality demos including the 1990 one, 'Into Battle'. Whether they can survive the intense competition to be found in the metal genre remains to be seen.

COUNTRY BOB AND THE BLOOD FARMERS

Album
1   To Hell In A Hand Basket   (Monster/Metro-America MA 1019) 1985

EP
1   The Blood Farmers   (Gravel Voice   ) 1985

No data available. Nice name though!

COVEN

Albums
1( ) Witchcraft - Destroys Minds And Reaps Souls   (Mercury 61239) 1970
2( ) Coven   (MGM SE 4801) 1971
3(B) Blood On The Snow   (Buddah DBS 5614) 1974

The Singles		Peak Position
I Shall Be Released/I've Come Too Far	(SGC 003) 1968	-
Wicked Woman/White Witch Of Rose Hall (PS)	(Mercury 72973) 1969	-
One Tin Soldier/I Think You Always Know	(Warner Bros 7509) 1971	26
One Tin Soldier/I Guess It's A Beautiful Day	(MGM 14308) 1972	79
Nightingale/Jailhouse Rock	(MGM 14348) 1972	-
Nightingale/Jailhouse Rock	(Lion 102) 1972	-
One Tin Soldier/Johnnie	(Warner Bros 0101) 1973	73
I Need A Hundred Of You/ ?	(Buddah 440) 1974	
One Tin Soldier/Say Goodbye...	(Warner Bros 0332) 1975	-

Personnel			Ex	To
JINX DAWSON	voc	AB	HIM, HER & THEM	EQUALIZERS
CHRIS NEILSEN	gtr	B		
JOHN HOBBS	KB	B		session/FREEWAY
GREG OSBORNE	bs	AB	HIM, HER & THEM	
STEVE ROSS	dr	AB		EQUALIZERS
DAVE WILKERSON	gtr	A		
DAVID LARMAN	gtr		HIM, HER & THEM	

This Chicago-based band, which originated from Indianapolis, covered Bob Dylan's 'I Shall Be Released' for their debut 45 in 1968. (1) was a complete recording of a 'black' mass suggesting that they started off in the Black Sabbath mould. They had to wait three more years for their sole Top 30 US hit, 'One Tin Soldier (The Legend of Billy Jack)' from (2), which was brought to the attention of a wider audience by virtue of its inclusion in the Tom Laughlin movie, 'Billy Jack'. Their two subsequent chart appearances were actually with the same song. In July 1973 they charted with a new version of the song and they made the charts again at the end of that year when the original version was reissued. Keyboardist John Hobbs went on to do session work and also played for Freeway and Mike Nesmith. Later in the late '80s Jinx Dawson and Steve Ross went to LA where they are currently working with The Equalizers.

THE CRACKERJACKS

Personnel		Ex	To
GARY BEDELL			
LARRY GOSHEN	dr	THE FIVE CHECKS	KENNY LEE AND THE ROYALS
PAUL HUTCHINSON		THE FIVE CHECKS	THE EPICS
JACK SCOTT		MARDEN BAKER QUINTET	
GENE WITTHERHOLT			

An early '60s rock outfit from Indianapolis who had no recording output.

LARRY CRANE

Album
1   An Eye For An Eye   (   ) 1991

Crane was lead guitarist in Trash, an early John Cougar Mellencamp band and followed John to fame as the lead guitarist in his road band. He left Mellencamp to chart a solo course but so far has only produced (1), an obscure album about which we know nothing.

CREPE SOUL

Personnel incl:	Ex	To
JOHN MELLENCAMP		SNAKEPIT BANANA BARN

This Seymour High School outfit which lasted for 18 months during 1965/66 was Mellencamp's first band. They mimed the hits of the day and obviously didn't make it onto vinyl. Mellencamp was just 15 when he joined.

DAMASCUS ROAD

A new-wave band from Kokomo who operated in 1979. They had previously used the name The Socks and in a later incarnation in the early '80s became The Port Raisin Band.

THE DANCING CIGARETTES

EP
1   Dancing Cigarettes   (Gulcher 007) 1981

Personnel			Ex	To
EMILY BONUS	bs	A		
MICHAEL GITLIN	gtr	A	STRANGE EVENT	
TIMOTHY NOE	KB	A	STRANGE EVENT	
JACLYN ODDI	syn	A		
JOHN TERRILL	dr	A	FORCES OF EVIL	
G. DON TRUBOY	gtr	A	STRANGE EVENT	

Formed in Bloomington in February 1980 the band became very popular locally for a time. In many ways an extension of **Strange Event** and an even earlier incarnation **The Barn Boys**. As well as the cuts on the EP (Puppies In A Sack/Mr. Morose/Pop Doormat/Best Friend), the band contributed 'Broken Windows' to Gulcher's 'Red Snerts' compilation (Gulcher 102) in 1981. The following year saw the inclusion of their 'Burn In Heaven' on 'Segments', a compilation on Sirius. Also in 1982, a 45 rpm EP, 'Razorhand/Burn In Heaven' was issued on Big Strike records.

DATURA SEEDS

Album
1( ) Who Do You Want It To Be   (Toxic Shock   ) 1990

Compilation Appearances
1(A) Black Brittle Frizbee   (Hit City HCR 001) 1988
2( ) Children Of The Corn   (Sonic Iguana   ) 1990

Personnel			Ex	To
JONEE QUEST	bs	A		
LEE CUTHBERT	gtrs	A		
PAUL MAHERN	voc,gtr	A	ZERO BOYS	
TOM DOWNS	dr	A		
VESS RUHTENBERG	gtr			

An Indianapolis outfit most famous for the inclusion of Mahern who doubles as a producer of local bands (he also produced the 'Black Brittle Frizbee' compilation). Essentially the band play commercial pop music, breaking no new ground. The album has nice artwork though. They disbanded in 1991.

THE DAWNBEATS

Personnel		Ex	To
BOB CARRIE	A	THE DOWNBEATS	
DICK DONAHUE	A		THE CLASSMEN
DON HERALD	A	THE DOWNBEATS	
PHIL RAMEY	A		
MORGAN SCHUMACHER	AB	THE DOWNBEATS	EDDIE WALKER AND THE DEMONS
DAVE ELLMAN	B	KEETIE AND THE KATS	CLASSMEN
LARRY (WAZOO) GARDNER	B	KEETIE AND THE KATS	EDDIE WALKER AND THE DEMONS
LARRY LEE	B	KEETIE AND THE KATS	INNER CIRCLE
TONY NASSER	B		

An instrumental quintet who were based in Indianapolis and evolved in 1959 out of an earlier trio The Downbeats who had been playing since 1957. They recorded one 45, 'Drifting/Midnight Express' for Amp Records.

THE DAWNELLS

Bloomfield was their base and this garage band released one 45, 'Little Egypt/Scorpion' on the Bogun label in the mid-'60s.

THE DAWN FIVE

Personnel	Ex	To
STEVE BENHAM		
DAVE DUNNE		
DAVE McKOWN		
GREG NICOLOFF		
MIKE NICOLOFF		

A popular local attraction in Indianpolis, the Dawn Five formed in 1965. They released one 45, 'A Necessary Evil/Mike's Bag' (Bee Gee 4690).

DAZE

A garage band who released one 45, 'Dirty 'Ol Sam/Slightly Reminiscent Of Her' (King 6171) in the mid-'60s.

DEAD CENTRE

A Bloomington rock band who distributed a demo tape, 'Hate Rex' in the Spring of 1992.

DECREPIT

Album
1( ) Infinite Falling   (   ) 1990

A rock band from Carmel.

DEL AND THE ROAD RUNNERS

Personnel		Ex	To
DEL BAILEY	gtr,voc	See THE FIVE CHECKS	also JIMMY + EXCEPTIONS
JIM BOWERS	gtr		also JIMMY + EXCEPTIONS
RAMON LOPEZ	dr		STAN KENTON ORCHESTRA
JERRY COLLINS			See KENNY LEE + ROYALS
AL FICKLIN			
EDDIE GREEN			See KENNY LEE + ROYALS
WILLIE PHILIPS			See JIMMY + EXCEPTIONS
DALLAS REYNOLDS			

An early '60s country-rock outfit from Indianpolis. They didn't make it onto vinyl.

DELIRIUM

Another of Indianpolis' many hardcore bands. They can be heard on the 'Children Of The Corn' compilation on Sonic Iguana Records which emerged in mid-1990.

DANNY DOLLAR AND THE COINS

Personnel		Ex	To
TOMMY ADAMS			
CHARLIE (BROWN) CLARK			
DANNY DOLLAR			
RALPH MEYER			
?	dr		

This quintet were a popular attraction around Indiana's nightclubs in the 1960s.

THE DOMINOS

Personnel	Ex	To
PAUL GRAY	KENNY LEE AND THE ROYALS	
HARVEY GROVE		
FRED LAWSON		
RONDO LOSCHKY	SPORTSMEN	
BILL ROBERTS	SPORTSMEN	See FIVE CHECKS

A popular nightclub act around Indianapolis in the mid-'60s. They did not record.

DOW JONES AND THE INDUSTRIALS

Album
1(A) Hoosier Hysteria   (Gulcher GULCH   101) 1980

EP
1(A) Dow Jones And The Industrials   (Hardly Music 000002) 1980

Personnel			Ex	To
CHRIS CLARK	voc,gtr,bs	A		
BRAD GARTON	syn,KB,tapes	A		
GREG HORN	voc,gtr,sax,KB,	AB		
	tapes, syn			
TIM NORTH	dr,voc,syn,KB	AB		
DAVE BEHNKE	o	B		
JENNY SWEANY	bs	B		

A strange combo from West Lafayette. (1) is shared with The Gizmos. The band includes a cut on the 'Red Snerts' (Gulcher 102) in 1981 (line-up B).

DON DRASICH

EP
1   Don Drasich   (Staff BP-376) 1979

Don 'Jackhammer' Drasich is a singer-songwriter and multi-instrumentalist from Gary (whence came The Jackson Five et al!!). (1) is a four track disc, two of which also appeared on a 45.

DRYROT

Cassettes
1(A)	Collapse Of Morals	(9 tracks)	(	) 1989
2(B)	Technology	(9 tracks - 5 live)	(	) 1990
3( )	Shift	(11 tracks)	(	) 1991

Personnel			Ex	To
CHRIS SMITH	gtr	ABCD	MALIGNANT PIGS	
STEVE BAHNWEG	dr,voc	ABCDE	MALIGNANT PIGS	
WILLIE HODGES	bs,voc	ABCDE	MALIGNANT PIGS	
DAVE BLUE	gtr	A		
DENNY HOWARD	gtr	BC		
BRIAN ANSELL	gtr	CDE		

Evolved out of the Malignant Pigs in November 1988 in Richmond. 1991 also saw a 45 on 12 x 12 and a cut on the Shredder Records compilation EP, 'World's In Shreds'.

THE DUKES

Personnel	Ex	To
GARY BEDELL		CRACKERJACKS
BOB CRABTREE		
JIM HICKMAN		
JIM SONDAY		
FRED WILLIAMS		
CHUCK BEST	EUGENE + NIGHTBEATS	
AL OFFICER		
DICK WALKER		

A live attraction around the Indianapolis clubs circa 1963. They didn't record as far as we know.

THE DUKES (aka ROYAL JONES AND THE DUKES)

The Singles
Take Your Love/The First Time I Saw Her	(Signett 3265)	196?
I Don't Love You Anymore/Do It Now	(Fujimo)	196?
Walking The Dog/Please Come Home	(Fujimo)	196?

Personnel incl:			Ex	To
GARY JONES	gtr	A		
GENE JONES	ld.voc,o	ABC		
KEITH KILMER	dr	ABC		
SKIP WALTERS	bs	AB		
DAVE WORKMAN	sax	ABC		
JAY PURVIS	gtr,voc	BC		
MIKE KISER	bs	C		

This was Goshen, Indiana's top band in the mid-'60s. Formed in 1963 by the Jones brothers, they underwent several personnel changes but their most stable line-ups are shown above. They recorded a few 45s for Fujimo and the Chicago-based Signett label. Gary Jones left the band in 1966 and was replaced by Jay Purvis who wrote 'Take Your Love' which has recently got another airing on the 'Hoosier Hotshots' (Epilogue EP1 001) compilation in 1992. It's very much in the folk-garage mould and worth a listen. They later signed to Columbia who clearly wanted to turn them into a Midwest version of Paul Revere and The Raiders and fitted them with navy uniforms and a new moniker Gene Paul Jones and The American Navy. When the band made it clear they didn't want to know, Columbia simply didn't record them and they soon were no more.

ECLIPSE

Album
1( ) Eclipse	(Sweetwood)	1983

A band from Camby. We have no other details at all.

THE ELLMAN-JAMES DUO

Personnel	Ex	To
DAVE ELLMAN	THE CLASSMEN	
MEL JAMES	THE CLASSMEN	

A late '60s duo from Indianapolis who didn't make it onto vinyl.

THE ELYSIANS

Cassette
1 The Elysians	( )	1989

New psychedelia..

EMERGENCY EXIT

A garage band who released a 45, 'Wild Illusions/ ? ' on (Snap 006) in the mid-'60s.

THE ENDD

The Singles
* So Sad/Emancipation	(Seascape SS-500)	1965
Project Blue/Out Of My Hands	(Seascape SS-501)	1966

Don't It Make You Feel Like Crying/Gonna Send You Back To Your Mother   (Seascape SS-503) 1966
Come On In To My World/This Really Is The Zoo, Plus Two   (Seascape SS-504) 1966

* as by The End.

Personnel incl:		Ex	To
RUSS SANDERS	voc		
LARRY ANDERSON	bs		

Hailed from La Porte, Indiana and were originally known as The End. Their finest moment, 'Out Of My Hands' can be heard on 'Pebbles, Vol.9' (BFD BFD-5026) 1980 and 'The Best Of Pebbles, Vol.2' (Ubik Records TAKE-2) 198?. Larry Anderson died in the '80s.

THE ENEMY

EP
1   School Lunch Victim   (   ) 1988

A hardcore band from Indianapolis who evolved into **The Wombats** and later to **Strike Three**. Apart from the EP, a 6-track affair, the band can also be heard on the Flush Tapes compilation, 'Baby Thru The Windshield' issued in 1989.

THE EPICS

Personnel	Ex	To
ART ADAMS		
PAUL HUTCHINSON	THE CRACKERJACKS	WILDFIRE
GUY TARRENTS		INNER CIRCLE
GARY THAXTON	THE MARDEN BAKER QUINTET	
BILL STEWART	THE MARDEN BAKER QUINTET	

A quintet from Indianapolis who were a popular club act in the mid-'60s.

EUGENE AND THE NIGHTBEATS

Personnel		Ex	To
RICHARD BOLING	A		
TOM BRENHAM	A		
EUGENE SMITH	A		THE TRAVELS
TOM SPENCER	A		THE TRAVELS
CHUCK BEST			THE DUKES
JOE JACKSON			

An Indianapolis outfit who formed in 1959 and were a popular attraction at teen dances. During the 1960s they were a nightclub act. We know of no recording output.

THE EVICERATERS

A hardcore band who released a demo cassette in 1988 called, 'The Best Of Buff Yuk'.

THE FAITH BAND

Albums
1(A) The Faith Band   (Brown Bag   085) 1973
2(A) The Faith Band 2   (Village   ) 1976
3(A) Excuse Me, I Just Cut An Album   (Village   VR 7703) 1977
4(A) Rock 'n' Romance   (Village/Mercury SRM 1-3759) 1978
5(A) Face To Face   (Mercury SRM 1-3770) 1979
6( ) Vital Signs   (Mercury SRM 1-3807) 1979

The Singles (on Mercury)				Peak Position
Dancin' Shoes/Desire		(Mercury 74037) 1978		54
You're My Weakness/Forever		(Mercury 74068) 1979		76
Big City Lights/Touchy Situation		(Mercury 74090) 1979		-

Personnel			Ex	To
JOHN CASCELLA	sax,KB	A	LIMOUSINE	JOHN COUGAR MELLENCAMP
CARL STORIE	voc	A	LIMOUSINE	See solo
DAVE BARNES	dr	A	LIMOUSINE	
DAVE BENNETT	gtr	A	LIMOUSINE	
MARK CAWLEY	bs	A	LIMOUSINE	

One of the longest running bands ever to emerge from Indianapolis. Formed as **The Chosen Few** they evolved into **Limousine** in 1971. They recorded albums under both names before evolving again into their most successful incarnation. Under this name they actually scored a couple of minor hits, 'Dancin' Shoes' which reached 54, and 'You're My Weakness' which peaked at 76. Cascella joined the roadband of **Mellencamp**, one of Indiana's biggest successes, but died of a heart attack whilst driving his car on 16th November 1992.

FALKANS

A garage band out of South Bend whose sole release was 'Why Marianne/Kiss Me When You're Glad' (Fujimo 2521) in the mid-'60s.

FEEBEE AND THE RAGWEED PATCH

A New Haven-based garage band whose sole platter was 'Burn The Midnight Oil/Monkey Man' on the Ben label in the mid-'60s.

THE FERRIS WHEEL

Came from the small town of Winchester. They recorded just one 45, 'Come Baby Back/Cherrie-42533' (Randolph 004) in 1966. The 'A' side, a garage punker, later resurfaced on the 'Hoosier Hotshots' (Epilogue EP1 001) 1992 compilation. The flip was more pop-oriented.

FESTIVAL

A band remembered, if at all, for their friendship with the late Tom Fogerty. He eventually joined the band, who were based in Lafayette and took them into the studios in July 1981. No known output.

FIRE HYDRANT MAN

Personnel incl:		Ex	To
MATT HART	gtr	F.O.N.	

An up and coming hardcore band. As well as an association with **F.O.N.**, Hart also works with the **Rasta Snowhounds**. Fire Hydrant Man can be heard on the Indiana hardcore compilation, 'Children Of The Corn' issued in 1990 through Sonic Iguana Records.

THE FIVE CHECKS

Personnel		Ex	To
DELBERT BAILEY		DEL + ROADRUNNERS	
BOB EDWARDS			
LARRY GOSHEN	dr	THE MARDEN BAKER QUINTET	THE CRACKERJACKS
PAUL HUTCHINSON			THE CRACKERJACKS
BILL ROBERTS		See SPORTSMEN/DOMINOS	

A popular early '60s nightclub act not just in their home state of Indiana but throughout the Midwest. The heart of the band became **The Crackerjacks**. Much later in the late '80s Hutchinson played in a country outfit, **Wildfire**.

THE FIVE CHORDS

Personnel	Ex	To
RON DERKS		
HARRY KETTLE		
JACK LEWIS		
ARLEY PRICE		
JERRY WOODWARD		

An early '60s quintet from Indianapolis who were popular around the clubs.

DAVE FLANNERY

Flannery came from the delightfully-named Santa Claus and put out one garage 45, 'Someday Baby/Tears' (Skoop 1005), in the mid-'60s.

F.O.N.

Demos
1	Think	(12 track)	(	) 1987
2	Care	(11 track)	(	) 1988

Album
1( )	Same Difference	(Sonic Iguana	) 1989

Personnel		Ex	To
GLEN CLEWLOW	voc,gtr	A	
DARYL FRAME	bs	AB	
PETE JANIDLO	dr	AB	
GILES DAVIS	voc,gtr	B	
MATT HART	gtr		FIRE HYDRANT MAN

F.O.N. (Freaks Of Nature) who formed in November 1987, are based in Muncie and can also be heard on the Family Fest compilation, 'The Great Outdoors' issued in 1989. Hart is also a member of The Rasta Snowhounds.

FOURTH ROOM

A garage band whose sole mid-'60s platter, 'Vote/You Better Do Right' (MOQ 1100) came in a picture sleeve.

THE FOUR WHEELS

Personnel	Ex	To
JIM ADAMS		THE BOYS NEXT DOOR
SKEET BUSHOR		THE BOYS NEXT DOOR
STEVE DRYBREAD		THE BOYS NEXT DOOR
JIM KOSS		THE BOYS NEXT DOOR
STEVE LESTER		THE BOYS NEXT DOOR

Indianapolis was the home of The Four Wheels in the mid-'60s. They released one 45, 'Central High Playmate/Cold 45' (Soma 1428), in 1965, before changing their name to The Boys Next Door later that year. You'll find 'Central High Playmate' on the 'Hipsville, Vol.3' (Kramden KRAN-MAR 103) 1986 compilation.

FREDDY AND THE FRUIT LOOPS

This band feature with one cut, 'Right And Wrong' on the 'Red Snerts' compilation on Gulcher Records (GULCH 102), from 1981.

GADFLY

<u>EP</u>
1( ) Gadfly   (Flux 5.5) 1992

A hardcore band who also have a cut on 'Children Of The Corn', a compilation released through Sonic Iguana Records in 1990. Not to be confused with another similarly named hardcore quartet from Rhode Island.

GALABOOCHES

Hailed from Gary in the mid-'60s and were fronted by a 16-year old singer. They released one Stones-influenced teen rock 45, 'I'll Never Work Out/She Doesn't Care' (Staff 188) and the 'A' side later resurfaced on the 1985 compilation 'Garage Punk Unknowns Vol.4' (Stone Age Records 664). It's a pretty routine teen effort for this era.

LISA GERMANO

<u>Albums</u>
1   On The Way Down From The Moon Palace   (Major Bill 191) 1991
2   Happiness   (Capitol 98691) 1993

Germano is the fiddle player in **John Cougar Mellencamp's** roadband. Impressed by the debut album Capitol Records offered her a development deal in 1992. This led to (2) which was critically acclaimed.

GHOST RIDERS

A surf outfit who released an instrumental 45, 'Mental Revenge/Ghost Riders Theme' (Newland 1001), on an Indianapolis label.

GARY GILLESPI

From Indianapolis he recorded his first 45 backed by The Playboys, 'Honest I Do/Dancing Girl' for Delta Records in 1961. He later played on the nightclub circuit with bands which included The Katalinas and By Chantz Operation. Later recordings were 'Blue Lover' and 'My Sweet Cindy' with the By Chantz Operation on BCO Records.

GIRLS CAN TOUCH

<u>Cassette</u>
1(A) Happy Dreams   (8 track)   (   ) 1989

<u>Personnel</u>			<u>Ex</u>	<u>To</u>
PATRICK SMITH	gtr,voc	A		
ROBERT SMITH	bs,voc	A		
TODD KEFFABER	dr	A		

A trio from West Lafayette. The band recorded the cassette themselves at Westbank Sound Studios in Minneapolis. The music is mid-tempo pop-rock. The title cut is excellent, as are 'Running In Circles' and 'Raising Something', both of which would feel quite at home on a REM album. Where the pace drops, interest drops off too, but even so, a band with promise.

THE GIZMOS

<u>Album</u>
1(B) Hoosier Hysteria *   (Gulcher GULCH-101) 1980
* They contributed to half of this album. The other side was by **Dow Jones And The Industrials**.

<u>EPs</u>
1(A) Muff Divin' ('Mean Screen', 'Chicken Queen', 'Muff Divin', 'That's Cool') (Gulcher GULCH-001) 1976
2( ) No.2 Amerika First   (7 track)   (Gulcher GULCH-002) 1977

```
3( ) Gizmos World Tour ('Gizmos World Tour', 'We're Gonna Rumble',
        'Hey Beat Man', 'Gimme Back My Foreskin')                    (Gulcher GULCH-004) 1978
4( ) Never Mind The Sex Pistols Here's The Gizmos                     (Gulcher GULCH-006) 1978
```

Personnel			Ex	To
KEN HIGHLAND	ld.gtr,voc	A		MARINES/HOPELESSLY OBSCURE
RICH COFFEE	gtr,voc	A		UNCLAIMED
RICK CZAJKA	gtr	A		
DAVEY MEDLOCK	voc	A		
DAVE SVLAK	bs	A		
TED NIEMIEC	voc	A		
EDDY FLOWERS	voc	A		CRAWLSPACE
JIM DEVRIES	dr	A		
PHIL HUNDLEY				solo
BILLY NIGHTSHADE	voc,bs	B		
ROBBIE WISE	dr	B		
DALE LAWRENCE	gtr	B		VULGAR BOATMEN
TIM CARROLL	gtr,voc	B		DICKS

Line-up A from 1976. B is from 1981.

Formed in Bloominton in 1976 cutting EP (1) the same year. They followed this with EP (2) in 1977. The seven tracks were: 'Amerika First'. 'Human Garbage Disposal', 'Ballad Of The Gizmos', 'Kiss Of The Rat', 'Pumpkin To Playboy', 'Cave Woman' and 'I'm Just A Regular Dude'. EPs (3) and (4) followed in 1978. (3) was a 7" and came in a picture sleeve. Side 1 of (4) was recorded live at Max's Kansas City.   In 1980, they contributed one side to the 'Hoosier Hysteria' album (a 'Hoosier' is a native of Indiana) and they broke up in 1981 - their final recording being a cut, 'The Midwest Can Be Alright' on the 'Red Snerts' (Gulcher GULCH-102) compilation LP of that year. Some members later relocated to the New York/New Jersey area. By the time of their demise none of their original line-up remained.

GOOD SEED

```
Albums
1    Good Seed                                            (Almond Tree   ) 197?
2    Rooted And Grounded                                  (Seedling 3576 ) 1974
3    Good Seed                                            (Village VR 7602) 1977
```

A little known combo from Indianapolis.

G.O.O.L.

Personnel incl:		Ex	To
JESSE HOTTLE	gtr		

An Indianapolis hardcore band formed late in 1989. The name stands for Generation Out Of Luck and they have a demo out called 'Eroded Away'.

LARRY GOSHEN

Larry was one of the State's top drummers during the '50s and '60s. Born in Bedford he moved to Indianapolis when he was 10 and graduated from Tech High School in 1959. During the late '50s and early '60s he played drums for The Crowns (1958), Jerry Lee Williams and The Crowns (1959) and The Sounds Of The Crowns (1959). In the '60s he was with The Marden Baker Quintet (1960), The Five Checkes (1962), The Crackerjacks (1963), Kenny Lee And The Royals (1963) and The Sportsmen (1964). Larry is still involved in the Indianapolis music scene today. He writes a monthly column called 'Indiana Gold' for 'Steppin' Out Indianapolis', an arts and entertainment publication and has written a book, 'Indy's Heart Of Rock 'n' Roll' about the Indianapolis music scene in the late '50s and early '60s.

GRAPES

This La Porte-based garage band put out one 45, 'You Come Home/When The Four Winds Blow' (Purple 101) in the mid-'60s.

GREMLINS

The Singles
Wait/Everybody Needs A Love   (Fujimo ?) 196?
We've Found A Love/Corrections   (Fujimo ?) 196?

A garage band from Elkhart.

GROUP INC

The Singles
Like A Woman/Just Call Me   (Staff   177) 196?
Like A Woman/Just Call Me   (Freeport 1008) 196?

A mid-'60s garage band from Gary, originally. However, we included them in our 'Chicago/Illinois' volume and 'Like A Woman' was later included on 'Highs In The Mid-Sixties, Vol.4: Chicago' (AIP 10006) 1983.

THE GYNECOLOGISTS

EPs
1( ) Feces And Psychopaths   (Vomit PYR-22681) 1981
2( ) Kinder, Gentler Nation   (6 tracks)   (Gyno   ) 1990

Cassette
1   Auto-Erotica Asphyxia   (13 tracks)   (   ) 1991

Personnel	Ex	To
MILBURN DRYSDALE		
JOHN WILKES BOOTH		
TOMMY AFTERBIRTH		
SIMON SCROTUM		

Tasteless trash from Columbus (northeast of Bloomington). They also appear on the 1983 Affirmation compilation, 'Master Tapes Two'. In 1990 they reappeared on their own Gyno label and seem to have relocated to Martinsville.

RONNIE HAIG (HEGE)

Based in Indianapolis Ronnie had a local hit with 'Don't You Hear Me Calling Baby/Traveler Of Love' (Note ?) back in the late '50s. After a few more recordings he slipped into retirement, re-emerging much later in 1984 with two country records:- 'Comin' On Home/Listen To My Music' (Acts ?) and 'Solitaire/Grandpa Fed' (Acts ?). More recently he's been reviving old rock 'n' roll sounds.

JULIANNA HATFIELD (THREE)

Albums
1   Hey Baby   (Mammoth   0035-2) 1992
2(A) Become What You Are (as Julianna Hatfield Three)   (Matador-Atlantic 92278) 1993

EP
1   I See You   CD5   (Mammoth   ) 1992

Personnel			Ex	To
JULIANNA HATFIELD	gtr,voc	A	BLAKE BABIES	

DEAN FISHER	bs	A	
TODD PHILLIPS	dr	A	BULLET LA VOLTA
CLAY CARVER	gtr		BULLET LA VOLTA

Hatfield was a key member of the highly-rated **Blake Babies**. She can also be heard on 'Spew 3' on Atlantic issued in 1993.

HEADSTONE

Album
1(A) Still Looking   (Starr SLP 1056) 1971

The Singles
What People Say/Carry Me On   (Rome   ) 196?
Buying Time/Snake Dance   (Rome   ) 196?

Personnel		Ex	To
TOM APPLEGATE	A		
DAVID APPLEGATE	A		
BARRY APPLEGATE	A		
BRUCE FLYNN	A		

(1), a predominantly heavy rock album which does contain some softer interludes and some psychedelic overtones, has aroused considerable interest among collectors in recent years. It was repressed a few years back and is worth a listen on account of the fine guitar work and vocals it contains. The two 45s feature non-LP tracks and all bar 'Snake Dance' feature on the 'Filling The Gap' (Obscure World 001) 1989, four LP box set compilation.

THE HEAVY

Personnel	Ex	To
LARRY INGLE		
PHIL THOMPSON	LOST SOULS	
FRANKIE WATTERS		
JEFF WILLIAMS		

Operated out of Kokomo and became known for wild clothes and stage antics.

HERD

An Indianapolis garage band whose sole mid-'60s platter was one 45, 'Lovelight/Daddy's Little Angel' (Jan Eden ?).

JOHN HIATT

Albums
1	Hanging 'Round The Observatory	(Epic KE 32688)	1974
2	Overcoats	(Epic KE 33190)	1975
3	Slug Line	(MCA 3088)	1979
4	Two Bit Monsters	(MCA 5123)	1980
5	All Of A Sudden	(Geffen GHS 2009)	1982
6	Riding With The King	(Geffen GHS 4017)	1983
7	Warming Up To The Ice Age	(Geffen 24055)	1985
8	Riot With Hiatt (live - promo only)	(Geffen A 2288)	1985
9	Bring The Family	(A&M SP 5158)	1987
10	Slow Turning	(A&M SP 5206)	1988
11	Y'All Caught? The One That Got Away (dbl - best of 1979-1985)	(Geffen 24247)	1989
12	Stolen Moments	(A&M 5310)	1990
13	Perfectly Good Guitar	(A&M)	1993

The first I ever heard about Indiana songwriter Hiatt was that he was connected in some way, (I never did discover in what way), to White Duck. That would have been in 1972. Since that time he has offered us a dozen fine albums, all without producing a hit single. Many people are more familiar with his work through the likes of Rosanne Cash, Tracey Nelson, Katy Moffatt, etc. They all seek out his songs like pearls, as well they might.

Hiatt was born on 20th August in 1952 in Indianapolis. He was brought up there drinking in his influences, primarily black music, including The Isley Brothers, James and Bobby Purify and Otis Redding. Much of this he heard on WLAC, a black music station broadcasting out of Nashville. He could only actually pick up the station at night; he was eleven at the time. He also enjoyed gospel music and tended to hang around local Baptist churches which was probably a curious experience for a young white Catholic boy. Hiatt didn't buy records in those days, and even then was something of a loner, an intense and rather fat teenager, in fact at age 12 he weighed some 260 pounds! Even so, he bought a guitar, taught himself to play, and began to form his own bands.

Within the embrace of these early bands (including The Four Fifths and Joe Lynch and Hangmen) Hiatt remained a shy plump adolescent; but on stage, a new side of his character began to emerge. By the late '60s he was into Sam and Dave and Michigan rocker Mitch Ryder and The Detroit Wheels. In his bands he mixed their material with the inevitable Beatles' covers and a smattering of his own songs.

Hiatt began running away from home although he always returned in the end. He took a job as a stock boy to gather some cash together. Using this nest-egg he travelled to New York to form a band with some friends. They based themselves upstate but Hiatt took an unwise chemical trip and ended up in hospital for three days. He returned home when he was discharged. In the early '70s he travelled to Nashville, aged just 18, and began songwriting for the famous Tree Publishing House. He stayed for five years. He began by obtaining an apartment which was spartan to say the least. Naked light, car tyres for bed legs - you get the picture? He lived on cheap food (eg. boloni and beans) and began smoking heavily. By 1971 Tree raised his wages from $25 to $50 a week!

So far, no-one had recorded any of his songs. Hiatt began playing at the Exit Inn in Nashville. He worked as a result with the likes of Rodney Crowell, Guy Clark and Chris Gantry. Almost immediately one of his songs, 'Thinking Of You' (written back in Indianapolis when he was 17) was picked up by (then) country-rocker Tracey Nelson for one of the Mother Earth albums. This wasn't placed by Tree (who, bless them, never placed any of his songs but continued to pay him), he did it all himself. In his five years in Nashville as a writer/performer, only two other songs were picked up, both by Tracey Nelson: 'As Sure As I'm Sitting Here' and 'An Arm And A Leg' - both appeared on her solo albums. The former was from his first LP for Epic. His contract with the recording giant came about following an introduction by Travis Rivers (Tracey's manager) to Columbia Nashville staff producer, Don Ellis. Having had one potential deal (with Elliot Mazer) fall through, Hiatt wasn't expecting too much from this new contract. In fact he was offered an immediate 45 deal and cut 'We Make Spirit (Dancing In The Moonlight)'. Unfortunately its release coincided with a huge similarly titled hit by Eastern band, King Harvest, and stations shied away from it. (1) was produced by Glen Spreen and Chips Moman who cut nine tracks with the budget for the 45. Don Ellis was prepared to throw in another $2,000 (totalling $6,000) and (1) was released in January 1974 almost as an accident. It sold only 15,000 copies and is not especially representative of his overall style. It was somewhat rock and roll orientated by his present standards. It also included a number of different styles which rather confused the wider audience. Finally, Epic failed to promote it at all despite some degree of critical acclaim. 'The Village Voice' for example called it the best new album in early '74. Almost 30% of sales were in Minneapolis and it was no coincidence that he had done the only promotional gigs there. Later that year he toured Wisconsin but even this small trip was a disaster (not least because of Hiatt's increasing experimentation with drugs including heroin).

Leaving narcotis behind him, he abandoned rock and roll for his second effort for Epic. Halfway through recording (2) he fell ill with hepatitis and his relationship with his label had taken a turn for the worse too. Epic said they wouldn't issue the album at all unless he toured to promote it. In a vicious circle the tour agents refused to set up a tour circuit if there was no album to promote. After a six-month impasse the album escaped in June of 1975 and died on the racks. Reviews were poor and when Don Ellis left Epic Hiatt's days there were numbered too. Epic gave him another chance and he returned to the studios. Only three cuts were recorded (including his own version of 'An Arm And A Leg') when he quit by mutual agreement. Simultaneously, Tree Publishing (who were now paying him $200 a week) fired him. Reeling under these blows Hiatt returned to Indiana.

In 1976, back in Indianapolis, he began working on his stage act, gigging solo and working the clubs with the likes of Tom Waits, Leon Redbone, Sonny Terry and Brownie McGhee. He worked on the road too, covering thirty three states in three years honing his craft. He didn't pull in much money but his personal appearance simply got better and better. One night he was working with guitarist Leo Kottke at The Caves, a club in Santa Monica. Kottke had told his producer/manager, Denny Bruce, to try and catch

Hiatt's set. Bruce was duly impressed and offered Hiatt finance to write some new songs and put a band together. The ultimate consequence of this arrangement was to be (3) which Bruce subsequently produced. Initially though, four rough cuts were sent to MCA who snapped him up in May 1978. Hiatt moved from San Francisco (where he had been living) to Los Angeles and the album was released in May 1979. Once again the reviews were excellent and once again his label failed to promote it. His style had changed dramatically since his Epic days. On (3) he was likened by the (enthusiastic) critics to UK art-rockers like Elvis Costello and Joe Jackson. (3) was full of influences - R & B and African included. His vocals were more nasal, his lyrics more biting, even vitriolic at times although the romantic always lurked in the wings.

(4), also badly promoted, followed the same basic path and Hiatt's reputation was growing. The production was a touch better and there was some mellowing out but those waspish observations remained. Even so, MCA dropped him.

In 1981 he worked with his friend Jack Nitzsche's wife, Buffe St. Marie in Scandinavia as part of her road band. Additionally he worked with Ry Cooder on his 'Borderline' album, and toured with him too. In 1982 he was also involved with Cooder's 'Slide Area' album and the soundtrack of 'The Border'. He also signed to Geffen records. (5) was a fine album, produced (in a rather over-complicated fashion) by Tony Visconti. It had less impact than his two MCA albums with the critics. (6) was produced by Nick Lowe (side one) and Scott Matthews/Ron Nagle (side two). It was a return to his peak - more keen observations from a working man living in the real world. His songs reflect emotions and happenings that we can all relate to whilst often placing them in fresh settings and looking at them from odd angles.

(7) was an odd album but still excellent. Produced by Nashville (and Area Code 615) veteran Norbert Putnam. It was very much a "rock" album and included a duet with Elvis Costello on 'Livin' A Little, Laughin' A Little'. It also included 'When We Ran', later so awesomely interpreted by Texan singer Katy Moffatt. 1985 also saw a live promotional album on Geffen which displays his considerable live skills. In the Summer of 1984, Hiatt began to deal with an accumulated alcohol problem by booking himself into a detox clinic for thirty days. He toured to promote (7) but in early 1985, his wife died. More touring followed and in that year he also worked on the 'Alamo Bay' soundtrack with Ry Cooder, and later on the soundtrack to 'White Nights'. Towards the end of the year he moved from California back to Nashville with his daughter. He concentrated on his songwriting.

Hiatt married his second wife in June 1986. This added to his family, too - his own daughter of seven, and a new stepson of thirteen. In the autumn of 1986 he flew into Los Angeles to talk to Geffen about a new album only to discover they had dropped him. He was not too put out about this; he did not like the label hierarchy much and in any event they, like his previous labels, had no idea how to market his work. The UK-based Demon label expressed some interest but nothing came of it. He did a brief tour of California which quite to his surprise, led to a deal with locally-based A & M after half a dozen labels expressed interest in 'Bring The Family'. It was cut quickly in the studios with a small band including Hiatt (guitar), Ry Cooder (slide guitar), Jim Keltner (drums) and Nick Lowe (bass). It emerged rapidly, a haunting autobiographical work in many ways. Lean, realistic and emotional rather than intellectual. The title cut has smoking slide from Cooder who also shines on 'Lipstick Sunset'. Every track is excellent including the six minute 'Tip Of My Tongue'.

(10) follows the same pattern - simple, cutting, and full of naked emotion. A fine example of the skills of a modern songwriter. (11) was a good collection of his MCA/Geffen material. (12) also appeared in a hail of critical acclaim. Sadly, Hiatt still remains better known for his songs as interpreted by others than his own work. His albums are respectable but unspectacular sellers and it seems unlikely that the majors will keep giving him contracts if he can't give them hits. In 1991 the studio group which had recorded the 'Bring The Family' album toured extensively and put out an album on Warner Brothers/Reprise (26713) using the group name Little Village. This was a respectable seller and bridged the gap nicely until (13) emerged. As ever, the critis raved: as ever sales were limited. When will we ever learn!?

HICKORY WIND

Album
1(A) Hickory Wind   (Gigantic   ) 1969

Personnel incl:			Ex	To
ALAN JONES	bs,voc	A		B.F. TRIKE
MIKE McGUYER	gtr,voc	A		B.F. TRIKE
BOBBY STREHL	dr	A		B.F. TRIKE

An Evansville late '60s outfit, the core of which evolved into B.F. Trike. Just 100 copies of their album were pressed up making it one of those ultra rare releases which are very sought-after by some. The highlight is 'Time And Changes', a late '60s psychedelic offering with great vocals and fuzz guitar. They recorded it again when they evolved into **B.F. Trike**. 'Father Come With Me' is a successful mixture of vocals and droning keyboards; 'Mr. Man' effectively superimposes spoken lyrics over a piano backing and 'I Don't Believe' and 'Judy' are pleasant laid back, melodic efforts. Certainly the album's worth hearing but don't mortgage your home to buy a copy!

HIGH GROUND

Album
1   Bending Moment   (Redbud   ) 1982

A blue-grass and country band.

HIM HER AND THEM

Personnel	Ex	To
BOB DAWSON		
JINX DAWSON		COVEN
STEVE FARBER		
GREG JOHNSON		
DAVID LARMAN		
GREG OSBORNE		COVEN

Operated in Indianapolis during 1964 and were perhaps most significant for the inclusion of Dawson and Osborne who went on to play for Coven, who later moved to Chicago where they met with some commercial success.

THE HITCH-HIKERS

Emerged from somewhere in Indiana with a 45, 'Beaver Shot/ ? ' (HH 1) during the 1960s.

PHIL HUNDLEY

A former member of The Gizmos, who had a cut ('30 Second Affair') on the 'Red Snerts' compilation (Gulcher 102) issued in 1981.

SKIPPER HUNT COMBO

Hammond was this garage outfit's home town and they recorded one 45, 'What Am I Gonna Do?/Scalded' (Glenn 1900).

ICED EARTH

Album
1(B) Iced Earth   (Century Media CM 9714) 1990

Personnel			Ex	To
JON SCHAFFER	gtr	AB		
GREG SEYMOUR	dr	AB		
GENE ADAM	voc	AB		
DAVE ABELL	bs	AB		
RANDY SAWYER	ld.gtr	A		
MICHAEL McGILL	ld.gtr	B		
RICHARD BATEMAN				AGENT STEEL/NASTY SAVAGE

A heavy metal quintet formed in Fort Wayne as **Pergutory**. Using the Iced Earth, (line-up A), name they cut a six track demo ('Enter The Realm') which resulted in interest from Century Media Records who signed them in 1990. The band had by that time relocated to Tampa in sunny Florida. Seems reasonable!

ARE YOU A SMART ASS?

IF YOU CAN SUPPLY MISSING INFO,
CORRECT ERRORS OR MAKE SUGGESTIONS TO
IMPROVE OUR BOOK, WE WANT TO HEAR FROM

YOU!

CONTACT US CARE OF:-

BORDERLINE PRODUCTIONS,
P.O.BOX 93
TELFORD, TF1 1UE
ENGLAND

IDLE FEW

<u>The Singles</u>

People That's Why/ ?	(Blue Rock) 196?
Farmer John/Another World	(Soma 1457) 1966
Farmer John/Another World	(Dunwich 127) 196?

<u>Personnel</u>	<u>Ex</u>	<u>To</u>
RON BENNETH		
RON KNOOP		
DAN McLEAN		
PAUL ROMINE		
RICK WEBSTER		

This Indianapolis outfit formed back in 1958 as The Kingsmen but changed their name after the similarly named Portland, Oregon outfit had their 'Louie Louie' hit. They were one of the city's top mid-'60s acts with a fine live reputation and opened for the likes of The Byrds, Beach Boys and McCoys when they visited Indianapolis. They recorded a cover of 'Farmer John' in 1966 which can now be heard on the 'Hoosier Hotshots' (Epilogue EP1 001) 1992 compilation. They had a second 45, 'Letter To Santa/Splishin' And Splashin'' (Label Unknown) in 1967.

THE IMPACTS

From Anderson, they released one surf-style 45 in the early '60s, 'Summer/Lindae' (Anderson 104).

THE IMPOSTERS

A garage band from Fort Wayne who recorded a version of 'Respect' on the Gateway label in the mid-'60s.

THE INNER CIRCLE

<u>Personnel</u>	<u>Ex</u>	<u>To</u>
LARRY BURCH		
JOHN HURST		
LARRY LEE		DAWNBEATS
GUY TARRENTS	EPICS	

A 1967 club band based in Indianapolis.

THE INTRUDERS

<u>The Singles</u>

Wild Goose/Tambourine	(Sahara 101) 1963
Surfin' Green/The Intruder	(Anderson 103) 196?

Both these 45s were instrumental surf-style recordings. The second label was based in Anderson.

INVERTED NIPPLES

A hardcore band from Evansville who have a cut on the 'Children Of The Corn' compilation on Sonic Iguana Records which was released in mid-1990.

THE JACKSON 5

<u>Albums</u>

1(B) Diana Ross Presents The Jackson 5	(Motown 700) 1970
2(B) ABC	(Motown 709) 1970
3(B) Third Album	(Motown 718) 1970

4(B)	Maybe Tomorrow	(Motown 735) 1970
5(B)	Jackson 5 Greatest Hits	(Motown 741) 1971
6(B)	Goin' Back To Indiana	(Motown 742) 1971
7(B)	Lookin' Through The Windows	(Motown 750) 1972
8(B)	Skywriter	(Motown 761) 1973
9(B)	Get It Together	(Motown 783) 1973
10(B)	Dancing Machine	(Motown 780) 1974
11(B)	Moving Violation	(Motown 829) 1975
12(B)	Jackson Five Anthology * (triple)	(Motown 868) 1976
13(-)	Michael Jackson and The Jackson 5 +	(Mowtown) 1984

* includes solo hits by Michael and Jermaine. + picture disk.

The Singles		Peak Position
Big Boy/You've Changed	(Steeltown 681) 1968	-
You Don't Have To Be Over 21 To Fall In Love/Some Girls Want Me For Their Love	(Steeltown 684) 1968	-
I Want You Back/Who's Loving You	(Motown 1157) 1969	1
ABC/It's All In The Game	(Motown 1163) 1970	1
The Love You Save/I Found That Girl	(Motown 1166) 1970	1
I'll Be There/One More Chance	(Motown 1171) 1970	1
Santa Claus Is Coming To Town/Christmas Won't Be The Same This Year	(Motown 1174) 1970	-
Mama's Pearl/Darling Dear	(Motown 1177) 1971	2
Never Can Say Goodbye/She's Good	(Motown 1179) 1971	2
Maybe Tomorrow/I Will Find A Way	(Motown 1186) 1971	20
Sugar Daddy/I'm So Happy	(Motown 1194) 1972	10
Little Bit Pretty One/If I Have To Move A Mountain	(Motown 1199) 1972	13
Lookin' Through The Windows/Love Song	(Motown 1205) 1972	16
Corner Of The Sky/To Know	(Motown 1214) 1972	18
Hallelujah Day/You Make Me What I Am	(Motown 1224) 1973	28
Get It Together/Touch	(Motown 1277) 1973	23
Dancing Machine/It's Too Late To Change The Time	(Motown 1286) 1974	2
Whatever You Got, I Want/I Can't Quit Your Love	(Motown 1308) 1974	38
I Am Love (Part 1)/I Am Love (Part II)	(Motown 1310) 1975	15
Forever Came The Day/All I Do Is Think Of You	(Motown 1356) 1975	60
Body Language/Call Of The Wild *	(Motown 1375) 1975	-

* Cancelled.

Personnel			Ex	To
SIGMUND 'JACKIE' JACKSON	voc		AB	THE JACKSONS
TORIANA 'TITO' JACKSON	voc		AB	THE JACKSONS
JERMAINE JACKSON	voc		AB	solo
JOHNNY JACKSON	dr		A	
RONNIE RANCIFER	p		A	
MARLON JACKSON	voc		B	THE JACKSONS
MICHAEL JACKSON	voc		B	THE JACKSONS

More a soul than rock outfit these superstars are a marginal case for inclusion. Just a brief outline of their career is given here; readers wanting to know more about the band or its individual members should consult a biography.

The Jacksons are all natives of Gary, Indiana and they originally formed as a trio (Jackie, Tito and Jermaine) in 1963. Jackie had been born on 4 May 1951; Tito on 15 October 1953, and Jermaine on 11 December 1954. Initially known as The Jackson Family they recruited cousins Johnny Jackson and Ronnie Rancifer and played locally. In 1964 when younger brothers Marlon, who'd been born on 12 March 1957, and Michael, who was born on 29 August 1958 joined in place of the two cousins, who remained as backing musicians, they became known as The Jackson 5.

They soon began to make an impact, entering and winning a talent contest singing The Temptations' 'My Girl' at Gary's Roosevelt High School in 1965. Their father, Joe Jackson, a steelworks' crane driver and former guitarist with The Falcons, became their manager and drove them to gigs as far afield as Chicago and New York. Indeed later in 1966 they won another talent contest at

Harlem's Apollo Theatre. In 1968 they recorded a 45, 'Big Boy', for the Gary-based Steeltown label without success, but the following year following recommendations from Gladys Knight and Bobby Taylor and The Vancovers and seeing them perform at a campaign benefit for Gary's mayor, Richard Hatcher, Motown boss Berry Gordy Jr. signed them and relocated them to Hollywood for rehearsals. The Jackson family meanwhile moved to California.

On 18 October 1969 they performed on a bill with Diana Ross and The Supremes and others at The Hollywood Palace. This was their first live appearance as a Motown act. Their first Motown 45, 'I Want You Back', with Michael Jackson on lead vocals topped the US Charts for four weeks and became a million-seller. It also made No.2 in the UK. (1), which tried to convey the impression that Diana Ross had discovered the band, made No.5 in the US and No.16 in the UK. Gordy had found a new hit machine. 'ABC' topped the US Singles Chart for two weeks becoming their second million-seller and when 'The Love You Save' also topped the US Singles Chart for two weeks to become their third million-seller in June 1970 they became the first act to top the US Top 100 with their first three chart entries. On 26 September 1970 Motown announced that The Jackson 5 had sold 10 million disks in nine months. More was to follow - 'I'll Be There' topped the US charts for five weeks in the Autumn of 1970, selling in excess of four million copies, it was Motown's biggest selling single ever. (3), which included 'I'll Be There' climbed to No.4 in the US and in December of that year 'The Jackson 5 Christmas Album', a mixture of traditional and modern seasonal songs, became the year's top-selling Christmas disk.

The band remained extremely successful up until they left the Motown label in May 1975. (4) peaked at No.11 in the US in 1971 and on 11 September that year an animated 'Jackson 5' series appeared on ABC TV in the States. (6), a soundtrack to a TV Jackson 5 special, climbed to No.16 in the US and (5), which had preceeded it eventually made No.12 in the US and No.26 in the UK. The album was a compilation of the band's singles to date. The title track from (7), which made Nos.7 and 16 in the US and UK Album Charts respectively, also made No.9 the UK Singles Chart to give the band their first UK hit single for almost 18 months. Featuring some effective tempo changes this was arguably one of their most interesting recordings.

1972 saw both Jermaine and Michael make their first solo recordings and in 1973 (8) climbed to No.44 in the US. In July 1973 The Jackson 5 became the first major US black group to tour Australia. In September the title track to (8), not used as a US single, reached No.25 in the UK. November saw Motown trying out another brother, Jackie, as a soloist but when his LP, Jackie Jackson, failed the experiment was never repeated. On 15 December Jermaine married Berry Gordy's daughter, Hazel, in LA. This act would later have considerable implications when the band left Motown.

In February 1974 the band returned home from a tour of Africa after just one week when they couldn't adjust to the food and water, but they soon bounced right back when 'Dancing Machine', from (9), gave them a No.2 becoming their biggest selling US single since 'Never Can Say Goodbye'. In November 1974 (10) peaked at No.16 on the US Album Charts and the same month they sang backing vocals on Stevie Wonder's 'You Haven't Done Nothing'' that topped the US charts.

Finally in May 1975 in search of more recording freedom and better royalties (it transpired they were only receiving 2.7% royalties on Motown sales and could not write their own material), The Jackson 5 left Motown to sign for Epic. Motown filed a $20 million law suit for breach of contract which was not settled until 1980 with The Jacksons making a payment of $600,000 and the label retaining all rights to the use of The Jackson 5 name. (11), their final album for Motown, peaked at No.36 in the US but later they issued (12), a triple compilation which peaked at No.84 in the US. Jermaine, who had married Gordy's daughter back in December 1973, remained at Motown as a soloist and left the band. Since Motown owned The Jackson 5 name the band continued life as simply The Jacksons.

THE JACKSONS

Albums
1(A)	The Jacksons		(Epic 34229) 1976
2(A)	Goin' Places		(Epic 34835) 1977
3(A)	Destiny		(Epic 35552) 1978
4(A)	Triumph		(Epic 36424) 1980
5(A)	Jacksons Live	(dbl)	(Epic 37545) 1981
6(-)	18 Greatest Hits		(Telstar) 1983 - UK only
7(B)	Victory		(Epic 38946) 1984

The Singles
		Peak Positiion
Enjoy Yourself/Style Of Love	(Epic 50289) 1977	6
Show You The Way To Go/Blues Away	(Epic 50350) 1977	28

Goin' Places/Do What You Wanna	(Epic 50454)	1977	52
Different Kind Of Lady/Find Me A Girl	(Epic 50496)	1977	-
Blame It On The Boogie/Ease On Down The Road (with Diana Ross)	(Epic 50595)	1978	54
Shake Your Body (Down To The Ground)/That's What You Get (For Being Polite)	(Epic 50656)	1978	7
Lovely One/Bless His Soul	(Epic 50938)	1980	12
Heartbreak Hotel/Things I Do For You	(Epic 50959)	1980	22
Can You Feel It?/Everybody	(Epic 01032)	1981	77
Walk Right Now/Your Ways	(Epic 02132)	1981	73
The Things I Do For You/Working Day And Night	(Epic 02720)	198?	-
State Of Shock/Your Ways	(Epic 04503)	1984	3
Torture/Torture (instr.)	(Epic 04575)	1984	17
Body/Body (instr.)	(Epic 04673)	1984	47
Nothin' (That Compares 2U)/Alright With Me	(Epic 68688)	1990	77
2300 Jackson Street/When I Look At You	(Epic 69022)	198?	-

Personnel		Ex	To
SIGMUND 'JACKIE' JACKSON	AB	THE JACKSON 5	
TORIANO 'TITO' JACKSON	AB	THE JACKSON 5	
MARLON JACKSON	AB	THE JACKSON 5	solo
MICHAEL JACKSON	AB	THE JACKSON 5/solo	solo
RANDY JACKSON	AB		
(LA TOYA JACKSON	A)	See also solo	solo
(REBBIE JACKSON	A)		solo
JERMAINE JACKSON	B	See also solo	solo

In May 1975, after leaving Motown to sign for Epic, the **Jackson 5** regrouped as The Jacksons. Youngest brother, Randy Jackson, (who'd been born in Gary on 29 October 1962) replaced Jermaine (who'd remained with Motown having married into the Gordy family) and sisters La Toya and Rebbie Jackson also joined temporarily.

On 16 June 1976 'The Jacksons' started as a four week summer variety show on US CBS TV. La Toya, Rebbie and Janet Jackson appeared in the show along with the five boys, a regular comedy sketch team and various guests. The series later enjoyed a second and longer run between January-March 1977.

With the TV series ensuring the band was in the public eye (1), their debut for Epic, was released in February 1977. It peaked at No.36 in the US and No.54 in the UK. The first 45 taken from it, 'Enjoy Yourself', made the US Top Ten and crept to No.42 in the UK. In May the band embarked on its first tour (The Jackson 5 had last toured five years ago) and participated in the celebrations for Queen Elizabeth II's Silver Jubilee at the King's Theatre, Glasgow, Scotland. Boosted by their UK tour, their next 45 release, penned and produced by Kenny Gamble and Leon Huff, 'Show You The Way To Go', a modest success in the US, topped the UK charts for one week in June to give the group their first and only UK No.1 hit. 'Dreamer', a UK-only release from (1) also made No.22 in the UK in September.

As 1977 drew to a close, (2) was released in December. It peaked at No.63 in the US and No.45 in the UK. It spawned further 45 hits:- the title track, 'Blame It On The Boogie' and a UK-only success with 'Even Though You've Gone' which peaked at No.31 in the UK in February 1978.

February 1979 saw the release of (3) and with it their greatest success to date. This was The Jackson's first self-produced album. It peaked at No.11 in the US in May, going platinum and becoming a million-seller. No.33 was its peak position in the UK, where the title track (a UK-only release) had earlier peaked at No.39 back in February. The big 45 success from (3) was 'Shake Your Body (Down To The Ground)', which continued to reinforce the band's position at the forefront of the emerging dance craze. It made the Top Ten both in the US and UK. In the US it sold over two million copies, going platinum.

In October 1980 came (4), the band's second self-produced LP. It peaked at No.10 in the US in November, giving the group their second platinum LP; earlier in October it had made No.13 in the UK. The 45s from (4):- 'Lovely One' and 'Heartbreak Hotel' were fairly successful but follow-ups, 'Can You Feel It?' and 'Walk Right Now' enjoyed far greater success in the UK.

In July 1981 The Jacksons set out on a 36-city US tour. On the tour recordings were made for (5), which was released at the end of the year. It later peaked at No.30 in the US in January 1982 where the tour receipts grossed $5 1/2 million.

1982 was a quiet year for The Jacksons as members concentrated on their solo projects and 1983 began low key, too, although (6), an UK-only TV promoted compilation topped the UK Album Charts for three weeks during August. On 21 November 1983, their promoter, Don King, called a press conference at the Tavern On The Green in New York to announce that Jermaine would rejoin his brothers, after leaving Motown, and that they'd embark on an 18-city 40-date US tour the following summer. The 'Victory' tour, as it became known, opened in Kansas City, Missouri, on 6 July bringing the six brothers together on stage for the first time in eight years. (7), finally peaked at No.4 in the US in September 1984, winning the group their third platinum disk. It also brought them further 45 success. 'State Of Shock' was taken from (7) but released in advance of the album in June 1984. It featured Mick Jagger on guest vocals alongside Michael Jackson. The record was a great success - one LA radio station, K-1QQ played the record continuously for 22 hours! It went gold in the US reaching No.3 and also climbed to No.14 in the UK in September, where (7) peaked at No.3. (7) spawned two further hits, 'Torture' and 'Body', the latter was The Jacksons final hit as a group. On 9 December 1984 they played their final show together at LA's Dodger Stadium. With pretty much the whole family embarking on solo careers none of them needed the band anymore. Michael, Jackie, Marlon, La Toya, Randy and Tito did all come together to participate in the recording of USA For Africa's 'We Are The World' on 28 January 1985. The record, made to aid African famine relief, became a Worldwide No.1.

JACKIE JACKSON

Album

1	Jackie Jackson	(Motown)	1973

Born on 4 May 1951 in Gary, Jackie was the eldest of the Jackson brothers. He played with The Jackson 5 from 1964-75 when they became The Jacksons and was a member of The Jacksons from 1975 until their demise in December 1984. Motown tried to promote him as a solo artist (following their success with Michael and Jermaine) in November 1973. However, when (1) flopped they did not repeat the experiment.

JANET JACKSON

Albums

1	Janet Jackson	(A & M 4907)	1982
2	Dream Street	(A & M 4962)	1984
3	Control	(A & M 5106)	1986
4	Rhythm Nation 1814	(A & M 3920)	1989
5	janet	(Virgin 87825)	1993

The Singles			Peak Position
Young Love/The Magic Is Working	(A & M 2440)	1982	64
Come Give Your Love To Me/Forever Yours	(A & M 2522)	1983	58
Say You Do/You'll Never Find	(A & M 2545)	1983	-
Don't Stand Another Chance/Rock 'n' Roll	(A & M 2660)	1984	-
Dream Street/Love And My Best Friend	(A & M 2682)	1984	-
Fast Girls/Love And My Best Friend	(A & M 2693)	1984	-
What Have You Done For Me Lately?/He Doesn't Know I'm Alive	(A & M 2812)	1986	4
Nasty/You'll Never Find (Another Love Like Mine)	(A & M 2830)	1986	3
When I Think Of You/Second Emotion	(A & M 2835)	1986	1
Control/Fast Girls	(A & M 2877)	1986	5
Let's Wait Awhile/Pretty Boy	(A & M 2906)	1987	2
The Pleasure Principle/Fast Girls	(A & M 2927)	1987	14
Miss You Much/You Need Me	(A & M 1445)	1989	1
Rhythm Nation/Rhythm Nation (instr.)	(A & M 1455)	1989	2
Come Back To Me/Vuelve A Mi (Come Back To Me)	(A & M 1475)	1990	2
Black Cat/ ?	(A & M 1477)	1990	1
Alright (7" R&B Mix)/Alright (7" Remix)	(A & M 1479)	1990	4
Escapade/Escapade (instr.)	(A & M 1490)	1990	1
Love Will Never Do Without You/ ?	(A & M 1538)	1991	1
The Best Things In Life Are Free/ ?	(Perspective 0010)	1992	10
That's The Way Love Goes/ ?	(Virgin 12650)	1992	1
If/ ?	(Virgin 12676)	1933	4
Again/ ?	(Virgin 38404)	1993	1

Born in Gary on 16 May 1966 Janet was the youngest of the nine Jackson children. In 1973 she appeared in her brothers' stage show for the first time aged seven. She made her TV debut as Penny Gordon Woods in the CBS TV series 'Good Times' in 1977 and also appeared in 'Fame' and 'Different Strokes'. Having signed to A & M Records in 1982, she released (1) in November 1982. It made No.63. The following year she enjoyed minor US hits with 'Young Love' and 'Come Give Your Love To Me'.

For (2), she enlisted help from Cliff Richard among others. It peaked at No.147. Both albums proved she could sell records. Although only a fraction of the sales her famous brothers were enjoying at the time, they were sufficient to encourage her record company to keep faith in her. Janet had done much acting in her childhood and to prove she hadn't completely discarded the field got herself cast in the hi-energy dancing TV series 'Fame' in 1984. It not only provided her with a platform for her dancing skills, it also encouraged her to incorporate dance into her music. This would pay great dividends later.

Her progress was then interrupted by a short and unsuccessful marriage with James DeBarge - a singer with the Motown group DeBarge. DeBarge had a drug problem which Janet had felt she could help him to overcome. Her attempts failed - they were separated within two months and the marriage was annulled within one year.

(3) followed in January 1986. It was produced by Jimmy Jam and Terry Lewis. She embarked on a 13-city US promotional tour in March and enjoyed four US Top Ten hits from (3) over the next few months:- 'What Have You Done For Me Lately?', 'Nasty', 'When I Think Of You' (which made No.1) and 'Control'.

In November 1986 'Control - The Video' was released and the following month she set out on a US tour. By now she was a superstar, topping Billboard's 1986 year end survey in six categories:- Top Black Singles Artist, Top Black Artist, Top Pop Singles Artist, Top Pop Singles Artist female, Top Dance Club Play Artist and Top Dance Sales Artist. In January 1987 she won two awards:- Best R & B Single (for 'Nasty') and Best Female R & B Artist at the 14th annual American Music Awards at LA's Shrine Auditorium. In March 1987 a fifth single was released from (3) - 'Let's Wait Awhile'. It peaked at No.2 in the US to give her five US Top Ten hits from the album. In April A & M also issued a re-mix of the song on their dance-oriented Breakout label in the UK, where it peaked at No.3. In June she guested on vocals on Herb Alpert's 45, 'Diamonds' which peaked at No.5 in the US. In August 'The Pleasure Principle' climbed to No.14 in the National Charts. The same month saw the release of 'Control - The Video, Part II'.

In November 1988 she recorded a new album with producers Jimmy Jan and Terry Lewis. (4) was a handful of tracks laced together by extracts of news bulletins. Its message being 'In complete darkness we are all the same. It is only our knowledge and wisdom that separate us'. The album was full of thought-provoking, socially aware songs dealing with topics like teenage pregnancy, homelessness, runaways and the value of knowledge and education. Some stunning videos accompanied the album with intricate dance routines which display Janet's potential to the full. Within four months of its release 3 million copies had been sold and it soon surpassed the sales of 'Control'.

Janet's career has gone from strength to strength. In 1990 her Rhythn Nation World Tour brought her back to the UK where she played sell-out concerts at Wembley Arena in late September and she also played at Birmingham International Arena. A megastar, Janet has firmly established herself at the forefront of the dance movement. (4) produced seven hit singles - this was the first time one album has produced this number of hits and was certified five times platinum.

In 1991 she signed to Virgin for an estimated $35 million with $17 million up front and $6 million per LP for three albums. This was the most lucrative deal in history though Michael's subsequent deal with Sony and Madonna's deal with Warner were to eclipse it. Bridging the gap before her first Virgin output Janet enjoyed a Top Ten hit with a duet with soul star Luther Vandross. By May 1993 she was back at No.1 with an advance single from (5). It was to stay there for eight weeks. At the time of writing, the first Virgin album band topped four times platinum in domestic sales alone.

JERMAINE JACKSON

Albums

1	Jermaine	(Motown	752) 1972
2	Come Into My Life	(Motown	775) 1973
3	My Name Is Jermaine	(Motown	842) 1976
4	Feel The Fire	(Motown	888) 1977
5	Let's Get Serious	(Motown	928) 1980
6	Jermaine	(Motown	948) 1980
7	I Like Your Style	(Motown	952) 1981
8	Let Me Tickle Your Fancy	(Motown	6017) 1982

9   Jermaine Jackson   (Arista 8203) 1984

The Singles		Peak Position
That's How Love Goes/I Lost My Love In The Big City	(Motown 1201) 1972	46
Daddy's Home/Take Me In Your Arms	(Motown 1216) 1972	9
You're In Good Hands/Does Your Mama Know About Me	(Motown 1244) 1973	79
She's The Ideal Girl/I'm So Glad You Chose Me (a)	(Motown 1386) 1976	-
Let's Be Young Tonight/Bass Odyssey	(Motown 1401) 1976	55
Let's Get Serious/Je Vous Aime Beaucoup (I Love You)	(Motown 1469) 1980	9
You're Supposed To Keep Your Love For Me/Let It Ride	(Motown 1490) 1980	34
You Like Me, Don't You? (Part I)/(Part II)	(Motown 1503) 1981	50
I'm Just Too Shy/All Because Of You	(Motown 1525) 1981	60
I'm My Brother's Keeper/Paradise In Your Eyes (b)	(Motown 1600) 1982	-
Let Me Tickle Your Fancy/Maybe Next Time	(Motown 1628) 1982	18
Very Special Part/Giving Me The Runaround	(Motown 1649) 1982	-
Dynamite/Tell Me I'm Not Dreaming (Too Good To Be True)	(Arista 9190) 1984	15
Take Good Care Of My Heart/Tell Me I'm Not Dreaming (c)	(Arista 9275) 1985	-
Do What You Do/Tell Me I'm Not Dreaming	(Arista 9279) 1985	13
When The Rain Begins To Fall (d)/Come To Me	(Curb 52521) 1985	54
(Closest Thing To) Perfect/(Closest Thing To) Perfect (instr.)	(Arista 9356) 1985	67
I Think It's Love/Voices In The Dark	(Arista 9444) 1986	16
Words Into Action/Our Love Story	(Arista 9495) 1986	-
Do You Remember Me?/Whatcha Doin'	(Arista 9502) 1986	75
If You Say My Eyes Are Beautiful (c)/Just The Lonely Talking Again (h)	(Arista 9690) 198?	-
Clean Up Your Act/I'm Gonna Git U Sucka (e)	(Arista 9788) 198?	-
I'd Like To Get To Know You/Spare The Rod, Love The Child	(Arista 2029) 198?	-
When The Rain Begins To Fall (d)/Substitute (f)	(MCA 52521) 198?	-
Time Out For The Burglar/News At Eleven (g)	(MCA 53032) 198?	-
Don't Take It Personal/Clean Up Your Act	(Arista 9875) 1990	64
Two Ships In The Night/Next To You	(Arista 9933) 1990	-

(a) Cancelled.
(b) Devo provided the backing vocals.
(c) With Whitney Houston.
(d) This was recorded with Pia Zadora and taken from the film 'Voyage Of The Rock Aliens'.
(e) By The Gap Band.
(f) Zadora solo.
(g) By The Distants.
(h) Whitney Houston solo.

Born in Gary on 11 December 1954, Jermaine was the third son of the celebrated Jackson family. He became a member of The Jackson 5 in 1964 enjoying years of success with his brothers.

After enjoying solo success with his younger brother Michael Jackson Motown pushed Jermaine in 1972 re-releasing (1) which peaked at No.27 in the US and his debut 45, 'That's How Love Goes', which climbed to 46 in the US, in November 1972. In March 1973 a follow-up 45, 'Daddy's Home', which was a revival of Shep and The Limelites' 1961 doo-wop ballad, made the US Top Ten earning him a solo gold disk.

(2), released in the summer of 1973, was less successful peaking at only No.152 in the US Album Charts, and a 45 from it, 'You're In Good Hands' was only a minor hit. This would prove his last solo success for three years. However, in this period, he married Motown boss Berry Gordy's daughter Hazel in LA on 15 December 1973, The Jackson 5 left Motown to sign for Epic in May 1975, with Jermaine leaving the band and remaining with Motown as a solo artist.

His new solo effort (3) was released in late 1976 peaking at No.164. It also spawned a minor US hit with 'Let's Be Young Tonight'. (4) made No.174 in September 1975 but these were essentially quiet years for Jermaine in which he was overshadowed by his brothers. When he did return to the Charts in July 1980 with (5) it went gold in the US peaking at No.6 and it also made No.22 in the UK.

The title track, written and produced by Stevie Wonder, peaked at No.9 in the US and No.8 in the UK, earning him his first solo success there. A UK-only 45, 'Burnin' Hot' peaked at No.32, whilst in the US, another Stevie Wonder composition, 'You're Supposed To Keep Your Love For Me', was chosen for release and gave him a minor hit. Later, during 1981, 'You Like Me, Don't You?' brought him a minor hit in the US and UK.

(7) peaked at No.86 in the US in November 1981 and 'I'm Just Too Shy' extracted from it gave him a minor US hit.

(8), in the summer of 1982, was his last LP for Motown. It peaked at No.46 in the US, whilst the title track (on which Devo provided backing vocals) climbed to No.18 in the US Singles Charts.

On 16 May 1983 Jermaine reunited with **The Jacksons** to perform on Motown's 25th Anniversary Spectacular, which was shown on US NBC TV. This was a precursor of what was to come. For on 21 November 1983, Don King, the Jackson's promoter, called a press conference to announce an 18-city, 40-date tour by the band, which would be augmented by Jermaine, who was leaving Motown. Then in February 1974 Jermaine signed a new solo contract with Arista. Later in May that year he made a visit to the UK to promote his forthcoming album (9). On the tour he sang tracks from (9) to delegates at the World DJ Convention in London. To coincide with the UK visit, an UK-only 45, 'Sweetest, Sweetest' was released in June 1984. It climbed to No.57 in the UK, where the album was retitled, 'Dynamite'. In July 1984 Jermaine set out on the 'Victory' tour with the rest of **The Jacksons** to promote their latest album. This tour would be their swansong - they played their final date together at LA's Dodger Stadium on 9 December. Meanwhile Jermaine had consolidated his solo reputation when 'Dynamite', his first US 45 release on Arista, made No.15 back in September.

During 1985 Jermaine continued to make strides with his solo career, enjoying a big hit both sides of the Atlantic with 'Do What You Do'; a minor US and UK hit with 'When The Rain Begins To Fall', a duet he performed with actress/singer Pia Zadora taken from the film 'Voyage Of The Rock Aliens' and a further minor US hit with '(Closest Thing To) Perfect' from the Jamie Lee Curtis movie, 'Perfect'. He enjoyed two further US hits in 1986 'I Think It's Love' and 'Do You Remember Me?' and appears to have established his reputation as a solo artist beyond doubt.

La TOYA JACKSON

Albums

1	La Toya Jackson	(Polydor 6291) 1980
2	My Special Love	(Polydor 6328) 1981
3	Heart Don't Lie	(Private 1 39361) 1984

The Singles			Peak Position
Night Time Lover/Lonely Is She	(Polydor	1117) 1980	-
If You Feel The Funk/Lonely Is She	(Polydor	2137) 1980	103
Stay The Night/Camo Kucha Kaiai	(Polydor	2177) 1981	-
I Don't Want You To Go/Love Song	(Polydor	2188) 1981	-
Bet'cha Gonna Need My Lovin'/Bet'cha Gonna Need My Lovin' (instr.)	(Larc	81025) 198?	-
Heart Don't Lie/Without You	(Private 1 04439) 1984		56
Hot Potato/Think Twice	(Private 1 04572) 1984		-
He's A Pretender/How Do I Tell Them?	(Private 1 05783) 1984		-
Love Talk/Imagination (remix)	(Private 1 06040) 198?		-
You're Gonna Get Rocked/Does It Really Matter?	(RCA Victor 8689-7-R) 1988		-
Such A Wicked Love/Does It Really Matter?	(RCA Victor 8873-7-R) 1988		-

La Toya Jackson was born in Gary on 29 May 1956. She was the family's fifth oldest child and the second daughter. In May 1975 she joined **The Jacksons** temporarily after **The Jackson 5** left Motown and the band regrouped. Her solo career got under way when Polydor signed her in 1980 and (1) reached No.116 in the US Album Charts. 'If You Feel The Funk', from (1), also gave her a minor 45 hit. (2) followed in 1981. It peaked at No.175 in the US Album Charts. In June 1984 she signed to the Private 1 label and (3) rose to No.149 in the US Album Charts and 'Heart Don't Lie', taken from it, gave her more minor chart success. With **The Jacksons**' demise in 1984 La Toya still has to establish herself as a successful solo artist. She gained notoriety in 1992 with a book concerning life in the Jackson family including allegations of physical and psychological abuse, a theme later endorsed in an evasive fashion by brother Michael.

MARLON JACKSON

Album
1   Baby Tonight   (Capitol   ) 1987

The Singles
(Let Your Love Find) The Chosen One/Sardo And The Child   (Capitol 5675) 198?
Don't Go/Don't Go (instr.)   (Capitol 44047) 1987
Baby Tonight (video version)/Baby Tonight (radio edition)   (Capitol 44092) 1987
Lonely Eyes (Part 1)/(Part 2)   (Capitol 44122) 198?

Born in Gary on 12 March 1957, Marlon is the fourth of the Jackson brothers. From 1964-75 he was a member of **The Jackson 5** and from 1975 until their demise in December 1984 he played with The Jacksons. Since their demise he has been trying to establish himself as a solo artist. (1) peaked at No.188 in the US Album Charts and whilst 'Don't Go' and the title track met with success in the R & B chart they failed to make any impression nationally.

MICHAEL JACKSON

Albums
1	Got To Be There	(Motown 747) 1972
2	Ben	(Motown 755) 1972
3	Music and Me	(Motown 767) 1973
4	Forever, Michael	(Motown 825) 1975
5	The Best Of Michael Jackson	(Motown 851) 1975
6	Off The Wall	(Epic 35745) 1979
7	One Day In Your Life *	(Motown 956) 1981
8	Thriller	(Epic 38112) 1982
9	Farewell My Summer Love 1984 +	(Motown 6101) 1984
10	Michael Jackson and The Jackson 5 - 14 Greatest Hits o	(Motown 6099) 1984
11	Bad	(Epic 40600) 1987
12	The Michael Jackson Mix	(Epic) 1987 - UK only
13	Dangerous	(Epic 45400) 1991

* Comprised recordings from 1973-75. Four of the ten tracks are with **The Jackson 5**.
+ Features recordings from 1973.
o This picture disc featured nine cuts by **The Jackson 5** and five by Michael Jackson.
^ Featured old cuts by **The Jacksons** and **The Jackson 5**.

The Singles			Peak Position
Got To Be There/Maria	(Motown 1191) 1971	4
Rockin' Robin/Love Is Here And Now You're Gone	(Motown 1197) 1972	2
I Wanna Be Where You Are/We Got A Good Thing Goin'	(Motown 1202) 1972	16
Ben/You Can Cry On My Shoulder	(Motown 1207) 1972	1
With A Child's Heart/Morning Glow	(Motown 1218) 1973	50
We're Almost There/Take Me Back	(Motown 1341) 1975	54
Just A Little Bit Of You/Dear Michael	(Motown 1349) 1975	23
Ease On Down The Road/	(MCA 40947) 1978	41
You Can't Win (Part 1)/(Part 2)	(Epic 50654) 1979	81
Don't Stop 'Til You Get Enough/I Can't Help It	(Epic 50742) 1979	1
Rock With You/Working Day and Night	(Epic 50797) 1979	1
Off The Wall/Get On The Floor	(Epic 50838) 1980	10
She's Out Of My Life/Get On The Floor	(Epic 50871) 1980	10
One Day In Your Life/Take Me Back (a)	(Motown 1512) 1981	55
The Girl Is Mine/Can't Get Outta The Rain (b)(c)	(Epic 03288) 1982	2
Billie Jean/Can't Get Outta The Rain (c)	(Epic 03509) 1983	1
Beat It/Get On The Floor	(Epic 03759) 1983	1
Wanna Be Startin' Somethin' (Part 1)/(Part 2)	(Epic 03914) 1983	5

Human Nature/Baby Be Mine		(Epic 04026) 1983	7
P.Y.T. (Pretty Young Thing)/Working Day And Night		(Epic 04165) 1983	10
Say Say Say/Ode To A Koala Bear	(a)	(Columbia 04168) 1983	1
Thriller/Can't Get Outta The Rain		(Epic 04364) 1984	4
Farewell My Summer Love/Call On Me	(d)	(Motown 1739) 1984	38
I Just Can't Stop Loving You/Baby Be Mine		(Epic 07253) 1987	1
Bad/I Can't Help It		(Epic 07418) 1987	1
The Way You Make Me Feel/The Way You Make Me Feel (instr.)		(Epic 07645) 1987	1
Man In The Mirror/Man In The Mirror (instr.)		(Epic 07668) 1988	1
Get It/Get It (Instr.)	(e)	(Mowtown 1930) 1988	80
Dirty Diana/Dirty Diana (instr.)		(Epic 07739) 1988	1
Another Part Of Me/Another Part Of Me (instr.)		(Epic 07962) 1988	11
Smooth Criminal (Part 1)/ (Part 2)		(Epic 08044) 1988	7
Black Or White/ ?		(Epic 74100) 1991	1
Remember The Time/ ?		(Epic 74200) 1992	3
In The Closet/ ?		(Epic 74266) 1992	6
Jam/ ?		(Epic 74333) 1992	26
Heal The World/ ?		(Epic 74790) 1992	52
Who Is It?/ ?		(Epic 74406) 1992	14
Will You Be There/ ?		(Epic 77060) 1993	7

(a) Recorded back in 1975.   (b) With Paul McCartney.
(c) The 'A' sides were also issued as one-sided budget releases.
(d) A remix of a recording from 31 August 1973.
(e) A duet with Stevie Wonder taken from his 'Characters' LP.

Michael Jackson was born in Gary on 29 August 1958, the seventh of nine children. His parents were quick to note his musical ability and soon set about trying to promote it. By the age of 5 he was performing 'Climb Every Mountain' to his kindergarten class. In 1964 along with four of his brothers, Jackie, Tito, Jermaine and Marlon, he became a member of The Jackson 5.

Berry Gordy signed the group to his Motown label and the family relocated to Encino in California. In December 1971, with The Jackson 5 already enjoying phenomenal success, Motown signed him as a solo artist. His debut 45, a ballad, 'Got To Be There', brought him immediate chart success and Diana Ross was on hand to promote him - he appeared on her TV Special 'Diana' and the two became lifelong friends. In March 1972 his debut album (1) peaked at No. 14 in the US and later in May of the same year it climbed to No.37 in the UK. Meanwhile he enjoyed a hit with UK-only release, 'Ain't No Sunshine', which had previously flopped for Bill Withers.

Greater success was to follow. (2) made No.5 in the US and 17 in the UK. The title track, another ballad, had been written for a movie, 'Ben' (which was a film about a trained rat) by American composer Waller Scharf and UK lyricist Don Black, who had suggested that Michael Jackson should sing the vocals on the song.

(3) and (4) were disappointing in comparison peaking only at 92 and 101 in the US Album Charts. (4) was his last official Motown release and when The Jackson 5 left Motown for Epic Michael Jackson also signed a solo deal with Epic, although he did not record another album until 1979. Meanwhile Motown released the first of many Jackson compilation LPs, (5) which could only manage No. 156 in the US Charts. Motown also continued to issue relatively unsuccessful Michael Jackson singles.

In July 1977 Jackson was chosen to play the Scarecrow in a movie version of the musical 'The Wiz', which was itself a successful stage adaptation of The Wizard Of Oz. During filming Jackson stayed at his sister, La Toya's, Manhattan apartment. He also met producer, Quincy Jones professionally through the project. Jones was responsible for its soundtrack. The film soundtrack was released on MCA in October 1978 and his duet, 'Ease On Down The Road' with Diana Ross gave them another minor Transatlantic hit.

(6), which Jackson had spend six months recording, was produced by Quincy Jones and released in August 1979. Peaking at 3 in the US and 5 in the UK it went on to sell over ten million copies worldwide. It also spawned four massive hits:- 'Don't Stop 'Til You Get Enough', 'Rock With You', 'Off The Wall' and 'She's Out Of My Life'. (6) put Jackson at the forefront of a new dance craze. On 27 February 1980 he received his first Grammy Award when 'Don't Stop 'Til You Get Enough' won the Best R & B Performance Award.

In May 1981, on the wave of Jackson's success, Motown released (7), which was compiled of recordings from the 1973-75 era. The album peaked at only 144 in the US and the title track was only a minor hit but over in the UK the single received considerable airplay and actually became his first UK No.1 the following month. Meanwhile Jackson, who had rejoined **The Jacksons** for their 'Triumph' tour, collapsed from exhaustion whilst touring in New Orleans, Louisiana, but he soon recovered. Over in England his popularity continued to go from strength to strength. Motown released a follow-up 45, 'We're Almost There', which made No.46, (5) was remarketed in the UK and climbed to No.11 whilst (7) finally peaked at No.29. The year concluded with Michael Jackson calling Paul McCartney to propose that they write and record songs together. As a result McCartney travelled to LA to record 'The Girl Is Mine' with Jackson.

In August 1982 Jackson and producer, Quincy Jones, began work on (8) at Westlake Studios, LA, with an impressive array of session musicians. The title track was written by former Heatwave writer Rod Temperton who Jones had asked to write some material for the album. (8), which was produced by Jones and engineered by Bruce Swedien, was finally released in December 1982. If 'Off The Wall' was a mega-success, the world had seen nothing yet. 'Thriller' became the most successful record of all time, breaking all previous sales records along the way. It sold over 40 million copies worldwide, made the No.1 spot in all Western countries, including the UK and US (where it topped the charts for 37 weeks - another record). It also went on to receive a record 12 Grammy nominations.

For most of 1983 Jackson fed off its success. The first single taken from it was 'The Girl Is Mine', which Jackson had recorded with McCartney back in late December 1981. It peaked at No.2 in the US and 10 in the UK prompting Jackson to make a flying visit to London to record some songs for Paul McCartney's upcoming LP. Arguably, though, it was his next 45 release, 'Billie Jean', that transformed the fortunes of the album itself. Coming complete with a slick video featuring self-choreographed dancesteps, it spent seven weeks at No.1 in the US and, not only did it perhaps mark a giant leap in Jackson's own career, it had a significant and lasting impact on modern music. It also peaked at No.1 in the UK. His next bullet was 'Beat It', on which Eddie Van Halen played lead guitar at the invitation of Quincy Jones (in fact he played for free). Once again accompanied by a slick video featuring group dance routines it was a monster US No.1 and made No.3 in the UK. Other hits from the album were, 'Wanna Be Startin' Something', the ballad, 'Human Nature', 'Say Say Say' (which was recorded with Paul McCartney and taken from his 'Piper Of Peace' LP) and finally the title track itself, which made No.10 in the UK six months ahead of its US release.

1983 had also witnesses the release of the LP, 'E.T. - The Extra Terrestrial' on MCA back in February. Jackson and Jones had begun work on this Spielberg movie back in June 1982. Apart from containing a previously unreleased Jackson cut, the album came with a souvenir booklet including pictures of Jackson cuddling E.T. The album made No.82 in the UK. Motown had also dug deep in their archives of Michael Jackson material again releasing a 45, 'Happy' which bummed in the US but climbed to 52 in the UK.

1983 had been a stupendously successful year for Jackson and as it drew to a close the future looked decidedly rosy for him. On 2 December MTV screened the full length version of his 'Thriller' video for the first time and later that month he announced a $5 million sponsorship deal with Pepsi Cola that didn't even involve him having to hold or drink a can of Pepsi in any promotion. He also had a nine singles set released in the UK and these even peaked at No.66 in the UK chart.

He met with a reversal early in 1984 when he was admitted to hospital on 26 January after his scalp got burnt following an accidental flare explosion whilst filming a Pepsi commercial. The ad was premiered on US MTV on 27 February that year. Meanwhile, Jackson was raking in the awards. He received an unprecedented eight Grammy awards linked to 'Thriller' projects the next day having received several Guinness World Records for sales of the album earlier in the month. He also won several Best Video awards at the second annual American Video Awards ceremony on 5 April and to coincide with this a new video, 'The Making Of Michael Jackson's Thriller' was released in the US and UK which featured the full length 'Thriller' video, produced by Jon Landis, as well as 'Beat It', 'Billie Jean' and hitherto unseen rehearsal clips. It soon became the best selling video to date. Indeed Jackson had become so successful some people were getting thoroughly sick and tired of him. On 27 April 1984 W-WSH, a Philadelphia radio station, broadcast a 'No Michael Jackson Weekend'. Around the same time Jackson went back to hospital to get further scalp and facial laser surgery following his accident back in January. However, he was soon back in the limelight visiting the White House in June to receive a Presidential Award from President and Mrs. Reagan. For the ceremony Jackson wore a jacket he'd been given by New York elevator operator, Hector Cormana. Meanwhile Motown, continuing their search for old material to re-release, came up with 'Farewell My Summer Love', (a re-mix of a recording from 31 August 1973), which was actually a bigger hit in the UK where it make the Top Ten and (9), an album of the same name which again did better in the UK, where it peaked at No.9 as against No.46 in the US. They also put out (10) which made No.168 in the US.

For the remainder of 1984 Jackson effectively put his solo career on ice to rejoin **The Jacksons** for their 'Victory' LP and related tour. Plagued with financial and organisational problems it brought him considerable hassle and a number of death threats. He enjoyed a minor UK hit in August with another Motown release, 'Girl You're So Together' which made No.33 and also appeared on his brother Jermaine's latest LP, 'Jermaine Jackson' sharing vocals with him on 'Tell Me I'm Not Dreaming'.

On the recording front 1985 was a quiet year for Jackson, witnessing no new singles or album releases. However, he still attracted plenty of publicity. After the success of the Band Aid single in the UK he co-wrote the US version with Lionel Richie, 'We Are The World', for star collection USA For Africa in the January. On 3 March he visited London to see the inauguration of his waxwork lookalike in Madame Tussauds, bringing traffic to a standstill as he jumped on to his car to wave to crowds. He also called in on the Abbey Road recording studios. In July he began work on a 15-minute space fantasy film, with George Lucas as his producer, in California. Called 'Captain Ed' with Jackson playing the star role, Disneyland/World were given exclusive distribution rights and built new movie theatres at both the Disneyland and Disneyworld sites to show the film. It was eventually premiered at Disneyland in September 1986 and featured Jackson performing a previously unreleased dance number he had written called, 'We Are Just Here To Save The World'. On 14 August 1985 he outbid all comers (including Paul McCartney and Yoko Ono) to secure the ATV music publishing catalogue at a cost of $47.5 million. This gave him the rights over 250 Lennon and McCartney song which was thought to cool his relationship with McCartney.

1986 began quietly for Jackson, too, but in March a second deal was struck with Pepsi for 15 million dollars. The terms included two further commercials and sponsorship of a world solo tour. Then on 4 August he went along with his co-producer, Quincy Jones, his pet 300-pound snake, Crusher, and Bubbles, his chimpanzee into Westlake studios to record (11). In November he shot a 17-minute video mini-film at various locations in New York for the title cut from (11).

As he'd become increasingly successful Jackson had become more eccentric. In September 1986 he bought his own oxygen chamber to prolong his life span. Then on 29 May 1987 he offered the London Hospital $50,000 (an offer he later doubled) to buy the remains of the 'Elephant Man', John Merrick. The hospital held firm rejecting all his offers. Jackson has consistently and vehemently denied both of these stories. When (11) was finally previewed on 13 July 1987 fifty of the biggest record retail heads were invited to his mansion at Encino to a dinner and tour of his home hosted mainly by La Toya Jackson and Joe Jackson. Michael himself just made a brief appearance to pose for photographers.

In August, the first single from the LP, a ballad duet with Siedah Garrett, 'I Just Can't Stop Loving You' was released. It went on to top both the US and UK charts. Later on 31 August the 17-minute 'Bad' video was shown on a US CBS TV special, 'Michael Jackson - The Magic Returns'. When (11) was finally released on the same day it entered both the US and UK charts at No.1. To help promote the album Jackson embarked on a solo world tour which commenced with a concert at the 38,000-capacity Korakuen Stadium in Tokyo on 12 September 1987. The tour went on to Australia (where some concerts were cancelled due to poor ticket sales), the US, Canada, the UK and Europe. Lasting over a year it became the biggest grossing tour of all time. Jackson's staff for this tour numbered over 250, including his own chef and hairdresser! The tour kept Jackson in the news and the hits continued to flow. The title cut from (11), which Jackson had written and co-produced himself, and follow-up, 'The Way You Make Me Feel' both made No.1 in the US and No.3 in the UK. In the UK also a TV compilation, 'Love Songs', credited to Michael Jackson and Diana Ross, peaked at No.15. Another UK-only release was (12), which consisted of old solo and Jackson 5 hits. It peaked at No.27.

On 26 March 1988 Jackson was topping the US charts again with 'Man In The Mirror', which had been written by Siedah Garrett. This was his fourth US No.1 from (11) although it didn't quite make the UK Top 20. He enjoyed more minor chart success in May 1988 with a duet, 'Get It', which he'd recorded with Stevie Wonder, which was taken from Stevie's 'Characters' LP. On 2 July 1988 he became the first artist ever to enjoy five US No.1 singles from one album when 'Dirty Diana' became his fifth No.1 from (11). The month before, incidentally, his Video compilation, 'The Legend Continues' had become the best-selling UK music video ever at that time outselling 'The Making Of Michael Jackson's Thriller'. On top of this, all his Epic LPs re-entered the UK charts and his autobiography, 'Moonwalk', in which Jackson stated his belief that he was one of the loneliest people in the world, was published. Now phenominally popular in the UK, Jackson played a record seven sell-out concerts at Wembley Stadium in July and presented Prince Charles and Princess Diana with a substantive sum towards The Prince's Trust Charity at one of them. During his stay he also visited Hamleys toy store, (where he bought a doll of himself), and the HMV record store. He returned again in September to play a further series of concerts, including one at Aintree Race Course. A limited UK-only five singles souvenir pack, 'Bad', was released amidst this Jacksonmania and it crept into the UK charts at No.99. Before the year was over Jackson had released two further 45s from (11), 'Another Part Of Me' and 'Smooth Criminal' and a film, 'Moonwalker' in which Jackson starred opened in December 1988 for general release in the US and UK. US sales of (11) topped six million.

Following this blaze of publicity Jackson withdrew to regroup. Always reclusive he continued to be a focus for tabloid speculation, especially in the UK. An obvious target was his plastic surgery operations. Jackson persists in asserting he has had very little done though his nose is clearly revised. In 1991 he released (13) amidst great hype. The first single, 'Black Or White', including lead guitar from Guns & Roses guitarist, Izzy Stradlin, was an enormous hit world-wide. Supported by a superb video it shot to No.1 in the US and remained there for seven weeks picking up a platinum award along the way. The video caused considerable controversy highlighting as it did Jackson's new 'white' skin. Accusations flew that Jackson was turning himself into a white man, (ironic given the title of the single). Jackson claims that he has a rare pigmentation disease which causes blacks to become increasingly pale. Whatever the reality, the fans didn't care - the hits flowed as ever from the new album, six in all, of which three made the Top Ten. The album sold over five million in America alone.

1993 was to be a difficult year for Jackson. After lengthy preparations the 'Dangerous' world tour commenced. The tour was dogged by illness and cancellations reaching a peak when stories broke in the American and European press concerning his personal life. Jackson was accused by a young boy of sexual abuse. The allegations have led to a series of conflicting outbursts and statements by members of the family. La Toya has joined the ranks of the accusers and other members of the family say she's a liar and are lending their support to Michael. His record label (Epic) and sponsor (Pepsi) both made supportive statements though Jackson's deal with Pepsi was to lapse in any event after the 'Dangerous' tour. As pressure mounted Jackson's health deteriorated and the tour was finally cancelled amidst stories of Jackson's addiction to pain killing drugs. At the time of writing the world was waiting with bated breath for Jackson to return to America where police investigations continue.

All this speculation notwithstanding, Jackson has become the most successful solo artist ever in the history of popular music. His talent and creativity are beyond question and his leanings toward rock over the past decade pose further interesting questions for Jackson's direction as the '90s progress, always assuming he weathers the present storms in his life.

REBBIE JACKSON

Album
1   Centipede   (Columbia 39238) 1984

Born Maureen Jackson in Gary on 29 May 1950, 'Rebbie' was the eldest of the Jackson children. (1) peaked at No.63 in the US Album Charts and the title cut (Columbia 04547), which was written and produced by Michael Jackson, made No.24 in the US Singles Charts the same year.

JERICHO

A '70s outfit from Mishawaka. Their sole vinyl offering was one 45, 'Possessed/People Of Lies' (Royal Knight 187). It came in a picture sleeve.

JESSIE AND THE JOKERS

Personnel	Ex	To
BOB BROWN		
FURMAN BROWN		
JESSIE COBURN		
DAVE HALL		
JERRY HALL		
LARRY SCOTT		
CHUCK WALLACE		

An early '60s Indianapolis act which didn't make it onto vinyl.

THE JETSONS

EP
1(A)   The Jetsons   (Gulcher GULCH 202) 1981

Personnel			Ex	To
MO JETSON	dr	A		
ASTRO JETSON	gtr	A		
JAMIE JETSON	voc	A		UNATTACHED
MANON JETSON	gtr	A		
CREEP JETSON	bs	A		

A new-wave band unconnected with the later punk band from Missouri. (1) was a three track affair and included the cute title, 'Genetically Stupid'. A different track from these three also appears on the 'Red Snerts' compilation (GULCH 102) issued in 1981.

JEWEL

<u>Album</u>
1   Cut 'n' Polished   (Erect   ) 1982

A cutting rhythm and blues band who are a popular club act.

THE JIANTS

Came out of Marion with 'Tornado/She's My Woman' (Claudra CL-112) during the 1960s. The 'A' side has since resurfaced on the 1990 compilation, 'The Madness Invasion, Vol.3'(GMG 75036) 1988.

JIMMY AND THE EXCEPTIONS

Personnel	Ex	To
JIMMY BOWERS	DEL & THE ROADRUNNERS	
DEL BAILEY	See DEL & THE ROADRUNNERS	
WILLIE PHILIPS	DEL & THE ROADRUNNERS	
GUY TARRENTS	See EPICS/INNER CIRCLE	

Hailed from Indianapolis in the mid-'60s where they were a popular live attraction. No recording output.

J.O.T.

<u>Album</u>
1(A) Hooray, J.O.T. - Live and Tasty   (   ) 1988

<u>Cassette</u>
1(A) Your Pals   (   ) 1986

Personnel			Ex	To
TOM WATTS	voc	A		
VESS RUHTENBERG	gtr	A		ANTENNA
ANDY ANGRICK	bs	A		
JIM BLACK	dr	A		

These rockers also appear on the Hit City Records compilation, 'Black Brittle Frizbee' with a couple of cuts.

THE KASTAWAYS

This was actually La Porte's Rivieras recording under another name. One 45 resulted, 'Sweets For My Sweet/You Never Say' (Riviera 1404) circa 1964.

THE KATALINAS

Personnel		Ex	To
DICK NEAT	AB		
RONNIE SCHROCK	AB		
GIL WORK	AB		
GARY GILLESPIE	B	solo	

A popular Indianapolis club act in the early '60s. Gillespie later joined as a vocalist.

KEETIE AND THE KASUALS

Personnel		Ex	To
DAVE KELLIE	AB	KEETIE AND THE KATS	

GARY LeMASTER	AB	
KEITH PHILLIPS	AB	KEETIE AND THE KATS
BILL SETTLES	AB	KEETIE AND THE KATS
DONNY SANDERS	AB	KEETIE AND THE KATS
BOB SNYDER	B	TOMMY DORSEY ORCHESTRA

A later version of the Indianapolis-based **Keetie And The Kats** dating from 1963. This mob didn't make it onto vinyl. Keith Phillips is no longer involved in the music business - he owns an English-style pub and restaurant in Anaheim, California. Donny Sanders later relocated to Nashville where he works in recording studios.

KEETIE AND THE KATS

Personnel		Ex	To
DAVE ELLMAN	ABC		THE DAWNBEATS
LARRY LEE	ABCD		THE DAWNBEATS
KEITH PHILIPS	ABCD		KEETIE AND THE KASUALS
BILL ROOKER	A		
NORM SHAFEY	B		
LARRY (WAZOO) GARDNER	C		THE DAWNBEATS
JOHN SCOTT	C		THE SPORTSMEN
DAVE KELLIE	D		KEETIE AND THE KASUALS
BILL SETTLES	D		KEETIE AND THE KASUALS
DONNY SANDERS	D		KEETIE AND THE KASUALS

Line-up A 1958: Line-up B 1959: Line-up C 1959: Line-up D 1960.

This Indianapolis-based instrumental combo started out in 1958. Keetie was a great showman on the drums and they were a popular live attraction. They later made it onto vinyl recording three 45s during the '60s:- 'That's The Way/Dreamer's Romance' (K-W 503); 'Move Part One/Move Part Two' for K-Records and 'Way Out/Crossties' (Huron 22007). The first was recorded with vocalist Jimmy Clendening. They later evolved into **Keetie And The Kasuals**.

JIM KENNEDY AND THE SATANS

Personnel incl:	Ex	To
JIM KENNEDY		

Released one 45, 'Hey Baby/Always Searching' (Skoop 1064) in the 1960s.

KHAZAD DOOM

Album
1(A) Level 6 1/2   (LPL 892) 1970
NB. This was repressed in the late '80s.

Personnel			Ex	To
JACK EADON	ld.gtr,voc,perc	A		
STEVE 'CROW' HILKIN	perc,voc	A		
TOM SIEVERS	bs,voc	A		
AL YATES	voc,KB	A		

This group was based in Gary and its progressive album (which dealers often misleadingly present as psychedelic), was very rare, although its limited repress a few years back should make it easier to get hold of a copy. It's worth a listen but don't pay megabucks for the pleasure. The better tracks are 'Nothing To Fear', quite a commercial song with appealing vocals and lots of atmosphere; 'In This World', a harmonic soft rock song and 'Excerpt From The Hunters, The Prelude', a long progressive piece with lots of keyboards. The group actually formed back in 1963 and took their name from the city in Middle Earth created in J.R.R. Tolkien's 'Lord Of The Rings'.

KILLING CHILDREN

<u>EP</u>
1( ) Certain Death   (Gravel Voice   ) 1983

A band from Columbus who can also be heard on a Gravel Voice compilation album, 'Columbus Compilation' issued in 1983.

THE KINSEY REPORT

<u>Albums</u>
1(A) Edge Of The City   (Alligator AL 4758) 1987
2(A) Midnight Drive   (Alligator AL 4775) 1989
3(A) Powerhouse   (Point Blank/Charisma 91421) 1991
4(A) Crossing Bridges   (Point Blank/Charisma 87004) 1993

<u>Personnel</u>			<u>Ex</u>	<u>To</u>
DONALD KINSEY	gtr	A	WHITE LIGHTNIN'	
KENNETH KINSEY	bs	A		
RALPH KINSEY	dr	A		

A blend of funk and blues/rock from the sons of the Chicago blues-man, Big Daddy Kinsey. They are based in Gary (best known for the Jackson family) and work regularly in New York clubs. After two albums for the successful Alligator label they signed with Point Blank, distributed by the resurrected Charisma label. Good stuff if you like whiskey in your music.

KNIGHTSMEN

<u>Personnel</u>		<u>Ex</u>	<u>To</u>
ROB McCOY	voc,dr		
GARY IRWIN	dr		
TOM REA	ld.gtr		
DONALD LEE	gtr		
KARL HINKLE	bs		
DAVID LEE	o		

Came out of Indianapolis with 'Let Love Come Between Us/Gimme A Little Sign' (Irwin Productions 135) during the 1960s. Just 500 copies were pressed.

THE KNOTS

A Muncie-based '60s outfit whose sole release was one 45, 'What A Shame/You Girl' (Baus 855).

THE KURSED

<u>Cassette</u>
1   The Kursed   (   ) 1989

Formed in Hobart as The Astral Zombies. Hardcore outfit of limited appeal.

TOMMY LAM

A popular Indianapolis-based singer during the '50s and '60s who fronted his own band and sang with many local groups.

THE LAMBERTS

A New Haven band whose sole platter was, 'Darling Now You're Gone/ ? ' (Ben 6739) in the 1960s.

LAST FOUR (4) DIGITS

EP
1(A) Big Picture   (Hardly Records 000001-R) 1981

Personnel			Ex	To
S.V. GRIDGESBY	gtr	A		
J. KOSS	dr	AB		
M. SHEETS	bs,gtr	AB		
R. WORTH	gtr	A		
A. XAX	syn	AB		solo/JOHN WAYNE BAND
MR. SCIENCE	gtr	B	DOW JONES & THE INDUSTRIALS	
J. HUFFAKER	gtr	B		

An Indianapolis-based band. (1) has four cuts, 'Fast Friends/City Streets/Coughing Up Blood/Another Sex Crime'. In addition they appear on the 'Red Snerts' compilation (Gulcher GULCH 102) also in 1981, with another cut, 'Diddy Wah Diddy'. They worked for a time latterly as The Last Five Digits.

LAUGHTERHOUSE

Nicely named hardcore band who can be found on the 'Children Of The Corn' compilation on Sonic Iguana Records issued in 1990.

THE LAZY COWGIRLS

Albums
1( )	The Lazy Cowgirls	(Restless	72078) 1985
2(A)	Tapping The Source	(Bomp	BLP 4025) 1987
3( )	Third Time's The Charm (mini LP - live in Australia)	(Grown Up Wrong	) 1988
4( )	Radio Cowgirl (live)	(Sympathy	001) 1988
5( )	How It Looks, How It Is	(Sympathy	039) 1990
6( )	Another Long Goodbye	(Sympathy	) 1993

EPs
1	The Long Goodbye	(Sympathy	025) 1989
2	There's A New Girl In Town	(Sympathy	122) 1991

NB: Sympathy = Sympathy For The Record Industry Records.
NB2: (3) later issued by Dog Meat as a CD including unissued stuff.

Personnel			Ex	To
DOUG PHILLIPS	gtr,slg	AB	COTTONWOOD	
PAT TODD	voc	AB		
ALLEN CLARK	dr,voc	A		DIZBUSTER/FEARLESS LEADER
KEITH TELLIGMAN	gtr,voc	A		ENEMIES/DIZBUSTER
ED HUERTA	dr	B	JACK BREWER BAND	
MICHAEL LEIGH	bs	B		

In reality a male quartet, and certainly not lazy, the band were formed in Vincennes in Southern Indiana but moved to Culver City, California in the early days. In a perfect world they would have appeared in 'Volume 1' of the 'Rock History' but slipped through the net. In addition to the above, there are non-LP 45s on Bomp and Sub Pop, an EP on IK Records as well as a cut on 'Sounds Of Now', a compilation on Dionysus (ID1-23305) issued in 1987. At least one of the band went on to the delightfully named Sacred Miracle Cave. If you are looking for influences, try The Stooges, New York Dolls, MC 5 et al. The band have a hot live reputation but have yet to catch quite the same spirit on their studio albums.

KENNY LEE AND THE ROYALS

Personnel				Ex	To
JERRY COLLINS	gtr		AB	See DEL & THE ROADRUNNERS	
PAUL GRAY	gtr		AB		DOMINOS
EDDIE GREEN	dr		A	See DEL & THE ROADRUNNERS	
KENNY LEE KERNOLDE	voc		AB		
LARRY GOSHEN	dr		B	THE CRACKERJACKS	THE SPORTSMEN

A popular live attraction around the Indianapolis nightclubs in the early '60s.

BOBBY LEWIS

Title		Peak Position
Tossin' And Turnin'/Oh Yes I Love You	(Beltone 1002) 1961	1
One Track Mind/Are You Ready?	(Beltone 1012) 1961	9
What A Walk/Cry No More	(Beltone 1015) 1961	77
Mamie In The Afternoon/Yes, Oh Yes It Did	(Beltone 1016) 1962	110
I'm Tossin' And Turnin' Again/Nothin' But The Blues	(Beltone 2023) 1962	98
A Man's Gotta Be A Man/Day By Day I Need Your Love	(Beltone 2018) 1962	-
Lonely Teardrops/Boom A Chick Chick	(Beltone 2026) 1962	-
Intermission/Nothin' But The Blues	(Beltone 2035) 1963	-

Born in Indianapolis on 17 February 1933 Bobby stayed there until he was 12 when he was adopted and taken from the orphanage he had grown up in by a Detroit family. He first recorded for the Parrot label in 1956. He enjoyed four hit singles - the number one topped the charts for seven weeks.

LIGHT

Albums		
1( ) Keys	(Abintra) 1981	
2( ) Light	(Abintra 13731) 198?	

An Indianapolis band. No other data available.

LIMOUSINE

Album	
1(A) Limousine	(GSF 1002) 1972

Personnel			Ex	To
JOHN CASCELLA	sax,KB	A	CHOSEN FEW	FAITH BAND
CARL STORIE	voc	A	CHOSEN FEW	FAITH BAND
DAVE BARNES	dr	A	CHOSEN FEW	FAITH BAND
DAVE BENNETT	gtr	A	CHOSEN FEW	FAITH BAND
MARK CAWLEY	bs	A		FAITH BAND

An Indianapolis quintet who, for the most part, had been **The Chosen Few**. (1) is fairly pedestrian stuff (no pun intended!), and they changed their name yet again and enjoyed some national success as **The Faith Band**.

BRAD LONG

This '60s style rocker had a 45, 'Love Me Again/Come To Me' on Music Stand Records in 1978 and also appeared on the Voxx compilation, 'Battle Of The Garages' (200.006) in 1982. An album was rumoured for Bomp/Voxx but never appeared. Brad was based in Logansport and worked extensively with bassist, Chuck De Ford. He later worked with a band called Tobias.

LORD AND THE FLIES

This '60s outfit seems to have spent time in both Indiana and Chicago. They released two 45s: 'You Made A Fool Of Me/Come What May' (USA 828) 1966 and 'Echoes/Come What May' (USA 857) 1967. 'Echoes' can be found on 'Mindrockers, Vol.5' (Line LLP 5207 AS).

THE LORDS OF LONDON

Personnel	Ex	To
HARRY CANGANY		
MARTY LAMBERT		
MIKE LEKSE		
RICHIE MEDVESCEK		
FRANK WECHSLER		

Formed in 1966 this combo made two unsuccessful stabs for stardom:- 'Time Waits For No One/Cornflakes And Ice Cream' (Decca 32196) 1967 and 'Broken Heart Of C.O.D./Sit Down Dance' (Domain 1421), probably circa 1966/67.

THE LOST SOULS

Personnel	Ex	To
DANNY DAIN		
CHARLEY HINKLE		
JOHN MOORE		
PHIL THOMPSON		THE HEAVY
DAVE TRUEBLOOD		

A 1967 combo with no recording output.

LYNYRDS INNARDS

Cassette
1( )	Hell Clown		( )	1989

EP
1( )	Swimsuit Issue EP		(Full On)	1991

An amusingly named rock band from Valparaiso who frequently worked the Bloomingdale/Chicago clubs. They can also be heard on the Sockeye tribute album, 'We Suck Worse' (Thought Balloon Records) issued in 1993.

LONNIE MACK

Albums
1	The Wham Of The Memphis Man	(Fraternity 1014)	1963
2	Memphis Sound	(Spin)	19??
3	Glad I'm In The Band	(Elektra 74040)	1969
4	Whatever's Right	(Elektra 74050)	1969
5	For Collectors Only (The Wham...) (reissue of (1))	(Elektra 74077)	1970
6	The Hills Of Indiana	(Elektra 74102)	1971
7	Home At Last	(Capitol ST 11619)	1977
8	Lonnie Mack And Pismo	(Capitol ST 11703)	1977
9	Strike Like Lightning (incl. S.R. Vaughn)	(Alligator 4739)	1985
10	Second Sight	(Alligator 4750)	1986
11	Roadhouses And Dance Halls	(Alligator/Epic)	1988
12	Live - Attack Of The Killer 'V'	(Alligator 4786)	1990

Lonnie was born Lonnie McIntosh on 18 July 1941 in Aurora. He first came to prominence in the Summer of 1963 when, at the end of someone else's recording session at King Studios in Cincinnati, Ohio, he recorded an instrumental version of 'Memphis', a Chuck

Berry composition. Its rhythmic guitar style took him straight into the Top Ten and he subsequently enjoyed a number of lesser hits. Full details of his 45s for Fraternity are set out below:-

Title			Peak Position
Memphis/Down In The Dumps	(Fraternity 906)	1963	5
Wham!/Susie-Q	(Fraternity 912)	1963	24
Baby, What's Wrong/Where There's A Will	(Fraternity 918)	1963	93/113
Lonnie On The Move/Say Something Nice To Me	(Fraternity 920)	1964	117
I've Had It/Nashville	(Fraternity 925)	1964	128
Chicken Pickin'/Sa-Ba-Hoola	(Fraternity 932)	1964	-
Don't Make Me Baby Blue/Georgia Boy	(Fraternity 938)	1964	-
Honky Tonk '65/Chicken Pickin'	(Fraternity 951)	1965	78
Crying Over You/Coastin'	(Fraternity 942)	1965	-
Tonky Go Go/When I'm Alone	(Fraternity 946)	1965	-
Crying Over You/Are You Guilty?	(Fraternity 957)	1965	-
Bucaroo/The Circus	(Fraternity 959)	1966	-
Tension (Part 1)/(Part 2)	(Fraternity 967)	1966	-
Wildwood Flower/Snow On The Mountain	(Fraternity 969)	1966	-
I Left My Heart In San Francisco/Omaha	(Fraternity 981)	1967	-
Save Your Money/Snow On The Mountain	(Fraternity 986)	1967	-
Soul Express/Down And Out	(Fraternity 1004)	1968	-
All We Need Is Love You And Me/Highway 56	(Roulette 7175)	1975	-

They were mostly rockabilly-styled instrumentals and an album (1) in a similar genre was also released in 1963. It made No.103 in the Billboard Album Charts. After enjoying a few months in the limelight Lonnie vanished from prominence for a five year period during which time he played one-nighters around the Midwest and South. Following a review of his album in 'Rolling Stone' Elektra bought the rights to it and also paid for him to record (3) and (4), which added funk to his raunchy rockabilly style with vocals that owed much to black gospel influences. For (6) he befriended Don Nix, the producer and former Mar-keys sax man, and the resulting album was in a softer, country style. Essentially, a shy man, though, Lonnie bowed out of the music business for what he described as 'religious' reasons and retreated back to Indiana where he drove a truck for a while. During this period he continued to cut various singles including one for Roulette, 'Highway 56' in 1975, which was produced by Troy Seals (now a country star). He recorded two albums for Capitol in 1977 - on the first he was assisted by former members of Area Code 615.

After an eight year lay off he returned in 1985 and began a string of albums for Alligator. This shy, retiring, figure has nonetheless guaranteed himself a place in rock history as an interesting guitarist and vocalist.

MADSON

This was actually Indiana's Olivers, who recorded in Chicago using a different name. They have one cut, 'I Saw What You Did', dating from July 1967, on the 'Colour Dreams' (Antar GONE 1) 1986 compilation.

MALIGNANT PIGS

Personnel		Ex	To
CHRIS SMITH	gtr		DRY ROT
STEVE BAHNWEG	dr,voc		DRY ROT
WILLIE HODGES	bs,voc		DRY ROT

A punk band from Richmond operating during mid-1990. Changed their name to Dry Rot.

MASON PROFFIT

Emerged out of Sounds Unlimited who were originally from Indiana. Sounds Unlimited later relocated to Chicago, Illinois and both bands are covered in our 'Chicago/Illinois' volume.

MATH BATS

<u>Albums</u>
1( )	Bat Day	(Private Pressing)	1984
2( )	Math Bats	(Private Pressing)	1985

An '80s new psych outfit who briefly attracted some attention from connoisseurs of the genre.

JEFF McDONALD

<u>Albums</u>
1	Thank You Lonesome Picker	(Homecoming	) 1986
2	Characters	(Hoot Mon	) 1987

A singer-songwriter. (2) may have been a cassette-only release.

ME AND THEM GUYS

<u>Personnel</u>		<u>Ex</u>	<u>To</u>
MARTY BAKER	o		
ROD KERSEY	dr		
STEVE MICHAEL	gtr		
STEVE PRITCHARD	gtr		
CRAIG TERRY	bs		

This mid-'60s high school combo formed in Greencastle in 1965, where they soon became a local dance hall attraction. They also played regularly at nearby Perdue and Depaux universities and recorded their only single, 'I Love Her So/Somethin' Else' (Gre-TTe 101) at Jan Eden Studios in Indianapolis in 1966. The flip was apparently a Kinks-influenced instrumental. You can check out the 'A' side on 'Back From The Grave, Vol.3' (Crypt CR-003) 1986. It has a rather nice organ backing with spoken vocals.

MECHT MENSCH

A punk bank from Columbus who can be heard on the 'Master Tapes 2' compilation on Affirmation issued in 1983.

JOHN COUGAR MELLENCAMP

<u>Albums</u>
1	Chestnut Street Incident	(MCA	2225) 1976
2	A Biography	(Riva	) 1978
3	Johnny Cougar (with Streetheart)	(Riva	RVLP 6) 1979
4	Night Dancing - John Cougar	(Riva	7401) 1979
5	Nothing Matters, And What If It Did	(Riva	7403) 1980
6	American Fool (With Zone)	(Riva	7501) 1982
7	The Kid Inside	(Main Man	601) 1983
8	Uh-Huh (1st as John Cougar Mellencamp)	(Riva	7504) 1983
9	Scarecrow	(Riva	824.865) 1985
10	The Lonesome Jubilee	(Mercury	832.465) 1987
11	Big Daddy	(Mercury	883.220) 1989
12	Whenever We Wanted	(Mercury	510.151) 1991
13	Falling From Grace (original Soundtrack)	(Mercury	451.200) 1992
14	Human Wheels	(Mercury	518.088) 1993

<u>EP</u>
1	U.S. Male	(Gulcher	) 1975

<u>The Singles</u>		<u>Peak Position</u>
I Need A Lover/Welcome To Chinatown (as John Cougar)	(Riva 202) 1979	28

Small Paradise/Sugar Marie	(Riva 203) 1980		87
A Little Night Dancin'/Pray For Me	(Riva 204) 1980		-
This Time/Don't Misunderstand Me	(Riva 205) 1980		27
Ain't Even Done With The Night/Make Me Feel	(Riva 207) 1981		17
Hurts So Good/Close Enough	(Riva 209) 1982		2
Jack And Diane/Can You Take It	(Riva 210) 1982		1
Hand To Hold On To/Small Paradise	(Riva 211) 1982		19
Crumblin' Down/Golden Gater (first as John Cougar Mellencamp)	(Riva 214) 1983		9
Pink Houses/Serious Business	(Riva 215) 1983		8
Authority Song/Pink Houses (acoustic)	(Riva 216) 1984		15
Lonely Ol' Night/ ?	(Riva	880.984) 1985	6
Small Town/ ?	(Riva	884.202) 1985	6
R.O.C.K. In The USA/ ?	(Riva	884.455) 1986	2
Rain On The Scarecrow/ ?	(Riva	884.635) 1986	21
Rumbleseat/ ?	(Riva	884.856) 1986	28
Paper In Fire/ ?	(Mercury	888.763) 1987	9
Cherry Bomb/ ?	(Mercury	888.934) 1988	8
Check It Out/ ?	(Mercury	870.126) 1988	14
Rooty Toot Toot/ ?	(Mercury	870.327) 1988	61
Jackie Brown/ ?	(Mercury	874.644) 1989	48
Pop Singer/ ?	(Mercury	874.012) 1989	15
Get A Leg Up/ ?	(Mercury	867.890) 1991	14
Again Tonight/ ?	(Mercury	866.414) 1992	36
Human Wheels/ ?	(Mercury	862.704) 1993	48

NB: (1) - (8) recorded as John Cougar. (9) onwards recorded as John Cougar Mellencamp. (5) - (12) produced by Mellencamp and Don Gehman.

Personnel

			Ex	To
JOHN COUGAR MELLENCAMP	gtr,voc	ABC	TRASH	
MIKE WANCHIC	gtr	ABC		
TOBY MYERS	bs	ABC	ROADMASTER	
LARRY CRANE	ld.gtr	AB	TRASH	solo
KENNY ARONOFF	dr	ABC		JEFFERSON AIRPLANE
JOHN CASCELLA	syn,acc	ABC	FAITH BAND	Died Nov. 1992
LIZA GERMANO	f	BC		See solo
DAVE GRISSOM	gtr.	C	JOE ELY	

A = 1984   B - 1988

Mellencamp was born on 7 October 1951 in Seymour. He came from a big family - being the second of five children. By the age of nine he had joined a school band miming the hits of the day and when he was just 15 in 1965 he'd joined his first live band, **Crepe Soul**, with whom he remained for 18 months. Later he joined another outfit, **Snakepit Banana Barn** only to be sacked by them soon after because he couldn't sing. In 1970 he graduated from Seymour High School, left home and moved into an apartment in the small town of Valonia. Within a year he had become both a husband and a father and had taken a job as a carpenter's helper. The following year he formed a glitter-rock group called **Trash** with Larry Crane, a friend, on guitars. They mainly covered '60s hits but did not make it onto vinyl. After graduating from Vincennes University, Mellencamp took a job with a telephone company. By now his marriage had failed and collecting a year's severance pay he headed for New York with a demo he'd recorded of the Paul Revere and The Raiders hit, 'Kicks'. In New York he met Tony De Fries who recorded him and negotiated a deal on his behalf with MCA Records. De Fries soon set about trying to launch Mellencamp's career and whilst (1) was still in demo form he had renamed Mellencamp as Johnny Cougar and in 1976 arranged for him to drive through his hometown of Seymour, Indiana in an open-top motorcade. The album comprised mostly cover versions.

The relationship with Tony De Fries did not work out and by 1977 Mellencamp had returned to Indiana - this time to Bloomington - where he'd formed a new band, The Zone, and was rehearsing material for a second LP with them. He met Billy Gaff (Rod Stewart's manager) and President of Riva Records who signed him to his label and released (3). To coincide with a UK tour (2) was released in the UK only and accompanied by a massive publicity campaign in which 'Cougar' was heralded as the next Bruce Springsteen, a reference to his blue-collar background. However, both the disk and the hype proved a big flop. Returning to the US to pick up the pieces in 1979 he enjoyed his first significant commercial success when (3) (which contained some material from (2)) climbed to No.64 in the US Album Charts in August of that year and later in December he enjoyed his first 45 success when 'I Need A Lover' peaked at No.28 to give him his first in a long series of hit singles. The song was also recorded by Pat Benator who helped to popularise it.

In February 1980, after nearly three years on the road, he returned to the studio to record (5), which was produced by Steve Cropper, and climbed to No.37 in the Album Charts. He also continued to enjoy 45 successes.

He remarried in 1982 and embarked on a major US tour with his own band (line-up A), supporting Heart initially, although later in the year he headlined the tour in his own right. On 3 July 1982, following Indiana's worst flood crisis, he gave a free concert in Fort Wayne, Indiana, for 20,000 high school students who had been sandbagged from the flood waters for eight days back in March 1982. In August 'Hurts So Good' stayed at No.2 in the US Singles Charts for four weeks to give him his first million seller and then on 11 September with LP (6) out (it had been produced by Jem and Don Gehman) and at No.1, he became the first male artist to have two Top Ten hits and a No.1 LP simultaneously. For by the time 'Hurts So Good' had dropped to No.8, his next 45, 'Jack And Diane' had entered at No.4 and would go on to spend four weeks at No.1 and to reach No.25 in the UK. Meanwhile (6) spent nine weeks at No.1 in the US becoming the biggest selling US LP of the year - over three million copies were sold.

During 1983 he enjoyed two further hit singles with 'Hand To Hold On To' and 'Crumblin' Down'. To coincide with the latter he changed his name from John Cougar to John Cougar Mellencamp and released (8) under his new name which peaked at No.9 in the US Album Charts to give him his second platinum-seller. It managed to climb to No.92 in the UK the following year. During 1983 he also produced, and contributed songs to 'Never Kick A Sleeping Dog', an album by Detroit rocker Mitch Ryder.

During 1984 he enjoyed further 45 Chart success in the US with 'Pink Houses' and 'Authority Song' and wrote a screenplay 'Ridin' The Cage' in which Warner Brothers showed some interest. The following year he turned his hand to production, producing 'Colored Lights' on The Blasters' 'Hard Line' LP. Having turned down the opportunity to participate in Live Aid in July 1985, he organised Farm Aid (along with Neil Young and Willie Nelson) on 22 September that year and appealed to the audience to write to their congressmen to demand action to help US farmers. 'Lonely Ol' Night' gave him another Top Ten hit in October of that year and close on its heels (9) was released. He had recorded it in his own recently-constructed studio. Some insight into why so many people like the guy so much was apparent from events during a concert he was playing in New York's Madison Square Garden on 6 December 1985. After the sound system had broken down twice, he returned to play for two hours and informed the audience that anyone with a ticket stub could get their money back if they wanted.

1986 saw him enjoy three more US 45 hits and two of them, 'Small Town' and 'R.O.C.K. In The USA' climbed to Nos.53 and 67 respectively in the UK. On 4 July that year he took part in Farm Aid II, which was held at Manor Downs, Austin, Texas. Later in September he embarked on a new LP (11) with producer Don Gehman at Belmont Hall Studio, Belmont, Indiana.

Farm Aid was becoming a regular fixture for Mellencamp. On 19 September 1987 he played in Farm Aid III with Joe Walsh, Lou Reed, Neil Young and others at the University of Nebraska Memorial Stadium. When (10) emerged it made No.6 in the US and 31 in the UK and he enjoyed further 45 success with 'Paper In Fire', which was taken from it. On 30 October 1987 he embarked on a six-week US tour commencing at Terre Haute (Indiana). It lasted through until 15 December. Where most people would have wanted to rest, Mellencamp was out the next day playing two free concerts for the people of Chilicothe, Ohio, after a local radio station W-FBC had arranged a petition. December 1987 also saw him contribute one cut, 'Run Rudolph Run', to the Various Artists' Special Olympics charity LP, 'A Very Special Christmas'.

Much of 1988 was spent on the road. He played two concerts at London's Hammersmith Odeon on 25 and 26 January and then back in the US embarked on a nationwide tour at Irvine Meadows, LA on 26 May which terminated on 3 July in Milwaukee, Wisconsin. In August he was one of the artists featured on the Woody Guthrie/Leadbelly tribute LP, 'Folkways: A Vision Shared' and the following month he appeared alongside Paul Simon on NBC TV's 'Coca Cola Presents Live: The Hard Rock'.

In 1989 (11) came out and it was one of his best. He also spent part of the year working on the original soundtrack to 'Souvenirs'. He painted the sleeve to (12), which came out in October 1991. He previewed in with a concert at Carnegie Hall September 16th and people queued before dawn for tickets. Even before its release Larry Crane departed for a solo career and was replaced by Dave Grissom from Joe Ely's band. Musically (12) was a melodic, charming mix of macho and youthful innocence. It's full of evocative, storyline songs of little America. Mellencamp had also started work directing a movie, 'Falling From Grace' in which he starred with Claude Akins, Mariel Hemingway, Larry Crane and John Prine. He also wrote the original soundtrack (13) which emerged in late 1992 and had a cut on the soundtrack of 'Honeymoon In Vegas' (Epic 52845) in 1992. (14) emerged in mid-1993 and peaked at 7 on the Album Charts going platinum in the process. The title cut gave him another hit single.

One of the biggest selling artists to come out of the state his reputation shows no sign of diminishing. Indeed, his career is going from strength to strength. During the '80s alone he had seventeen Top 40 hits and sold over twenty-five million albums.

MIKE'S HOUSE

Personnel			Ex	To
CHARLES HOPPER	KB,voc	A		
JOHN SCOTT SHEETS	gtr,voc	A		
VAN ROBINSON	dr	A		

This band has a cut on 'Black Brittle Frizbee', a compilation (Hit City HCR-001) issued in 1988.

MOBIUS STRIP

Album
1( ) Mobius Strip   (Nervous   ) 1983

A heavy metal band. No other data available.

MODERN VENDING

Album
1( ) One Bad Peccary   (Ajax 005) 1990

EP
1( ) Modern Vending   (Ajax   ) 1989

A quintet who first came to light in 1988 on the 'Black Brittle Frizbee' compilation (Hit City HCR-001), which exposed a number of in-state bands to a wider public.

MUSHROOM FARM

A '60s band from Evansville who released one 45, 'Why Can't I See/Get Lost' (Gigantic 3726).

MX 80

A new wave band from Bloomington. Given that all of their album output was recorded after a move to San Francisco they were included in 'An American Rock History, Volume 1: California, The Golden State'.

NATCHEZ TRACE

Put out one 45, 'Beautiful Girl/Got To Move' (Nato 194), during the 1960s.

ND WITNESSES

Personnel	Ex	To
GARY DRAPER		
DON ELLIS		
DOUG METCIK		
DOUG STERNS		
JIM TUTTEROW		
DENNY WILSON		

An early '60s outfit from Indianapolis who didn't make it onto vinyl.

THE NIDS

<u>Cassettes</u>

1	Mr. Pooh Picks The Hits		(	)	1989
2	Music To De-Tassle Corn By		(	)	1989
3	Fashionable Revolution		(	)	1990

<u>Personnel</u>			<u>Ex</u>	<u>To</u>
PAUL	dr	AB		
DAVE	gtr,voc	AB		
SEAN	voc,gtr	AB		
JULIE	bs	A		
JAKE	bs,voc	B		

A band from Bloomington. No data held as to the style of their music. Formed October 1986.

NO LABELS

A new wave group from Columbus with a cut on the 'Master Tapes' compilation issued by Affirmation in 1983.

JOHN O'BANION

<u>Albums</u>

1	John O'Banion	(Elektra 6E 342)	1981
2	Danger	(Elektra)	1982

<u>The Singles</u>

I Love You Like I Never Loved Before/She's Not For You	(Elektra 47125)	1981
Love Is Blind/If You Love Me	(Elektra 47163)	1981

A singer-songwriter born in Kokomo. (1) produced a hit single, 'I Love You Like I Never Loved Before' which peaked at No.24 on the Hot 100 in the Spring of 1981.

OBSERVERS OBSERVING OBSERVABLES

<u>EP</u>

1( )	Observers Observing Observables	(Hardly Music HM 000003) 1981

This combo also used the name 'The Three Os Band'. (1) had five cuts.

OLIVERS

This outfit recorded their sole 45 in Chicago - 'Bleeker Street/I Saw What You Did' (Phalanx 1022) in 1966. It was later leased to RCA Victor (47-9113) for nationwide distribution in 1967. The release has since received wide compilation coverage with 'Bleeker Street' appearing on 'The Psychedelic Sixties, Vol.1' (Cicadelic 1001) 1982 and the flip resurfacing on 'Garage Music For Psych Heads 1' (Psych Out PSY 102) 198?, 'Mind Blowers' (White Rabbit WR-LP 001) 1983 and 'The 60's Choice Collection Of Scarce Garage Records, Vol.1' (Venus In Furs GMG 75021) 1987. The flip is a pretty good architypal garage recording from this era with some catchy organ and effective guitar. See also **Madson**.

PHIL ORSI AND THE LITTLE KINGS

We included this outfit in 'Volume 3' of the series, which dealt with Chicago and Illinois, but they were originally from Gary.

OSCAR AND THE MAJESTICS

This was another '60s outfit orignally from Gary but later based in Chicago, which was also included in 'Volume 3' of this series. They had one additional 45, which wasn't listed in the earlier volume, 'My Girl Is Waiting/Jungle Beat' (Ark 7638).

OTHER FIVE

A garage combo from Muncie who put out two cover versions on a 45, 'You Really Got Me/Better Come Home' (Baus 5887) in 1967. 'Better Come Home' would be better without the brass and their version of 'You Really Got Me' is an unusually restrained rendition of the 'Kinks' song.

THE OUTSIDERS

Personnel		Ex	To
DAN HAILEY			
MIKE RAY			
ROB SWEENY			
WAYNE WILSON			
?			

A quintet which formed in Indianapolis in 1965.

THE PANICS

EP
1(A)   The Panics   (Gulcher 201) 1980

Personnel			Ex	To
ERIC WHITE	bs	A		
JOHN BARGE	voc	A		
MIKE OST	dr	A		
JOHNNY CARSON	gtr	A		

A quartet from Bloomington who can also be heard doing 'Drugs Are For Thugs' on the 'Red Snerts' compilation album from 1981 (Gulcher GULCH 102).

PATTERN

A combo from Columbus who were included on 'Columbus Compilation' on Gravel Voice Records in 1983.

PEACE AND LOVE

It is no surprise that a '60s outfit chose a name that summed up what it was all about. Their sole stab for fame and fortune was one 45, 'I've Got News For You/Gotta Go Back' (L.F.001).

RAY PIERLE

Album
1   Rhythm Of The Highway   (private pressing   ) 197?

Indianapolis-based. (1) is said to be the third album! Connected to the group McKay.

PERPETUAL MOTION

Hailed from New Albany with one 45, 'Necking Don't Make It/Get Ready' (Dial 9078) in May 1968. We can't confirm whether they were related to the Chicago-based band of the same name who appeared in 'Volume 3' of this series.

P. J. AND THE GENTRY

Released 'The Wounded Camel/Sing And Dance' (Beaver 7642) in the 1960s. They were based in Hammond.

PORT RAISIN BAND

Personnel			Ex	To
JIM TE RONDE	gtr	A		
SCOTT WOOLRIDGE	voc	A		WOOLRIDGE BROS
JEFF MARTIN	dr	A		
BRIAN WOOLRIDGE	bs	A		WOOLRIDGE BROS

A band from Kokoma who can be heard on the 'Red Snerts' compilation (Gulcher GULCH 102) issued in 1981. They formed as **Socks** and then used **Damascus Road** before settling on this name.

THE PRETENTIOUS WANKERS

Cassette
1( ) U Ain't Us   (   ) 1989

Delightfully-named hardcore band from Evansville.

PRIMEVIL

Album
1( ) Smokin' Bats At Compton   (700 West 740105) 1974

An obscure mid-'70s outfit from somewhere in Indiana. If anyone has any more information please send us details.

PRIMITIVE INFINITY

Cassette
1   Falling Apart   (   ) 1989

(1) is a demo by this thrash metal band.

PROFILES

A '60s outfit who put out one 45, 'Raindrops/ ? ' (Musicland 24004).

PURE FUNK

Formed in Indianapolis in 1971. They later became **Roadmaster**.

PURGATORY

A heavy metal band from Fort Wayne. They changed their name to **Iced Earth** but promptly fell apart.

RADIATION SICKNESS

Album
1( ) The Other Me ... A Journey Into Insanity   (Old World   ) 1991

EP
1( ) Bounds of Reality   (6-track)   (Putrefaction   ) 1990

Demo Tapes
1( ) We're All The Victims   1988
2( ) Elvis Ain't Dead   1989

Personnel		Ex	To
DOUG PALMER	voc		
MIKE J. HAROLD	dr		
RICK CALLOWAY	gtr		
BYRON JOLTON	bs		
RYAN ROLLINS			

An Indianapolis quartet making a push for the big-time.

RASTA SNOWHOUNDS

Personnel incl:		Ex	To
MATT HART	gtr		

A hardcore project featuring Fire Hydrant Man guitarist Hart. He has previously played with F.O.N.

THE RAVENS

A '60s punk outfit who had a 45, 'My Secret Girl/ ? ' on their own Raven label.

REDCOATS

Came out of New Albany with 'Cobra/Dance' (Mae   ) in June 1967.

THE RENEGADES

Originally known as JJ and the Dukes, this outfit was based in Logansport. Their sole vinyl offering was 'You Won't Do/Judy' (Trumph 671-A-2066) in 1967.

RICK AND THE RIOTS

'Garage Punk Unknowns, Vol.6' (Stone Age SA 666) 1986 includes a track called 'Big Murph' by this Indianapolis band which dates from 1961. It was originally issued on Shazzamm (III) and backed by 'Traffic Jam'.

RIGHT TO LEFT

This band can be heard on the 'Black Brittle Frizbee' compilation (Hit City HCR-001) which was issued in 1988.

THE RIVIERAS

Albums
1(A) Let's Have A Party	(USA	102) 1964
2( ) Campus Party	(Riviera 701) 1965	

Personnel			Ex	To
BILL DOBSLAW	voc	A		
PAUL DENNERT	dr	A		
OTTO NUSS	o	A		
DOUG GEAN	bs	A		
JIM BOAL	gtr	A		
WILLIE GAUT	gtr	A		

A fraternity rock band from South Bend, who enjoyed considerable commercial success in the mid-'60s. They issued a string of 45s on Riviera, all produced at the U.S.A. studios (which also distributed their first LP). Their 45s are listed below but only three made it nationally - 'California Sun/Played On' (Riviera 1401), an enormous hit reaching No.5 on the Top 100 and two lesser hits, 'Little Donna/Let's Have A Party' (reaching 93 and 99 respectively) (Riviera 1402) and 'Rockin' Robin/Battle Line' (Riviera 1403) which made 96 only. In Europe they are known pretty well exclusively for 'California Sun' which typified the 'surf and sun' Beach

Boys' influenced style with a catchy melody, piping organ and a meat hook chorus. The Dictators did a great cover of the song on their debut album 'Go Girl Crazy'.

<u>Singles</u>

Played On/California Sun	(Riviera 1401) 1963 (re-issued with H.B. Goosestep on B-side, this was the hit).
Let's Have A Party/Little Donna	(Riviera 1402) 1964
Rockin' Robin/Battle Line	(Riviera 1403) 1964
Rip It Up/Whole Lot Of Shakin'	(Riviera 1404) 1964
You Never Say/Sweets For My Sweet	(Riviera 1405) 1965 (as Kastaways)
Let's Go To Hawaii/Lake View Lane	(Riviera 1406) 1965
Somebody New/Somebody Asked Me	(Riviera 1407) 1965
Comin' Down/Pop Top	(Riviera 1408) 1966
Never Felt The Pain/ ?	(Riviera 1409) 1966

ROADMASTER

<u>Albums</u>

1(A)	Roadmaster	(Village	V.R. 7601) 1976
2(B)	Sweet Music	(Village/Mercury SRM 1-3760) 1978
3(B)	Hey World	(Mercury	SRM 1-3774) 1979
4(B)	Fortress	(Mercury	SRM 1-3814) 1980

<u>The Singles</u>

Circle Of Love/You Come See Me	(Mercury 74038) 1978
Hey World/I'm On My Way	(Mercury 74084) 1979

<u>Personnel</u>			<u>Ex</u>	<u>To</u>
RICK BENICK	gtr	ABC		HENRY LEE SUMMER
TOBY MYERS	bs	AB		JOHN COUGAR MELLENCAMP
MICHAEL REED	KB,bs	ABC		HENRY LEE SUMMER
ADAM SMASHER	voc	A		became a disc jockey
STEPHEN RILEY	dr	A		BZZ
STEPHEN McNALLY	voc	B		THE GAME
BOBBY JOHNS	dr	BC	DIAMOND REO	to construction business
?	bs	C		

Mainstream melodic rockers formed as Pure Funk (A), who recorded a three-track demo produced by Todd Rundgren in 1975 after he had caught them playing in a bar. The demo, recorded at the Bearsville Studio in upstate New York, led to a contract with Village and later Mercury and the band looked set. Musically the band were good news indeed - a spicy blend of synthesisers and guitars peculiar to the period in which they operated. They were undoubtedly influenced, as were most U.S. rock bands of the day, by the likes of Yes and Genesis. After (1) the line-up shifted with McNally, who had sung background on the first album, replacing Adam and former Diamond Reo drummer, Johns, joining in place of Riley. After (2) the band began to pick up a hot live reputation and consequently a lot of out of state gigs, playing with the likes of Ted Nugent, Blue Oyster Cult and Rush. (3) was to be the biggest seller (over 30,000) but by (4) things had begun to fall off. It was produced by former Turtles Flo and Eddy but sounded thin and tired. They were canned by Mercury. MCA displayed some interest, and indeed some money was forthcoming from the label; that, too went sour after some late demos, mainly because Toby Myers was offered, and accepted, a slot in John Cougar Mellencamp's band. And that, as they say, was that. Riley eventually went on to W.A.S.P. and L.A. Guns in Los Angeles.

FRANK RONDELL AND THE CHANCELLORS

<u>Personnel incl:</u>	<u>Ex</u>	<u>To</u>
FRANK RONDELL		

Cut one 45, 'The Bat/Last Laugh's On Me' (Fujimo 917 F 6138) circa 1963/64. Frank Rondell was originally from Canada.

RON-DE-VOOS

A garage quartet previously known as The Blue Flames and The Rendezvous. They cut their own 45, 'The Maid/Pipeline' on their own Cycle label circa 1965/66 and the 'A' side, a routine rock 'n' roller, has since resurfaced on 'Back From The Grave, Vol.7' (Crypt 013) 1988. They finally quit in 1968. The 1983 compilation 'Psychedelic Unknowns, Vol.5' (Starglow-Neon SN-00001) 1983 includes a cut called 'Trip So Wild' by an outfit called Ron-De-Voos, which we think is probably a different band.

SALT AND PEPPER

Personnel		Ex	To
BILL BOGBY	AB		
BILL LYNCH	A		
DAN HAILEY	B	THE OUTSIDERS	

Forming originally in 1962 this Indianapolis-based duo was a popular live act around the clubs throughout the '60s.

SANGRALADS

Personnel		Ex	To
LLOYD AMOS			
PHIL ARMSTRONG	o		
RICK INGLE	dr		
ROCKY LILLARD			
DANNY OBERLANDER			
BILL THOMPSON			

They were also known as Sun Lighting Incorporated and emerged from the Sangralea Valley with two 45s:- 'Think Of What You're Sayin'/Mary's Kidd' (Whap WH-318) 1968 and 'Quasar 45/There Must Be Light' (Whap WH-319) in 1969.

SANZ INC

The Singles
I'm Gonna Leave You/My Baby's Eyes   (Skoop 1069) 196?
I Just Want You/I'll Never Forget   (Skoop 1072) 196?

A garage band from Santa Claus.

SCOURGIN' ZOMBIES

A hardcore band who can be heard on 'Children Of The Corn', a compilation of hardcore music issued in 1990 by Sonic Iguana Records.

SCREAMIN' GYPSY BANDITS

Albums
1( ) In The Eye   (BRBQ 03) 1973
2( ) The Dancer Inside You   (BRBQ 04) 1974

Personnel incl:		Ex	To
MARK BINGHAM	gtr		KAKA CALIENTE
TINA LANE	voc		
BOB LUCAS	dr		
DALE SOPHIEA	bs		MX 80
BRUCE ANDERSON	gtr	MRS. SEAMANS SOUND BAND	MX 80

An oddball outfit from Bloomington best remembered for the inclusion of Sophiea and Anderson who went on to form MX 80 then took it to San Francisco. (1) was preceded with a couple of 45s on BRBQ under the name Tina Lane And The Screamin' Gypsy Bandits.

SERAIAH

A Christian-metal band based in Marion which lies on State Highway 37 midway between Indianapolis and Fort Wayne. The band issued a four-track demo ('Soldier of Jehovah') in mid-1988, after an earlier and less successful effort.

THE SERFMEN

The Singles
A Man Can't Live Without Love/ ?	(Nemfres 101)	196?
Chills And Fever/Back Again	(Nemfres 102)	196?

This band later evolved into The Olivers.

SHAPES

The Singles
Send Him Home/ ?	(Fujimo ?)	196?
Santa Claus Is Coming To Town/Prancer's Got Some Red Spots	(Fujimo 9573)	196?

A garage band from South Bend.

SHAMROCK SHAKES

EP
1( ) House Of Jep	(Final Jeopardy)	1989

Personnel	Ex	To
ANDY LEVY		TOTAL PASSOVER

A hardcore combo from Ames who can also be heard on the compilation, 'It Came From The Cold' issued by Chef Music Records in 1989.

SHOOTING STARS

The Singles
I Love Her Anyway/ ?	(Sims no No.)	196?
I Watch The Clock/Donna	(Airtown 011)	196?

Winchester was this band's home turf.

SIGMA 5

This was actually La Porte's Rivieras who recorded a 45, 'Comin' Down/Pop Top' (Riviera 1408) under this name in 1966.

SIR CHARLES AND DAZE OF OLD

A '60s outfit who recorded one 45, 'Baby Come Back/ ? ' (Skoop 1071).

SIR WINSTON AND THE COMMONS

Personnel		Ex	To
DON BASORE	gtr,voc		drafted in 1967
HERBIE CRAWFORD	bs		
RONNIE MATELIC	ld.gtr		ANONYMOUS (via J. RIDER)
JOHNNY MEDVESCEK	dr		ANONYMOUS (via J. RIDER)
JOE STOUT	o		

This was a very popular Indianapolis band which grew out of an earlier combo called The Pickups in 1963. They once opened for The

Byrds at the Indianapolis Coliseum in July 1966 and their stage shows were reputedly pretty wild - they'd jump around and throw things. They made two vinyl excursions:- 'Not The Spirit Of India/One Last Chance' (Nauseating Butterfly 2207) and 'Come Back Again/We're Gonna Love' (Soma 1454) in 1965. 'We're Gonna Love' has also resurfaced on 'Back From The Grave, Vol.3' (Crypt CR-003) 1986. There's lots of fuzz on this garage grunger.

SKAFISH

Albums
1(B)	Skafish		(I.R.S./A&M XSP 008) 1980
2( )	Conversation		(I.R.S./A&M) 1983

Personnel			Ex	To
JIM SKAFISH	voc,KB	AB		
LARRY MAZALARI	ld.gtr,bs	AB		
GREG SARCHET	bs	A		
LARRY MYSLIWIEC	dr	AB		
KAREN WINNER	gtr,KB	A		
JAVIER CRUZ	KB,syn	B		
BARBIE GOODRICH	gtr,voc	B		
KEN PRONAZKA	gtr,bugle,voc	B		

A curious combo from Gary who moved to East Chicago, Indiana in 1977. As the name implies, the band were just across the state line from Illinois. Skafish was reported to be a hermaphrodite. Certainly a quirky band with odd instrumentation. Their first gig was at The Vibes in Chicago and by the time the first album was issued they were touring out of state. They opened for XTC at the Ritz in New York in August 1980 and also played dates around Detroit the same month.

Apart from the albums they appeared on a number of compilations. 'Disgracing The Family Name' which appeared on 'IRS Greatest Hits Vols.2 & 3' (IRS SP 70800) in 1981 was originally a 1979 45 coupled with 'Work Song' (Illegal ILS-0018). There is also a non-LP 45, 'Obsession With You/Sink Or Swim (IRS IR-9011) issued in June 1980. Most people in the UK who know of them probably heard them for the first time on the original soundtrack from 'Urgh - A Music War' (A&M SP 6019), with 'Sign Of The Cross'. (1) was an excellent album, the band fluid and complementary to the neurotic songs with their strange themes and dark moods. (2) was both a change in direction and a disappointment.

THE SLAMMERS

A new wave band who can be heard on 'The Master Tapes' compilation on Nimrod. The album was issued in 1982.

SLOPPY SECONDS

Albums
1( )	Destroyed	(Toxic Shock TXLP 17) 1989
2( )	And Them Some	(Taang) 1991
3( )	Christmas CDs	(Taang) 1992
4( )	Knock Yer Block Off	(Taang) 1993

EPs
1( )	Germany	( ) 1988
2(A)	First Seven Inches	(Alternative Testicles) 1988
3( )	Where Eagles Dare	(Roadkill) 1990

Personnel			Ex	To
STEVE BARRON	dr	A		
DANDY ROADKILL	gtr	A		
SHAZAM BO'BA	bs	A		
B.A.	voc	A		

An Indianapolis-based alternative rock band. Line-up (A) also appear on the 'Black Brittle Frizbee' compilation on Hit City

Records, issued in 1988, with 'Germany', 'The Men' and 'I Don't Want To Take You Home'. (2) is in fact the 'First Seven Inches' EP plus some previously unissued cuts.

SNAKEPIT BANANA BARN

Personnel incl:		Ex	To
JOHN MELLENCAMP	voc,gtr	CREPE SOUL	TRASH

Mellencamp was briefly a member of this Seymour-based band in 1966. When he was sacked the following year because they said he couldn't sing, he purchased his first acoustic guitar. The rest is history.

SNAKESKIN COWBOY

Personnel			Ex	To
SCOTT NEWBOLD	gtr	A		
JIMMY CAIN	voc	A		
JOHN D	bs	A		
DON WEBBER	dr	A		

A new Indianapolis-based metal band who have done time in studios so demos will exist.

SOCKS

A band from Kokomo. Formed in the early '80s they became first Damascus Road and later The Port Raisin Band.

THE SONS OF REGRET

Cassette
1( ) Strangelove   (own product   ) 1990

Moody, doom-laden music with very good vocals. Hints of The Cult. A promising beginning from this Bloomington outfit.

SONS OF SOUND

Hailed from Indiana with one 45, 'He's Gonna Ride/So Be It' (Bogan ?), circa 1966/67.

THE SOUND FARM

A '60s outfit who recorded a 45 for AMH.

SOUNDS UNLIMITED

Personnel	Ex	To
PHIL BRAEDT		
STEVE FOSTER		
KEN MAHCKE		
WAYNE WILSON		

Originally from Indiana they moved to Chicago and their discography was included in 'Volume 3' of this series. However, the line-up given in that volume was completely wrong and this is corrected above.

SOUTH SHORE

Personnel			Ex	To
STEVE GULYAS	gtr,bs,KB	A		
JOE ALAMILLO	dr	A		

A duo from Gary who issued one 45, 'Doing Alright Without You/Dreaming Of You', on Sosa (SS 0002) in 1981.

THE SPINNERS

Recorded a surf-styled 45, 'Surfing Monkey/Beetel Mania' (Lawson 324), in Mishawaka, in the early '60s.

SPLIT LIP

Album
1( ) Soul Kill   (New Start   ) 1992

A hardcore band. No other data.

THE SPORTSMEN

Personnel		Ex	To
RONDO LOSCHKY			
LARRY GOSHEN	dr	KENNY LEE AND THE ROYALS	
BILL ROBERTS		See DOMINOS	
JOHN SCOTT		KEETIE AND THE KATS	WILDFIRE

A popular band in the clubs of Indianapolis circa 1964. Much later in the late '80s Scott resurfaced in Wildfire, a country outfit.

RUBY STARR

Albums
1	Ruby Starr	(Curtom 8011) 1971
2	Ruby Starr	(Capitol 11417) 1975
3	Scene Stealer	(Capitol 11549) 1976
4	Smokey Places	(Capitol 11643) 1977

The Singles (on Capitol)
*	Did It Again/Long Wait	(Capitol 4190) 1975
	Who's Who/Maybe I'm Amazed	(Capitol 4301) 1975
	On Top/When You Walk In The Room	(Capitol 4435) 1976

* with Grey Ghost.

This vocalist was also a member of Arkansas-based band Grey Ghost/Grey Star and it is a moot point whether she should be in this volume or a later one. She worked in the studios with Black Oak Arkansas, toured with them extensively as a vocalist, and is probably best remembered as the screeching vocalist on 'Jim Dandy To The Rescue'.

STEVE KOWALSKI

EP
1   Can't Find London   (Rusty Cow   ) 1991

Personnel		Ex	To
TOM SHOVER	gtr,voc	ABC	
TIM BOLTER	dr	A	
ROB ROWE	bs	AB	
PAT SPURGEON	dr	BC	
JAKE SMITH	bs	C	

Not a man, but a band from Indianapolis. They can also be heard on the 'Children Of The Corn' hardcore compilation issued by Sonic Iguana Records in 1990.

BORDERLINE

ARE YOU A SMART ASS?

IF YOU CAN SUPPLY MISSING INFO,
CORRECT ERRORS OR MAKE SUGGESTIONS TO
IMPROVE OUR BOOK, WE WANT TO HEAR FROM

YOU!

CONTACT US CARE OF:-

BORDERLINE PRODUCTIONS,
P.O.BOX 93
TELFORD, TF1 1UE
ENGLAND

STRANGE EVENT

Personnel incl:		Ex	To
MICHAEL GITLIN	gtr	BARN BOYS	DANCING CIGARETTES
TIMOTHY NOE	KB	BARN BOYS	DANCING CIGARETTES
G. DON TRUBOY	gtr	BARN BOYS	DANCING CIGARETTES

Formed in Bloomington. A short-lived project with no known output.

STRIKE THREE

A hardcore band which operated under the name **Enemy** initially and then **The Wombats**. They share a drummer with **Clear Sight**.

STRONTIUM 90

Cassette
1( ) Strontium 90   (Sonic Iguana   ) 1992

Yet another of the many hardcore bands who can be heard on the Indiana compilation album, 'Children Of The Corn', issued in 1990 by Sonic Iguana Records.

HENRY LEE SUMMER

Albums
1	Henry Lee Summer	(CBS Associated BFZ 40895) 1988
2	I've Got Everything	(CBS Associated OZ 45124) 1989
3	Way Past Midnight	(Epic EK 47059) 1991
4	Slam Dunk	(Epic) 1993

Personnel		Ex	To
HENRY LEE SUMMER	voc,gtr		
RICK BENICK	ld.gtr	ROADMASTER	
MICHAEL REED	KB	ROADMASTER	
JIMMY RIP	gtr		
GRAHAM MABY	bs		
?	dr		

An Indianapolis-based singer-songwriter with a style akin to **John Cougar Mellencamp**, perhaps Indiana's favourite son. Summer has been working for around ten years, issuing his first single, 'Sweet Love/The Fool' as long ago as 1982 on First Step records. His signing to CBS Associated in late 1987 was a major move and he has already enjoyed chart success with all three albums and some hit singles.

THE SURF SUNS

Hailed from New Haven in the '60s with one 45, 'Still In Love With You Baby/I Can't Stop It Now' (Ben 6745).

THE SWAGMEN

Hailing from Mishawaka they issued one 45, 'Mendecino/So Long Baby' (Americana 1205) during the 1960s.

SWAY

Album
1( ) Spinning Dreams   (Mammoth   ) 1991

Personnel	Ex	To
JOHN STROHM	of BLAKE BABIES	

FREDA LOVE   of BLAKE BABIES

Another version of **Antenna Sway**.

SWEET F.A.

Albums
1(A) Stick To Your Guns   (MCA   6400) 1990
2(A) Temptation   (Charisma 91783) 1991

Personnel			Ex	To
STEVEN DAVID DE LONG	voc	A	VIOLATION	
JAMES 'J.T.' THUNDER	ld.gtr	A		
JOHN LIGHTNING	ld.gtr	A		
JIM QUICK	bs	A		
TRICKY LANE	dr	A	WHITE WRATH	

An unlikely set of names for this Indianapolis-based metal band. They have a hot reputation in the metal mags but have so far
failed to score in any significant way. (1) was produced by Howard Benson at Soundscape studios in Atlanta, Georgia.

THE SWINGIN' LADS

Personnel	Ex	To
JIM BRUHN	See CLASSMEN	
RON CARROLL		
DON KELLEY	THE FASCINATORS	
BILL LYNCH		
MANNY PARIS		

A mid-'60s Indianapolis act. Kelley had earlier played for a '50s band from Terre Haute, **The Fascinators**. The Swingin' Lads played
on local bills with many big names and also appeared on the Ed Sullivan television show.

SWINGIN' STING RAYS

A '60s band who issued one 45, 'Teen Queen/ ? ' on the Fujimo label.

TAKERS

A Hammond-based garage band who released one 45, 'I Can Say No More/ Wonder' (Takitics no No.), in the mid-'60s.

TEEN TONES

The Singles
Fortune Teller/Poison Ivy   (Don & Mira 6269) 196?
Do You Want To Dance/Long Cold Winter   (T. T.   2487) 196?

Hailed from South Bend. 'Fortune Teller' can also be found on 'Straight From The Garage, Vol.5' (Garageland EP 5) 1987.

THE TEMPESTS

The Singles
Prancer/Rockin' Xmas Goose   (Fujimo 4630) 196?
Look Away/Carousel Blues   (Fujimo 6946) 196?
Love I'm In/Pink Elephants   (Fujimo 7701) 196?
Boppin' The Blues/Whole Lotta Shakin'   (Fujimo ?) 196?
Searchin'/Come On Everybody   (Fujimo ?) 196?
Brainstorm/Love I'm In   (Fujimo ?) 196?

Zip A Dee Do Dah/Lookin' Out The Window   (Fujimo ?) 196?

Recorded for a North Indiana label, they are thought to have come from Elkhart, although 'Look Away' appears on 'Highs In The Mid-Sixties, Vol.19: Michigan, Part 3' (AIP 10028) 1985 which is where that series' sources place them. Who knows? 'Look Away' also appears, incidentally, on the 'Riot City' (Satan 1003) 1985 compilation. It's a pretty good early '60s rocker.

TERMINAL SOLUTION

Cassette
1( ) Force Of Life   (   ) 1990

A hardcore combo from New Albany.

TFH

A hardcore band to be heard on Sonic Iguana's compilation 'Children Of The Corn', issued in 1990.

THE TIKIS

Personnel		Ex	To
BOB FOLGER	bs		
DAVE WEBSTER	o		
RICK WORKMAN	voc,dr		
PAT WO	gtr		

A teen combo from Syracuse, northern Indiana who recorded a Stones-styled ballad, 'Show You Love' backed by 'Careful What You Say' (Fujimo 917 F 6139) at Chicago's RCA studios in late 1966. You can check out the 'A' side on 'Back From The Grave, Vol.5' (Crypt CR-005) 1985 and it's well worth a listen.

TOO COOL

Cassette
1( ) Too Young, Too Loose, Too Cool   (Chatterbox   ) 1991

A new band from Pennsylvania, Indiana.

TORKAYS

The Singles
* Little Loved One/Cindy Lou   (Stacy 958) 196?
  I Don't Like It/Karate   (Stacy 960) 196?
* as Keith O'Connor.

Nothing else known.

TOXIC REASONS

Albums
1   Independence   (Risky-Bitzcore   1655) 1982
2   Kill By Remote Control   (Alternative Tentacles 41) 1984
3   Within These Walls   (Treason   ) 1985
4   Bullets For You   (Alternative Tentacles 55) 1986
5   Dedication 1979-1988   (Funhouse   12-005) 1988
6   Toxic Reasons - Fashion For Facism   (Lone Wolf   009) 1990
7   Anything For Money   (Hellhound   ) 1990

EPs

					Ex	To		
1	Toxis Reasons	(3 track)				(Risky	)	1981
2	Ghost Town					(	)	1989
3	Nobody Tells Us	(the 1980 material)	(4 track)			(Selfless	)	1990

Personnel			Ex	To
ED PITTMAN	voc	AB		
BRUCE STUCKEY	ld.gtr	AB		RASTABILLY REBELS
ROB LUCJAK	ld.gtr	A		
GREG STORT	bs	AB		
J. J. PEARSON	dr	AB		
TERRY HOWE	gtr	B		

An Indianapolis-based band with punk origins who grew from those stripped down beginnings into something more. (1) contains slicing guitar pulsing at chainsaw speed with some variety shaken in via reggae rhythms and a rework of 'Shapes Of Things To Come'. (2) came complete with personnel changes and is an excellent album with ace original material and more sterling guitar work from Lucjak and Stuckey. (3) was even better but was followed by Lucjak's departure. This resulted in a degeneration into derivative thrash-metal. Shame! The band can also be heard on 'Process Of Elimination', a compilation (Touch & Go 13265) and 'Children Of The Corn' (Sonic Iguana). They disbanded in 1991.

TRADEWINDS

Released one 45, 'Floatin''/Oop Poo Pa Doo' (Destination 620), in the 1960s.

TRANSGRESSION

Album
1( ) Cold World   (Manic Ears 16) 1988

A hardcore band based in Indianapolis though they may have originated in Zionsville. In addition to (1), they appear on at least one compilation cassette from the area, and share an EP with Apocalypse.

TRASH

Personnel incl:		Ex	To
JOHNNY COUGAR MELLENCAMP	voc,gtr	SNAKEPIT BANANA BARN	solo
LARRY CRANE	ld.gtr		Mellencamp's band

A glitter-rock outfit formed by Mellencamp in Valonia which mostly covered '60s songs and did not make in onto vinyl.

THE TRAVELLS

Personnel		Ex	To
RONALD KHERT	A		
EUGENE SMITH	A	EUGENE & THE NIGHTBEATS	
KENNETH SMITH	A		
TOM SPENCER	A	EUGENE & THE NIGHTBEATS	
JACKIE JACOBSEN			WILDFIRE
GARY HAMILTON			
PAUL JACKSON			
DAVE JONES			
GARY JACOBSEN			WILDFIRE
EEDDIE JEFFERS			

An early '60s quartet which went through several line-up changes. At one time they included Jackie (Asher) Jacobsen, one of the state's best lady bassists. A popular club act they never made it onto vinyl. Jackie and Gary Jacobsen currently play with an Indianapolis-based country outfit called Wildfire.

TROJANS OF EVOL

Gary was the Indiana home for this band but they travelled to Chicago's Columbia studios in late 1966 to record a 45, 'Through The Night/Why Girl' (T.O.E. 125970), which they released on their own label. 'Through The Night', which contains quite a guitar break and lots of fuzz, can be heard on 'Back From The Grave, Vol.6' (Crypt CR-007) 1985.

TROUP

Came out of Pierceton with two 45s in 1967:- 'I'm Going Away/I'll Be Back' (RTB 3776) and 'Jungle Jive/Teenage Girl' (RTB 3778).

DUKE TUMATOE AND THE ALL STAR FROGS

Albums
1( )	Naughty Child	(Blind Pig 980)	1981
2( )	Duke Tumatoe And The All Star Frogs	(Blind Pig)	1982
3( )	Dukes Up	(Blind Pig 1584)	1984
4( )	I Like My Job	(Warner 25836)	1989

Personnel			Ex	To
DUKE TUMATOE	gtr,voc	A		
L. V. HAMMOND	bs,voc	A		
JAMES HILL	KB,voc	A		
ROBIN STEELE	dr	A		

A rock outfit. (4) was issued using the name Duke Tumatoe and The Power Trio.

UNION GROOVE

Another of the state's many hardcore bands easily sampled by picking up the 'Children Of The Corn' compilation issued on Sonic Iguana in 1990.

UNPREDICTABLES

Hailed from Evansville with one '60s 45, '99 1/2/Knock On Wood' (Guild Craft 203).

VAGUE ATMOSPHERE

Album
1	Words And Music	(Blue Cube)	1991

Actually a poet, K.C. Pocius, backed by rock music and sound-effects. Based in Mishawaka.

VIDICUS

Personnel		Ex	To
BRETT CRIPE	gtr,bs		
MARC COFFIN	gtr		
KEITH WELLS	dr		

A little known new-wave styled trio from Elkhart. They made a big name in their home-town with songs like, 'I Don't Care' and 'Let Our Rock And Roll Go', but never came to anything on the wider circuit.

THE VULGAR BOATMEN

Albums
1( )	You And Your Sister	(Record Collect 1171)	1989
2( )	Please Panic	(Safehouse/Rough Trade)	1992

Personnel incl:		Ex	To
DALE LAWRENCE	voc	GIZMOS	
(ROBERT RAY)			
MATT SPEAK			
ERIK BÉAADE			
ANDY RICHARDS			

A quintet, one of a number of bands using this name. Two of these outfits are directly related, and both worked on (1). Puzzled? Then read on. The band had a dual axis with feet in both Indianapolis and Gainesville, Florida. They were formed by Walter Sala-Humara in Florida in 1980 (he now fronts The Silos). Walter produced the album, which is full of mellow, laid back music, and subtle insidious lyrics. There is a control, almost a repression of emotion that keeps you on the edge of your seat, anticipating mayhem. Lawrence and Ray co-wrote most of the material and Ray co-produced the album. Lawrence lives in Indianapolis and Ray in Gainesville. The songwriting was done by mail, with the songs being worked out in gigs in both states by the local versions of the band. The record label is owned by Walter. Apart from the above they have a cut on the 'Hear No Evil' compilation on Longplay Records in 1992. The Florida version will be covered in a later volume.

EDDIE WALKER AND THE DEMONS

The Singles
Twistin' Your Life Away/Big D. Blues		(Keet 1000) 196?
Till I Have You/Night Train Twist		(Keet 1001) 196?

Personnel	Ex	To
GEORGE ABELL		
LARRY (WAZOO) GARDNER	DAWNBEATS	
GENE ROBINSON		
MORGAN SCHUMACHER	DAWNBEATS	
EDDIE WALKER		

An early '60s vocal group from North Indiana.

WALKING RUINS

Cassette
1( ) Going Down The Tubes	( ) 1989	

A hardcore band from Bloomington.

STEVE WARINER

Albums
1	Steve Wariner	(RCA AHI1-4154) 1982
2	Midnight Fire	(RCA AHL1-4859) 1983
3	One Good Night Deserves Another	(MCA 5545) 1985
4	Life's Highway	(MCA 5672) 1986
5	Down In Tennessee	(RCA AHL1-7164) 1986
6	It's A Crazy World	(MCA 5926) 1987
7	I Should Be With You	(MCA 42130) 1988
8	I Got Dreams	(MCA 42272) 1989
9	Laredo	(MCA 42335) 1990
10	Christmas Memories	(MCA 10067) 1990
11	I Am Ready	(Arista 1-8691) 1991
12	Drive	(Arista 1-8721) 1993

Wariner is one of the most successful of the new breed of country artists to have emerged during the '80s. He was born on Christmas Day 1954 in Noblesville, Indiana, though he is now based in Nashville. He began his musical career as a bass player in a country band when he was a teenager, moving on to play with Bob Luman and Chet Atkins. In 1971 aged just 17 he took up the bass slot in

Dottie West's band and remained with her until 1974. He was signed by RCA in 1978 and began a huge run of singles success on the country charts (detailed below though it may not be exhaustive). His switch to MCA gave him more say in the way he developed his direction and an association with producer Tony Brown strengthened his move away from country-rock into straight country music.

Country Hit Singles:

Title	Label/Cat.No./Year	Peak Position
I'm Already Taken	(RCA 11173) 1978	63
So Sad (To Watch Good Love Go Bad)	(RCA 11336) 1978	76
Marie	(RCA 11447) 1979	94
Beside Me	(RCA 11658) 1979	60
Forget Me Not	(RCA 11658) 1979	49
The Easy Part Is Over	(RCA 12029) 1980	41
Your Memory	(RCA 12139) 1980/1	7
By Now	(RCA 12204) 1981	6
All Roads Lead To You	(RCA 12307) 1981	1
Kansas City Lights	(RCA 13072) 1982	15
Don't It Break Your Heart	(RCA 13308) 1982	30
Don't Plan On Sleepin' Tonight	(RCA 13395) 1982/3	27
Don't Your Mem'ry Ever Sleep At Night	(RCA 13515) 1983	23
Midnight Fire	(RCA 13588) 1983	5
Lonely Women Make Good Lovers	(RCA 13691) 1983/4	4
Why Goodbye	(RCA 13768) 1984	12
Don't You Give Up On Love	(RCA 13862) 1984	49
What I Didn't Do	(MCA 52506) 1984/5	3
Heart Trouble	(MCA 52562) 1985	8
Some Fools Never Learn	(MCA 52644) 1985	1
You Can Dream Of Me	(MCA 52721) 1985/6	1
Life's Highway	(MCA 52786) 1986	1
Starting Over Again	(MCA 52837) 1986	4
Small Town Girl	(MCA 53006) 1986/7	1
The Weekend	(MCA 53068) 1987	1
The Hand That Rocks The Cradle (duet with Glen Campbell)	(MCA 53108) 1987	6
Lynda	(MCA 53160) 1987	1
Baby I'm Yours	(MCA 53287) 1988	2
I Should Be With You	(MCA 53347) 1988	2
Hold On A Little Longer	(MCA 53419) 1988/9	6
Where Did I Go Wrong	(MCA 53504) 1989	1
I Got Dreams	(MCA 53665) 1989	1
When I Could Come Home To You	(MCA 53738) 1989/90	5
The Domino Theory	(MCA 53733) 1990	7
Precious Thing	(MCA 79051) 1990	8
There For Awhile	(MCA 53936) 1990	17
Now It Belongs To You (Duo with Mark O'Connor)	(Warner 4913) 1991	72
Leave Him Out Of This	(Arista 2349) 1991	6
The Tips Of My Fingers	(Arista 2393) 1992	3
A Woman Loves	(Arista 12426) 1992	9
Crash Course In The Blues	(Arista 12461) 1992	32
Like A River To The Sea	(Arista 1-2510) 1993	30
Drivin' And Cryin'	(Arista 1-2578) 1993	48

WEE JUNS

Released one 45, 'Way Down/With Your Love' (Skoop 1068) in the 1960s.

WHAT'S IT TO YA

Album
1( ) What's It To Ya   (Huh 80-928.3989) 1975

A local act about which we have no details at all.

WHY ON EARTH

Albums
1( ) Feel It Comin'   (New World   ) 1983
2( ) Why On Earth   (New World   ) 1985

Based in Indianapolis but apart from the fact that they played heavy rock we have no data.

WILDFIRE

Personnel	Ex	To
GARY JACOBSEN	THE TRAVELLS	
JACKIE JACOBSEN	THE TRAVELLS	
PAUL HUTCHINSON	CRACKERJACKS	
JOHN SCOTT	THE SPORTSMEN	
DAVE ELMORE		
DAVE MARTIN		
BILL KIRKPATRICK		
MIKE BERRY		

An '80s country outfit from Indianapolis. John Scott had played with the late '50s/early '60s outfit, **Keetie and The Kats** prior to **The Sportsmen**. Hutchinson had played for **The Jewels** and **The Five Checks** prior to joining **Crackerjacks** back in the '60s.

WILD ONES

The Singles
Tale Of A City/ No. 5   (Orlyn 66791) 196?
Please/Just Me   (Tiger   608) 1967

A garage band from Fort Wayne.

WILD THINGS

Santa Claus (Indiana) was home base for The Wild Things who released one 45, 'Love Comes, Love Goes/I'm Not For You' (Showboat 670 (9685-1516)), in 1966. You can check out the 'A' side on the 'Follow That Munster' (Rock 1101) 1969 compilation. They have been described as a folk garage band.

BILL WILSON

Albums
1   Everchanging Minstrel   (Windfall   ) 1974
2   Made In The USA   (Red Bud   ) 1980

A singer-songwriter. There is a third LP, title unknown, on BRBQ Records, issued in 1975.

WITH AUTHORITY

A Bloomington-based band who issued an EP in 1990 and a live cassette more recently.

DEAN WOLFE

An Indianapolis-based vocalist who fronted The Red Men, The Second Chapter and The Wolfe Pack during the 1960s.

DEAN WOLFE AND THE RED MEN

Personnel incl:		Ex	To
DEAN WOLFE	voc		

One of Wolfe's Indianapolis-based '60s outfit. They did not record.

DEAN WOLFE AND THE SECOND CHAPTER

Personnel		Ex	To
DEAN WOLFE	voc		
DON JESSIE			
HARRY NEIDIGH			
KEITH PAYNE			

Another Indianapolis-based '60s band fronted by Wolfe. They also didn't record.

DEAN WOLFE AND THE WOLFE PACK

Personnel incl:	Ex	To
DEAN WOLFE		

The last in the trilogy of '60s band from Indianapolis which Wolfe fronted.

THE WOMBATS

A hardcore band operating in late 1989. They began life as Enemy and later changed names again to Strike Three.

THE WOOLRIDGE BROS

Personnel incl:		Ex	To
SCOTT WOOLRIDGE	voc	PORT RAISIN BAND	
BRIAN WOOLRIDGE	bs	PORT RAISIN BAND	

A combo based in Kokomo who issued a 45 on the Don't 2 record label in 1992.

THE XL'S

The Singles
Second Choice/Ruined World   (Paro 100) 196?
Mary Jane/Mixed With The Rain   (Paro 202) 196?

Personnel		Ex	To
TED BENNETH	o		
G.C. EGY	bs		
BILL EVANS	voc		
TIM FERGUSON	gtr		
GREG FUNK	dr		

A 1960s band from Terre Haute.

THE YOUNG LORDS

Album
1( )	Down	(GDR	) 1993

Cassettes
1( )	Sons Of Regret	(	) 1989
2( )	Bucket	(	) 1992

Hardcore from Lafayette. They can also be heard on 'Children Of The Corn', a compilation of punk bands on Sonic Iguana, which emerged in 1990. They signed to Behamoth late in 1990 and are may have an album out on that label. The band have frequently been linked to Chicago and may actually be an Illinois band.

THE ZERO BOYS

Albums
1( )	Vicious Circles	(Nimrod 001/Toxic Shock TXLP 11) 1982	
2( )	Make It Stop	(BitzCore	) 1991

EP
1( )	Livin' In The '80s	(5 tracks)	(Z Records	) 1981

Personnel			Ex	To
MARK CUTSINGER	dr	A		
TERRY HOLLYWOOD	gtr	A		
JOHN MITCHELL	bs	A		
PAUL Z (MAHERN)	voc	A		DATURA SEEDS
PETER DAVIS	voc,gtr			

An Indianapolis outfit. The Toxic Shock version of (1) was a 1989 re-issue. The EP contains 'Livin' In The Eighties', 'Stoned To Death (For Sexual Offences)', Stick To Your Guns', 'I'm Bored', and 'A Piece Of Me'. In addition they have a cut, 'New Generation' on the 'Red Snerts' compilation (Gulcher GULCH-102) issued in 1981, and appear on the 'Nimrod Master Tapes' and 'Master Tapes 2' compilations. There is also a split 45 on Selfless with the Toxic Reasons.

ZOO GODS

Cassette
1	Zoo Gods	(Levin Inc.	) 1991

A new Indianapolis quintet. (1) is a four-track demo with hooky melodies, wah wah lead guitars, power drumming with a thick slice of blues-based metal meandering throughout.

The following artists were also based in Indiana, but had no recording output that we know of of or that we have much detail of:-

Name	Comment	Time Frame
ANXIETY NEUROSIS	Hardcore punk.	1990
BIG TROUBLE	Hardcore punk.	1990
BIRDMEN OF ALCATRAZ	A rock band.	1990
BITCH HEAD	Hardcore punk.	1990
BLACKLISTED	Hardcore - once known as Seminal Explosion.	1990
CRYPTIC ROT	Hardcore punk.	1990
DROP DEAD	Metal band from Indianapolis.	1990
HERETIC LUNCH	Hardcore band.	1990
JACKDAW	'70s Rock. Demos produced.	1974
THE KRITTERS	Gary-based band.	1960s
MONKEYFISH	Hardcore band.	1990
NIGHTCHILD	Indianapolis metal. 45 recorded.	1988
OUTSPOKEN	No data.	1990
THE PRIMATES	Hardcore.	1990
PSYCHO REGGAE	Hardcore. Signed to Secret Records.	1990
RAMBLECREW	Rock band.	197?
RATZKRIEG	Heavy metal.	1990
REHAB SPLATZ	Hardcore.	1990
RIOTS	An all-girl band from Gary.	1960s
DAN ROSS AND THE BRUNETTES	Bloomington rock band.	1984
THE SLEEZE DOGS	Hardcore. They have cassettes out.	1990
THE SQUIRES	Gary-based band.	1960s
SUNDIBLUE	Studio time 1978. Indianapolis-based.	1978
TWO PENNY HANGOVER	Hardcore band.	1990
VBF	Hardcore band.	1990

John Mellencamp (Indiana)

Credit: Polygram Records

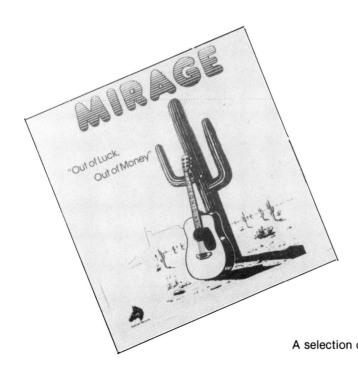

A selection of Iowa albums.

ANACRUSIS

2345 ERRINGER RD.
SUITE 108
SIMI VALLEY, CA. 93065

TCI
Talent Consultants Int'l
200 West 57th St. Suite 910
New York, NY 10019
FAX: (212) 974-9163
PHONE: (212) 582-9661

MISSOURI

ANTENNA

mammoth
RECORDS
CARR MILL 2ND FLOOR
CARRBORO, NC 27510
919·932·1882

INDIANA

Ike and Tina Turner (Missouri) during the seventies.
Courtesy of Record Collector.

Michael Jackson (Indiana)
Courtesy of Record Collector

Janet Jackson (Indiana). Courtesy of A & M Records.

The back cover of Pavlov's Dog's
'Pampered Menial' album.

The inside centrefold of Pavlov's Dog excellent debut 'Pampered Menial'. (Missouri).

BLAKE BABIES

mammoth
R E C O R D S
CARR MILL 2ND FLOOR
CARRBORO, NC 27510 919·932·1882

INDIANA

The Morells (Missouri)

The Daybreakers (Iowa)

The XLs (Iowa)

Tina Turner's 12 inch 'Let's Stay Together' single.

King of the Hill. Photo courtesy of Metal Hammer magazine.

The back cover of Brewer and Shipley's 'Shake Off The Demo album.

Brewer and Shipley. The inside centrefold from their 'Tarkio' album.

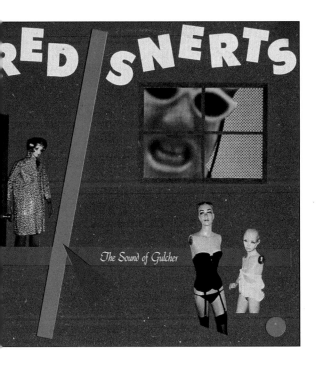

RED SNERTS

The Sound of Gulcher

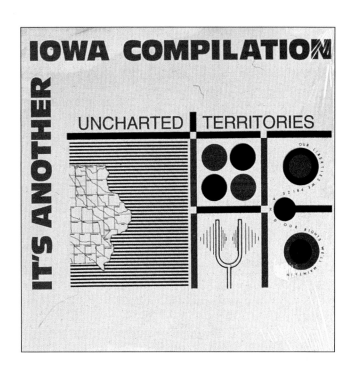

IT'S ANOTHER IOWA COMPILATION

UNCHARTED TERRITORIES

SHAKE AND PUSH

THE MORELLS

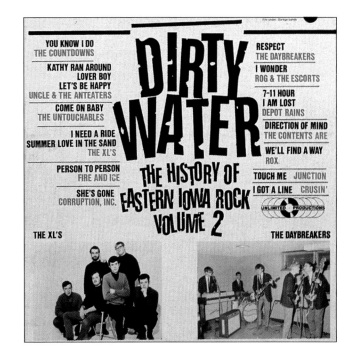

File under: Garage bands

YOU KNOW I DO
THE COUNTDOWNS

KATHY RAN AROUND
LOVER BOY
LET'S BE HAPPY
UNCLE & THE ANTEATERS

COME ON BABY
THE UNTOUCHABLES

I NEED A RIDE
SUMMER LOVE IN THE SAND
THE XL'S

PERSON TO PERSON
FIRE AND ICE

SHE'S GONE
CORRUPTION, INC.

THE XL'S

DIRTY WATER

THE HISTORY OF
EASTERN IOWA ROCK
VOLUME 2

RESPECT
THE DAYBREAKERS

I WONDER
ROG & THE ESCORTS

7-11 HOUR
I AM LOST
DEPOT RAINS

DIRECTION OF MIND
THE CONTENTS ARE

WE'LL FIND A WAY
ROX.

TOUCH ME JUNCTION

I GOT A LINE CRUSIN'

UNLIMITED PRODUCTIONS

THE DAYBREAKERS

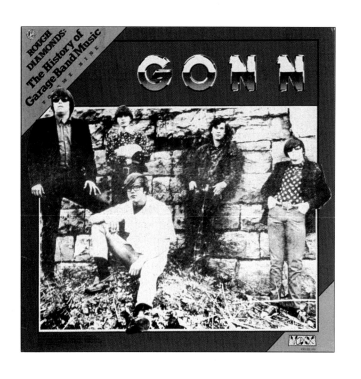

ROUGH DIAMONDS:
The History of
Garage Band Music
VOLUME NINE

GONN

VoXX

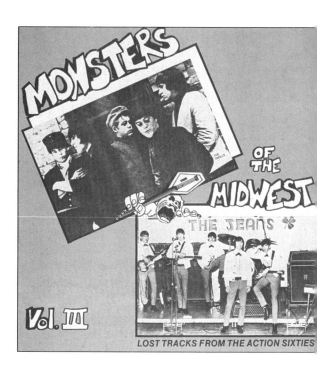

MONSTERS

OF THE

MIDWEST

THE JEANS

Vol. III

LOST TRACKS FROM THE ACTION SIXTIES

SHOOTING STARS · WILD THINGS · XL'S · IDLE FEW

SIR WINSTON & THE COMMONS · MERE IMAGE

HOOSIER
HOTSHOTS

BACKDOOR MEN · FERRIS WHEEL · THE ENDD

TEEN TONES · CIRKIT · DUKES · TIKIS · BLUES INC.

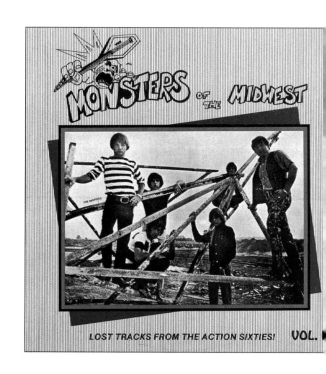

MONSTERS OF THE MIDWEST

LOST TRACKS FROM THE ACTION SIXTIES!   VOL.

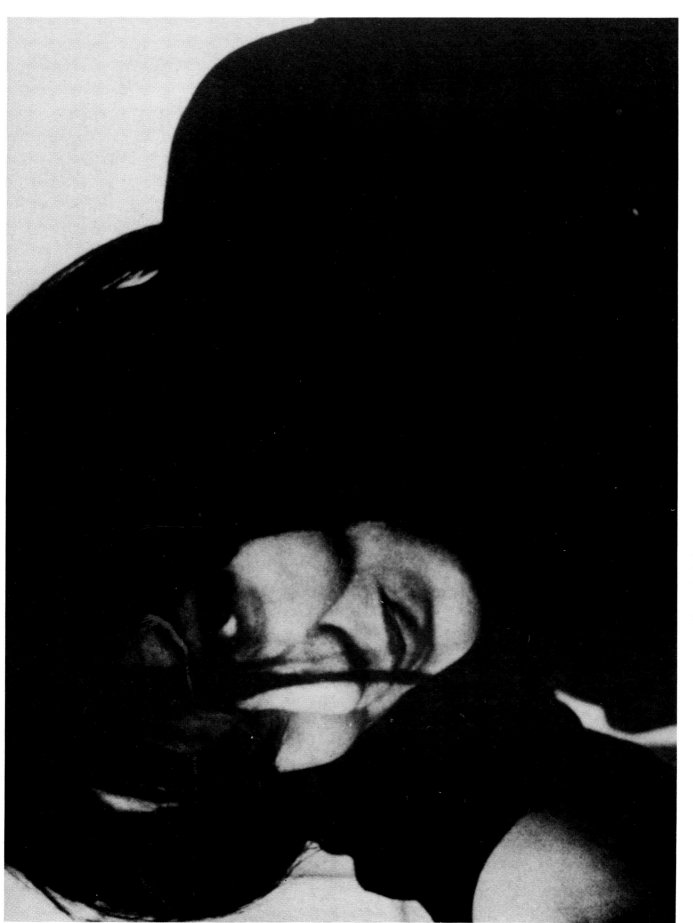

Juliana Hatfield (Indiana). Courtesy of Mammoth Records.

PRS 1001

BASS GUITAR & VOCALS — TIM McCORKLE

LEAD GUITAR & VOCALS — STEVE MEYERS

DRUMS — LEWIS McCORKLE

RECORDED AT LIBERTY SOUND

ENGINEER — BOB COLE

ROAD MANAGER — K.C. GEORGE FIELDS

ART DESIGN — CHANDRA HAMM

**Produced by Chris Fritz for Panama Records.
Special Thanks to Ron West, Bill Bergman,
Jeff Walker, Charlie Zych, Tim Miller,
and Stan Koron.**

SEITE-I

1) TAKE YOU AWAY — 4:41
2) U.S. IS COMING AROUND — 3:47
3) CRUMBLING TOWERS — 3:43
4) BANKERS BAR — 4:30
5) FIND A NEW DAY — 3:20

SEITE II

6) OUT ON THE TIDE — 3:56
7) CEILING WALL — 4:35
8) GLITTER BOOTS BOOGIE — 3:47
9) LET ME KNOW — 3:20
10) LETTERS TO MYSELF — 4:45

The Daybreakers (Iowa).

The Royal Flairs (Iowa).

Photo courtesy of Metal Hammer Magazine.

I O W A

Known as the Hawkeye State Iowa, which covers an area of 56,290 square miles, contains a quarter of the nation's best farmland. Herbert Hoover, the 31st President of the United States was born here in West Branch in 1874 in a two-room cottage that is now part of the National Historic Site, where he was buried in 1964. The story of his career is told by mementos and displays in the Hoover Presidential Library. Iowa became the 29th State to achieve Statehood on 28 December 1846. The state flower is the Wild Rose.

The gold leafed dome of the state capital in Des Moines towers above what is a prospering centre of manufacturing, finance, publishing and culture. Other main population centres are:-

Cedar Rapids at the rapids of the Cedar river as its name indicates. An industrial centre, it is particularly noted for meat and grain processing and farm equipment manufacturing.

Council Bluffs over in the West on the border with Nebraska. First a fur post, then an important Mormon town, it became something of a ghost town when Brigham Young led his followers west to Salt Lake City. The railroads brought it back to some prominence.

Davenport down in the South-East of the State is an important cultural centre.

Dubuque in the East beside the Mississippi offers rides on an incline railway and river steamers. It is named after Julian DuBuque who once mined lead with the Indians there.

Iowa City now houses the University of Iowa as well as the Old Capitol building, since it was once the capital of the Iowa territory.

Keokuk which takes its name from the Indian Chief Keokuk who was buried in Rand Park. The Keokuk Dam, built in 1913 runs for a mile across the Mississippi and the 'George M. Verity', an old towboat, is now a river museum.

Waterloo over in the West, on the border with Nebraska and South Dakota, is notable for a 100-foot shaft on the banks of the Missouri River, which commemorates the grave of Sergent Charles Floyd, who died of appendicitis on the Pioneering Lewis and Clark Expedition in 1804.

Iowa is really the heart of America's conservative Midwestern farming communities. It is possible to drive for miles upon miles through fields of corn and scattered farmhouses. Now what about its music?

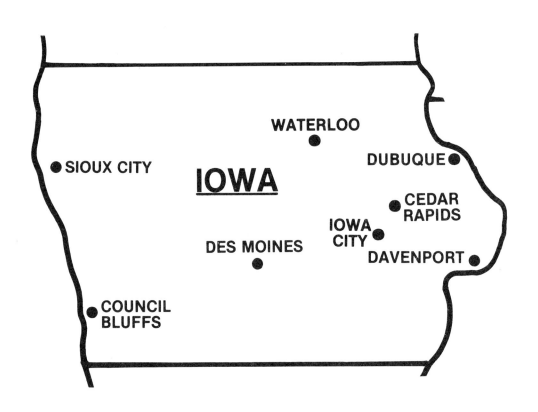

I O W A

23 LIES

Personnel			Ex	To
FARIS	gtr,voc	A		
JOEL MARAIS	gtr,voc	A		
TIM JOHNSON	bs,voc	A		
VINNE LUMSDON	dr	A		

Based in the state capital Des Moines, this quartet can be sampled on 'Another Iowa Compilation' (South East SER-006) issued in 1988.

THE ACTIVATORS

A '60s outfit from Spirit Lake who have one cut, 'Stormy Monday' on the 'Roof Garden Jamboree Album' (IGL 103) 1967.

ADELMUND BROTHERS AND THE COUNTRY KINGS

Country artists who recorded 'My Pride And I/Someone Told My Story' (IGL 163) on the Milford-based label in the late '60s.

AFTERFLASH

A late '60s outfit from Oelwein who recorded one 45, 'Cook Book/Leave Myself To Die' (Hawkeye 207).

AL'S UNTOUCHABLES

Personnel incl:		Ex	To
AL HUNTZINGER	dr		
TOM HAWKINS	bs		
RON BRESSLER	dr		
BRUCE NUNEMAKER	gtr		
DICKIE DOUGLAS	ld.gtr		

Both sides of this '60s Johnny and The Hurricanes-style instrumental band 45, 'Come On Baby/Stick Around' (Hunt 6007), later resurfaced on the 1982 'Boulders, Vol.4' (Max MLP.04) compilation. Al Huntzinger and Dickie Douglas were later in The Untouchables. In 1973 two previously unissued cuts emerged, 'No-one Left To Love' and 'Psychedelic Mantra'. These were issued, along with the 45 cuts, on an EP.

AMBER

Operated out of Denison in the early '70s. We know of one 45, 'Freedom/Cantasa' (Galaxy 1061).

AMERICAN LEGEND

Late '60s Beatles clones who made vinyl in 1968 with 'Back In The USSR/Sunshine Morning' (DJ101). It was recorded in Minneapolis.

ANCIENT BOYGIRLS

Cassette
1( ) The Horrible Monster Album   (   ) 1993

A curious combo from Grinel.

ANTELON

A '70s rock outfit based in Des Moines. Their sole vinyl excursion was 'Real Life/You May Be Surprised' (Icarus 594-25) in 1974.

ARTIFICIAL LIMB EMBRACE

Curiously named project which is actually just one man, Ed Ware. Perhaps there is something in the air in Iowa. Featured on the compilation, 'Another Iowa Compilation' on South East Records (SER.006) which emerged in 1988.

AUSTIN & GRAF

A rock/pop duo whose sole vinyl offering was 'Mary Neil Blair/Go Get 'Em Geo. Handy (Frekyl 0001) in 1970.

THE BANDITO'S

A covers band from Arnolds Park who gave their own country-rock interpretation of Buddy Holly's 'Peggy Sue' and Tom Jones' 'Green Green Grass Of Home' on IGL (189) in the early '70s.

BANDS OF GOLD

The architect of this project was Roger Hughes after he left **Dee Jay and The Runaways**. It produced one 45, 'You Won't Change Me/It's Over' (Smash 2058) in the late '60s.

JACK BARLOW

The Singles
All I Have Is You/ ?	(Golden Ring 3021)	196?
House Of Stone/Step Down	(Soma 1175)	196?
After All/49-51	(Soma 1420)	196?
After All/49-51	(Apex 76943)	197?

Hailing from Des Moines, Jack was a country rock artist whose career spanned the late '60s and early '70s.

MAX D. BARNES

Albums
1	Rough Around The Edges	(Ovation 1749)	1980
2	Pieces Of My Life	(Country Roads)	1981

A country rocker from Hardscratch who uprooted himself to Nashville in 1971. There was also a 1972 45 on Jed Records.

THE (SILVER HAIRED) BEACH NIKS

The Singles
Like Stoned/Good Things	(MMC 007)	1966
Last Night I Cried/It Was A Nightmare	(MMC 008)	1966
Last Night I Cried/It Was A Nightmare	(Sea Mist 1001)	1966

A highly-touted '60s punk outfit from Newell. 'Last Night I Cried' has resurfaced on the cassette compilation, 'Monsters Of The Midwest, Vol.1'. Some members ended up in **Dee Jay and the Runaways** and **The Coachmen**.

BELL AND SHORE

Albums
1(A)	Little Movies	(Flying Fish 460)	1988
2(A)	L Ranko Motel	(R.O.M. 26008)	1989

Personnel	Ex	To
NATHAN BELL	A	
SUSAN SHORE	A	

A fine Iowa-based country-rock folk duo who are well worth searching out.

THE BERRIES

Came out of Des Moines and recorded one 45, 'I've Been Looking/Baby, That's All' (IGL 133) in 1967. The flip can be found on 'Monsters Of The Midwest, Vol.4'. It's a Hollies cover with lots of ringing twelve-string hook-lines.

STEVE BLEDSOE

The Singles
Three-Thirty Blues/After Hours	(VEM 227)	19??
Green Cheese/Dumb Dumb Bunny	(Witch 102)	19??
Move On Down The Line/ ?	(Kahill 1050)	19??
Stan The Man/ ?	(Scope 1961)	19??
Cool Steppin' Baby/ ?	(Scope 8266)	19??

A rock artist whose recording career spanned the late '50s and early '60s.

BLUE WATER TRIO

A pop trio out of Spirit Lake who recorded 'Angel/Bus Driver Blues' (IGL 217) in the early '70s.

TOMMY BOLIN

Bolin was originally from Iowa and was of mixed white/Red Indian parentage. He later ended up in Colorado where he formed a band called Zephyr before joining The James Gang in 1973. He eventually settled in LA and his life and death was documented in 'Volume 1' of this series, 'California, The Golden State'.

BONESTEEL

Album
1( ) One More Hour	(Lazy Day Records no number) 197?

A '70s rock outfit based in Sioux City, this was a later version of The Lazy Day Band.

HANK BOWKER AND THE SUNNY BLUE TRIO

Personnel incl:	Ex	To
HANK BOWKER		

Country-popsters who recorded 'Just A Step Away/Tomorrow's An Empty Yesterday' (IGL 159) for the Milford-based label in the late '60s.

DEREK BRANDON

Based in Iowa City in the late '60s this pop artist recorded one 45, 'Now You Know/Tree In The Meadow' (Blessing 10002).

BYRON BREFFLE

Came from Lake Park and released 'Maybe Baby/Why Did It Happen' (IGL 112) in 1966. The 'A' side was a Buddy Holly number. Later in 1968 he revealed his true identity when he released 'Run For Your Life/Because I Love You' (IGL 145) under his true name, Brian Scott.

BRILLO AND THE FIREBIRDS

This rock outfit hailed from Quad Cities and their sole vinyl offering was 'Calling Red Rover/Some Place To Hide' (Golden Voice 834) in 1968.

BRIMSTONE

Issued 'Home Cooking/Visions Of Autumn' (Lanco 3122-23) in the early '70s.

DAVID BROOKS BAND

Appear on the 'Iowa Compilation' album on South East Records, issued in mid-1987.

GREG BROWN

Albums
1( )	One Big Town	(Red House	) 1990
2( )	Down In There	(Red House	) 1991

A singer-songwriter based in southern Iowa.

THE BY AND BYS

Mid-'60s rockers whose sole platter was 'Thanks To You/Keep It Free' (Holland 6730) in 1967.

CAPTAIN KIRK

Album
1	Captain Kirk	(Cognito 600) 1970?

This was actually Fort Dodge-based Kirk Kaufmann prior to the formation of **The Hawks** but after the demise of **Westminst'r**.

CAPT. AMERICAN JONES

A pop outfit from Spirit Lake who cut one side of a 45, 'No Guts, No Glory' (IGL 253) in the mid-'70s. The flip was by a different act - The Clay Country Band.

THE CASTELS

Came out of Milford with 'Look What Love Has Done/How Can You Tell' (IGL 107) in 1965.

CHANCE

Came out of Cedar Rapids in the late '60s/early '70s. Their sole vinyl epitaph was their cover of 'Heard It Through The Grapevine' backed by 'Little Valleys' (Jungle 131). They were a 7-piece.

THE CHEVELLES

A vocal sextet from Spirit Lake, some of whom were later in **Dee Jay And The Runaways**. Two 45s were released:- 'Blue Chevelle/Mala-Boo' (Bangar 0603) (in a picture sleeve) and 'Chevelle Stomp/Dear Sue' (Bangar 0616), both in 1963.

CHRONIC LOVE

Personnel			Ex	To
MARK BRUGGEMAN	dr,voc	A		DANGTRIPPERS
J. LARS FATLAND	voc	A		
DIRK PIERCE	gtr,voc	A		

| PAT POWERS | bs | A |
| BRENDA SYPAL | b/g,voc | (A) |

An Iowa-based quartet with a cut on 'Another Iowa Compilation' (South East SER-006) 1988.

DOYLE CLARK AND THE SUNDOWNERS

| Personnel incl: | | Ex | To |
| DOYLE CLARK | | | |

A country act from Jefferson who recorded 'It's Christmas/I Just Seen Santa Clause' (Ven-Jence 4) and 'Nothing/Am I Wasting My Teardrops' (IGL 231) in the early '70s.

CLAUDE PATE

Album
1   Situation   (Pravda   ) 1988

An Iowa trio who appeared on the 'Iowa Compilation' album on South East Records in 1987, the same year that their first 45, 'If You Will/Ain't There, It's Gone' was issued by Pravda. The band relocated to Minneapolis but fell apart in 1989. Pretty poor fare too, in the main!

CLE-SHAYS

Issued one 45, 'Spend All My Money/Annabelle Zodd' (Monex 5232) in 1968. They came from Des Moines and the 45 was a garage rocker.

THE COACHMEN

| Personnel incl: | | Ex | To |
| LENNY SWAT | gtr | | DEPOT RAINS |

An early Muscatine garage band with no vinyl output.

COLT .45

Album
1( ) Colt .45   (Fanfare 4080) 19??

A Des Moines rock band. Pretty rare stuff.

THE COMBINATION BRIDGE

A rock outfit who emerged from Sioux City with 'What A Night It's Been/I'm Just Pretending' (IGL 167) circa 1969.

CONCRETE FACE

EP
1   The Man With The Concrete Face   (South East   ) 1987

Nothing else known.

THE CONFEDERACY

From Belmond, this quintet recorded 'Feelin' Free/So Far Away' (United Artists 1139) in the late '60s. They were later known as Catch.

THE CONTENTS ARE

Hailing from Davenport this mob actually made an album (which we have no details of). Recorded at Fredlo it was possibly the only album released in eastern Iowa. It was reputedly full of Byrdish tunes like their track 'Direction Of Mind' on 'Dirty Water: The History Of Eastern Iowa Rock, Vol.2' (Unlimited Productions RRRLP-003) 1986. They released two 45s in 1967:- 'I Don't Know/Direction Of Mind' (ROK 6709) and 'Future Days/New Mexico' (ROK 6907).

CORRUPTION, INC.

Personnel			Ex	To
TOM HETZLER		A		THE DAYBREAKERS
THOM WESSELS	gtr	A	THE DUQUESNES	
JIM LOGEL	voc	A		
MIKE McCLEARY	gtr	A		
DAVE MEYERS	dr	A		

From Iowa City they recorded one 45, 'She's Gone/Somewhere' (Hunt 1201) in late 1966 or early '67 in the upstairs of an Iowa City store. The band were quite popular in Iowa City and also played in places like Cedar Rapids and Burlington. The 'A' side, a Seeds-style punk number with a screeching intro, can be heard on the compilation, 'Dirty Water: The History Of Eastern Iowa Rock, Vol.2' (Unlimited Productions RRRLP-003) 1986. Also impressive is Jim Logel's double track vocal.

COTTONWOOD

A '70s rock act from Sioux City who cut two 45s:- 'Sunshine Woman/No Feeling Left Inside' (Magic 45003) and 'It Feels So Good/Round And Round' (Magic 45005).

THE COUNTDOWNS

Personnel incl:		Ex	To
LARRY BARRETT	voc,gtr		UNCLE AND THE ANTEATERS

Hailed from Coralville, a suburb of Iowa City. Originally known as The Friars they recorded one 45, 'You Know I Do/Strange Are The Shadows' (Fiji 691) in 1965. It also got a release the same year on Bear (1968). This high school combo later changed their name to Uncle And The Anteaters (sometimes spelled Uncle Na Anteaters). Barrett, apart from singing and playing guitar on 'You Know I Do', also wrote it. You can hear it on the 'Dirty Water: The History Of Eastern Iowa Rock, Vol.2' (Unlimited Productions RRRLP-003) 1986 and on 'Monsters Of The Midwest, Vol.4' but it's not worth seeking out. Barrett was also later involved in The XL's.

THE COUNTRY LADS

A country outfit as their name suggests, from Davenport. They made vinyl in 1964 with 'The V. Spike Jones Boogie/Pick Me Up On Your Way Down' (Fredlo 6414).

COUNTRY SPICE

This country-rock outfit recorded a 45, 'Cajun Lady/Clouds' (Sonic 227), for the Milford-based label in the early '70s.

CRANK

A late '60s/early '70s act from western Iowa who made vinyl twice with 'Cloudburst/Sweet Iowa Woman' (Blue Rose 2,000,000) and 'Come One Come All/Hot Old Sun' (UA 1567).

BOB CREAGER AND THE WESTONES

Personnel incl:	Ex	To
BOB CREAGER		

Country-rockers from Shenandoah who released 'Back Again To Cry/Company Time' (IGL 144) in 1968.

BARRY CREES AND THE HAWKS

A late '60s pop act from Iowa City who made just one 45, 'Fall Is Here' (Falcon 101). The flip side was an instrumental version of the same song.

CRUSIN'

EP
1( ) Gold   (Rock 'n' Roll 0002) 1983

Personnel			Ex	To
MAX ALLAN COLLINS	voc,KB	AB	ROX	
PAUL THOMAS	bs	AB	ROX	THE ONES
RIC STEED	dr	AB	JUNCTION	THE ONES
LENNY SLOAT	gtr	A	DEPOT RAINS	
BRUCE PETERS	voc	B	ROX	THE ONES

Collins put this outfit together in Iowa City in 1976 as a '60s 'oldies' band in reaction to the emerging disco scene. Sloat soon departed to be replaced by Peters making the band almost a reincarnation of The Daybreakers. 'Dirty Water: The History Of Eastern Iowa Rock, Vol.2' (Unlimited Productions RRRLP-003) 1986, captures a live performance of the band singing 'I Got A Line' (with Peters on vocals) from 1977. 'The History Of Eastern Iowa Rock, Vol.1' (Unlimited Productions RRRLP-002) 1985 also features three of their cuts:- 'Bus Stop' and 'Twist And Shout' (with Bruce Peters on vocals) and 'Gimme Some Lovin'' (with Max Allan Collins doing the vocal honours).

An August 1983 one off reunion led to a five song EP, (1). It had a limited pressing of 1,000 and featured live performances of 'A Little Bit O' Soul', 'Little Latin Lupe Lu' and 'Wild Thing' plus two new studio tracks:- 'Her Rock And Roll Man' and 'Future Of Our Love'.

THE CURSING BIRDS

Average rock from Iowa who can be heard on 'Iowa Compilation', (the first of a series of such recordings) released by South East Records in 1987.

TED CUTLER AND BALL PEN REDEMPTION

Personnel		Ex	To
TED CUTLER	gtr,voc		
ZELEKE MOGOBO	dr		
KHAMPRASONG	bs		

This trio can be heard on 'Another Iowa Compilation' issued by South East Records (SER-006) in 1988. Based in the state capital, Des Moines.

DAHCOTAH

A quintet out of Cedar Rapids whose sole stab for stardom, 'Too Easy To Love/She's A Bore' (Cognito 006), came in a picture sleeve. The band spanned the late '60s and early '70s.

DALE AND THE DEVONAIRES

A '60s dance quintet from Fort Dodge, who released 'Never Be Free/Take A Look At A Fool' (IGL 116) and a folk-rock 45, 'Come Back To Me/Look Up' (DEB 8500) circa 1966/67.

DALE AND THE OPTIONS

A mid to late '60s act whose sole vinyl excursion was 'Teach Me Diana/You're So Fine' (B-Wolf 101).

THE DANGTRIPPERS

Album
1(B)   Days Between Stations   (Dog Gone 005) 1989

EPs
1(A)   Incantation   (3 tracks)   (South East   ) 1987
2(B)   Jack Knife   (4 tracks)   UK only   (Rocket   5) 1990

Compilation appearances
1( )   Iowa Compilation   (South East   ) 1987
2(A)   Another Iowa Compilation   (South East SER-006) 1988
3( )   Not The Songer But The Songs (an Alex Chilton tribute)   (Munster   012) 1993

Personnel			Ex	To
DEVIN HILL	gtr,voc	AB		
MOGO MITCHELL	dr	A		
SCOTT STRECKLEIN	bs	AB		
DOUG ROBERSON	voc,gtr	AB		
MARK BRUGGEMAN	dr	B	CHRONIC LOVE	

The Iowa City band debuted in 1987 with an EP, an 'artsy' sleeve housing jangle-pop full of '60s influences, not unlike REM. The disc was given excellent reviews. The second EP (the title cut is also on the first EP) was more of the same but, like the album, featured a new line-up. They really are rather good and have attracted attention in Europe, and even the U.S.A. majors are sniffing around. In 1992 they released 'Headhunter/Henry Slade' on Susstones. The band have connections with Head Candy and Voodoo Gearshift.

DANTES

Hailed from Des Plaines with 'Can't Get Enough/80-96' (Jamie 1314) in 1966.

THE DARK KNIGHTS

A garage quintet from Storm Lake who released 'Send Her To Me/Dark Knight' (IGL 111) in 1966.

THE DAYBREAKERS

Album
1(A)   The History Of Eastern Iowa Rock, Volume 1:   The Daybreakers   (Unlimited Productions RRRLP 0002) 1985

N.B.   This is a compilation of their 45s and previously unissued material.

Personnel incl:			Ex	To
MAX ALLAN COLLINS	voc,KB	A		ROX
TERRY BECKEY	bs,voc	A		JUNCTION
LARRY BARRETT	gtr,voc			
BRUCE PETERS	voc	A		ROX
PAUL THOMAS	bs	A		ROX
DENNY MAXWELL	gtr			JUNCTION
MIKE BRIDGES	gtr			
BUDDY BUSCH	KB			

Hailing from Iowa City in eastern Iowa, this outfit travelled to Nashville during 1967 to record a number of tracks, two of which,

'Psychedelic Siren/Afterthoughts' (Dial 45-4066) were released on a 45 the same year. 'Psychedelic Siren', notable for its screeching siren intro. and backing, is usually regarded as their finest moment and can also be found on two compilation collections (aside from (1)):- 'Psychedelic Unknowns' (Calico Records EP 00001A) - this was a double EP - and 'Psychedelic Unknowns' (Calico Records PSY 101) - an album which also contains nineteen cuts by various other artists. They hoped to have a song called 'Daybreak' released as a second 45, but Buddy Killen, who had produced their first session felt the lyrics should be redone. Other previously unreleased material from their Nashville session included 'If You Really Love Me' and 'Summertime'. After the session they returned to Iowa and continued to work on demo tapes at the Fredlo Recording Studio. 'Daybreak' was redone with new lyrics and sent to Killen but he never invited them back to Nashville to record another session. A later version of this haunting number is included on (1). 'Evil Woman', 'Show Me' and 'Woman', all fast punkers, also emerged from the Fredlo demo tapes. Aside from cuts from the Nashville and Fredlo sessions, (1) also includes four cuts from the band's twilight days in 1971 when they were known as Rox. These are all well crafted British-influenced rockers written by Bruce Peters on which he provides the vocals. Finally (1) contains three tracks:- 'Bus Stop', 'Twist And Shout' and 'Gimme Some Lovin'' - by Cruisin', which was a sort of partial reunion line-up from 1977.

'Dirty Water: The History Of Eastern Iowa Rock, Vol.2' (Unlimited Productions RRRLP-003) 1986, also includes a pretty rough live version from 1968 of 'Respect' by the band, which was guitarist, Mike Bridges', last performance with the band.

DEE JAY AND THE RUNAWAYS

The Singles			Peak Position
Jenny Jenny/Boney Moronie	(IGL	100) 1965	-
Love Bug Crawl/The Pickup	(Coulee	109) 1965	-
Peter Rabbit/Three Steps To Heaven	(IGL	103) 1965	-
Peter Rabbit/Are You Ready?	(Smash S-2034) 1966		45
Peter Rabbit/Three Steps To Heaven	(Smash S-2034) 1966		-
She's A Big Girl Now/He's Not Your Friend	(Smash S-2049) 1966		-
* Keep On Running/Don't You Ever	(Sonic	132) 1966	-
* Keep On Running/Don't You Ever	(Stone	45) 1967	-
My Gal/Doesn't Matter Anymore	(Sonic	148) 1967	-
Sunshine Morning/And I Know	(Sonic	158) 1967	-
Love Tender, Love/While You Were Sleeping	(Dee Jay	101) 1982	-

* With Terry Klein (ex-Templars and later solo act)

Personnel incl:		Ex	To
DENNY KINTZI	KB		solo
JOHNNY SENN (JAY)	voc		JOHN SENN & THE FORTUNES
DENNY STOREY (DEE)		DENNY + DUKES	solo
GARY LIND	voc		
BOB			
CURT POWELL	ld.gtr		solo
ROGER HUGHES		DENNY + DUKES	

Operated out of Spirit Lake where they enjoyed a good local reputation. Things began to look up for them when their vocalist, Johnny Senn, got together with Cliff Plagman and Roger Blunt from Milford to discuss setting up a local recording studio. The IGL studios were established and 'Jenny Jenny' became the label's debut recording in June 1964. Having a pressing of just 100 it is now extremely rare. Their follow-up, 'Peter Rabbit', a popish number, was the label's most successful recording. It was later picked up by the Chicago-based Smash label and distributed throughout the US and Canada. It also got the band an appearance on Dick Clark's 'Where The Action Is' TV show. After a further nationwide recording for Smash they reverted to the Sonic label for three further 45s. The first of these, 'Keep On Running' (the Spencer Davis number) which they recorded with Terry Klein, former vocalist with local band The Temptors, also got a release on the Stone label without the band even knowing.

Surprisingly none of the band's releases have appeared on the flurry of compilations of '60s material that have surfaced in recent years, although 'Don't You Ever' was included on the Various Artists LP 'Roof Garden Jamboree' (IGL 103) 1967 at the time. Kintzi, Storey and Powell all recorded solo 45s for IGL/Sonic as did Tim Smith, a South Dakotan who had written 'Peter Rabbit'. Senn recorded an album for IGL with a new band The Fortunes.

The later 45 release in 1982 included a picture and story insert.

DENNY AND THE DUKES

This project was the work of Roger Hughes and Denny Storey (later of **Dee Jay and The Runaways**) and operated out of Sioux City producing one 45, 'In A Thousand Cities/Is It Really Love?' (Sultan 1002) in the mid-'60s.

DEPOT RAINS

Personnel incl:			Ex	To
DENNY FRY	voc	A	THE ROGUES	
NICK RADCLIFFE	dr	A	THE ROGUES	
LENNY SLOAT	gtr	A	THE COACHMEN	CRUSIN'

This Muscatine folk-rock outfit emerged out of two of the town's earliest garage bands, The Rogues and The Coachmen. The compilation 'Dirty Water: The History of Eastern Iowa Rock, Vol.2' (Unlimited Productions RRRLP-003) 1986 features two cuts by the band which were the product of an early 1968 session at RCA studio in Chicago. They were '7-11 Hour (Whiskey Hollow)', a poetical folk-rock composition written and sung by Denny Fry and 'I Am Lost', a folk-tinged Lenny Sloat composition on which he does the vocal honours.

DEPUTY DOG BAND

A '70s band from Mason City who struck vinyl with 'Melinda Rose./S.O.L.' (Dawg-Gone 002).

THE DOGS

Personnel incl:	Ex	To
JUDY KOENIG		solo

Issued a 45, 'Teen Slime/Rot And Roll' on Rave-Up.

DONNA AND THE TENNESSEE MOONSHINERS

These country-rockers came out of Sioux City with 'Giesha Girl/The Root Of All Evil' (IGL 104) in 1965.

THE DO'S AND DON'TS

The Singles
Be Sure/Still Remember The Past	(Zorch 103)	196?
Cherry Lane/Girl In The Corner	(Zorch 10234-1)	1967
The Scrogg/Loving You The Way I Do	(Zorch 105)	196?
Woman/No One To Talk My Troubles To	(Zorch 106)	196?
Let The Sun Shine Free/She's Walking Out Of Life	(Zorch 107)	196?
I Wonder If She Loves Me/Our Love May Not Live Again	(Red Bird 10-072)	196?
Hot Rock And Roll To Go/Being With You Girl	(Zorch 108)	196?

Based in Ely and Cedar Rapids this rock outfit was formed out of the ashes of **The Escorts**. They were a quintet with a woman pianist.

LARRY DOWD AND THE ROCK-A-TONES

Late '50s rockers out of Des Moines. They made vinyl twice with 'Why, Oh Why/Forbidden Love' (Spinning 6004) and the highly regarded 'Blue Swinging Mama/Pink Cadillac' (Spinning 6009).

THE DOWNBEATS, WITH EDDIE RANDALL

Personnel incl:		Ex	To
EDDIE RANDALL			

Hailed from Cedar Rapids with just one 45, 'Fool's Paradise/Down Beat Rock' (QT 1629) in the late '50s/early '60s. It is reputed to be a fine early rocker.

DREDNEX

Featured on the 'Iowa Compilation' on South East Records from 1987. No other data available.

DRUNKEN BOAT

Album
1( ) See Ruby Falls   (First Warning 75714) 1992

EP
1( ) New Pop   (First Warning 75704) 1991

Personnel incl:		Ex	To
TODD COLBY	voc		

This Iowa combo relocated to New York City as early as 1987. The output noted was issued by Steve Wynn's label.

DUBONDI

A pop act which cut one 45, 'Call Me Back/Being Away' (RAP 27924) in the '60s.

THE DUQUESNES

Personnel incl:		Ex	To
THOM WESSELS	gtr		CORRUPTION INC.
CHUCK BUNN	bs		THE DAYBREAKERS

This Iowa City '60s mob did not record.

DVC

Album
1(A) DVC   (Alfa 11005) 1981

Personnel			Ex	To
JOHNNY BOLIN	dr	A	TOMMY BOLIN BAND	
JOHN BARTLE	gtr	A	JAN PARK BAND	
MAX PADILLA	bs	A		
ROB FOREST	gtr,voc	A		

This combo operated from around 1975 onwards. Johnny Bolin is indeed the brother of guitar virtuoso, the late Tommy Bolin and Tommy did actually cut some tapes with DVC in 1976.

THE ECLECTICS

Compilation Appearances:
1( ) Iowa Compilation   (South East   ) 1987
2(A) Another Iowa Compilation   (South East 006) 1988

Personnel			Ex	To
MARKY DEN HARTOG	voc,gtr	A		
DENNIS A VOLKERT	ld.gtr	A		
SCOTT HANNA	bs	A		
DON HISCOCKS	dr	A		

Local band. Local sound. There was a 45 on South East in 1988.

EDGE

A new wave band from Iowa who can be heard on the 'Music For No Man's Land' compilation with 'Not Foolin' Me' (Fly Girl CT-001) in August 1981.

EDISON EFFECT

This late '60s rock act from Quad Cities made vinyl with 'Happy Days/Important Things' (Thought 6945) in 1969.

EHLERS 4 PLUS MOORE

Popsters from Sioux Rapids who released 'My Heart Sings/You've Lost That Lovin' Feeling' (Sonic 183) in the early '70s. The flip was, of course, a hit for the Righteous Brothers back in 1965.

SCOTT ELSTON

A '70s popster who recorded 'Wipeout/Mama Don't Allow' (Ven Jence no number).

GENE ENO AND TOM WELLS

Personnel	Ex	To
GENE ENO		
TOM WELLS		

This country duo from Sioux City issued one 45, 'Old Joe's Rock Hound/Old Joe's Brag' (IGL 222), in the early '70s.

ENOCH SMOKEY

A hippie trio from Anamosa who released a version of 'Roll Over Beethoven' backed by 'It's Cruel' on Pumpkin Seed (83-4010) in the 1970s.

THE ESCORTS

Personnel incl:		Ex	To
ROGER BOOTH	voc		

The Singles
Main Drag/Judy Or Jo Ann	(Soma 1144)	19??
Space Walk/You're The One	(Zorch 101)	19??
I Wonder/Our Love May Not Live Again	(Zorch 102)	19??
I Found Love/I Wanna Do It	(Fredlo 6311)	1963
The Wobble Drum/On Top ...	(Fredlo 6403)	1964
Heart Of Mine/Twelfth Of Never	(Fredlo 6416)	1964

From Ely/Cedar Rapids The Escorts' career spanned the late '50s to the late '60s when they then reformed as The Do and Don'ts. A quartet, they featured a female pianist.

THE ESTABLISHMENT

Came out of Mason City in the late '60s with 'After The Lights Go Out/Don't Cry ...' (Exclusive no number).

THE FABULOUS PAWNS

Basing themselves in Cedar Falls they recorded 'Monkey Time/One More Heartache' (IGL 154) in 1968.

THE (FABULOUS) THUNDERBOLTS

Hailed from Harlan in the early '60s with 'My Girl Sue/I Wanna See You Again' (Poverty 1072). They were a quintet and their 45 was a pounding rocker.

THE (FABULOUS) TRAIDMARX

Horn rockers from Laurens who covered 'Higher And Higher/With A Little Help From My Friends' (UA 1105) in the late '60s. They were a seven piece.

RAY FABUS AND THE STRIKES

Personnel incl:	Ex	To
RAY FABUS		THE RAY FABUS FOUR

A '60s outfit from Des Moines who struck vinyl twice with 'Camel Walk/Please' (Soma 1158) and 'Please/Lulu Belle' (Soma 1191).

THE RAY FABUS FOUR

Album
1(A) What Four?   (Pizza Records 002) 196?

Personnel incl:	Ex	To
RAY FABUS	RAY FABUS AND THE STRIKES	

A later Fabus project also based in Des Moines.

FACTS OF LIFE

Based in Quad Cities their sole and unsuccessful bid for stardom was 'How Far Can The Future Be/He Is Finally On His Way' (Mystery 70-667) in 1970.

FEDERAL RESERVE (WITH TOMMY TUCKER)

Personnel incl:	Ex	To
TOMMY TUCKER		SALT RIVER

The Singles
Grow Up Someday/Take The Midnight Train   (Cadet 5584) 196?
Let's Go Down To The Park/Someday   (Cadet 5622) 196?
Get It Together/45 Sec. Blues   (R-Jay 6856) 1968

Recorded in Des Moines in the mid to late '60s.

BESS FIELDS

A pop artist from Paulina. Her sole platter was 'Song Of Joy/Auctioneer' (IGL 237) in the early '70s.

THE FIFTH GENERATION

A covers band from Carroll who released cover versions of 'Purple Haze/Caroline' (IGL 155) in 1968.

FIRE AND ICE

Personnel			Ex	To
JOE McCLEAN	bs,voc	A	THE XL's	
LES THEDE	dr	A	THE XL's	
LARRY BARRETT	voc,gtr	A	UNCLE AND THE ANTEATERS	
ANDY BAILEY	o	A	THE ROUSTABOUTS	

Emerged out of the ashes of The XL's, who were ripped apart by the draft. McClean provides the vocals on his composition 'Person To Person' recorded in 1968. This number, which features some fine instrumental breaks with McClean muttering in the background, can be heard on 'Dirty Water: The History Of Eastern Iowa Rock, Vol.2' (Unlimited Productions RRRLP-003) 1986. Line-up A disintegrated in late 1969 although manager, Martin, put together a later line-up involving Bailey and some Davenport musicians. Bailey, incidentally, still plays with current Iowa bands. Les Thede stood in on drums for The Daybreakers/Rox, during the summer of 1970 when their regular drummer, Busch, was sidelined through illness.

THE FIVE KEEYS

Based in Mason City in the mid to late '60s. Their sole platter was 'Run Around/I Tell My Heart' (Bangar 661).

THE FLAIRS

After a powerful version of 'Roll Over Beethoven' backed by 'Brazil' on Palms (726) this Sioux City outfit changed their name to The Velaires and re-recorded the song under this name.

FORGOTTEN TIMES

Cut a version of The Nightwalkers' 'Little Black Egg' backed by 'Won't You Be With Me' for Night Owl (678) in 1967. They came from Quad Cities.

FOUR MILLION

Local rockers who can be heard on 'Iowa Compilation' issued on South East Records in 1987.

FOWL

This rock outfit emerged from Ames with 'You Know/My Love Has Changed' (IGL 179) in the early '70s.

FREEDOM ROAD

A rock outfit from Algona who recorded a 45 in the early '70s, 'Hay Seed/You Ain't Goin' Nowhere' (IGL 193).

FREEDOM SUITE

Personnel incl:	Ex	To
LAWRENCE HARRELL		
? SCHROEDER		

A late '60s rock act from Sioux City who released 'Pregnant Woman/You've Got To Live For Yourself' on their own label (Freedom Suite 612).

FREEMAN AND LANGE

Album
1   Freeman And Lange   (Flying Fish 011) 1976

This duo produced one of the early items in the catalogue of Chicago-based Flying Fish records.

FRIARS

Came out of Iowa City with 'Set Up/Hitch Hyke' (Cardon 1007) in the mid-'60s.

FULL FATHOM FIVE

Albums
1(A) The Cry Of A Falling Nation   (South East   012) 1987
2( ) Paingiver   (mini-album)   (Link   018) 1988
3( ) Four A.M.   (Link   019) 1989
4( ) Multinational Pop Conglomerate   (Link   024) 1989

EPs
1( ) Four Song EP   (South East   ) 1987
2( ) Smoke Screen   (Link   ) 1989

Compilation Appearances:
1(A) Iowa Compilation   (South East   ) 1987
2(A) Another Iowa Compilation   (South East SER 006) 1988

Personnel		Ex	To
ERIC MELCHER	gtr,voc	A	
DAVE STEPHENSON	bs	A	
BRENT FOSTER	dr	A	

Aggressive rock trio from Iowa City (formerly known as The Weathermen), who seem poised for big things. EP(1) was good though Melcher's vocals were weak. Good quality garage grunge though and well worth hearing. Iowa does not, it must be said, breed many bands likely to succeed in wider arenas -this is one of the few.

THE GALLOWS

Personnel		Ex	To
CRAIG MOORE	bs		THE PAGANS
NICK BLOOM	sax		
GERRY GABEL	KB		THE PAGANS
GARY COOPER	dr		THE PAGANS
LARRY LA MASTER	gtr		THE PAGANS
DENNIS CHAMBERLAIN	voc		
AL MOANDER	gtr		

Formed initially as a surfing band in Keokuk circa 1963-64 although they later progressed onto 'Louie Louie' type songs and Rolling Stones and Dave Clark Five cover versions. The band recorded two 45s:- 'Slow Death/Come To The Party (IT 2307) in 1965 and 'Too Many Fish In The Sea/Remember Mary? (Maintain 2315) in 1967. In 1965 some of its core members left to join The Pagans and Moore, Gabel and La Master were all later in Gonn, but The Gallows soldiered on as a Young Rascals-style, blue-eyed soul band until well into 1967.

GARF

Hailed from Cedar Rapids with 'Why Is It Bad To Know You/Lavaleika' (Corrugated Rec 0001) in 1972.

THE GAS COMPANY

Album
1( ) Live At The Macombo Club   (UA 1523) 196?

Originally from Spirit Lake this pop fourpiece also cut one 45, 'Meaning Of Love/Love From Your Heart' (IGL 126) in the mid-'60s. The flip was also included on the various artists album, 'Roof Garden Jamboree' (IGL 103), released in 1967. They worked a great deal in Chicago.

GENOCIDE

A '70s rock act from Sioux City who made vinyl with 'I'll Be Around/Let's Go, Tonight's The Night' (Bucksnort 05).

GONN

Album
1(A/B) Rough Diamonds: The History Of Garage Band Music, Vol.9: Gonn   (Voxx VXS 200.029) 1985

The Singles
Blackout Of Gretely/Pain In My Heart   (Emir   9217) 1966
Come With Me (To The Stars)/You're Lookin' Fine   (Merry Jaine IT-2316) 1967

Personnel			Ex	To
BRENT COLVIN	dr	A		
CRAIG MOORE	bs	ABC	THE PAGANS	TRINITY
GERRY GABEL	KB	ABC	THE PAGANS	MOTHER HOOKER'S BLUES BAND
REX GARRETT	gtr	AB		
GARY STEPP	gtr	A		
LARRY LA MASTER	gtr	B	THE PAGANS	
DAVE JOHNSON	dr	BC		TRINITY
DANA GEORGES	ld.gtr	C		
ALFRED BOYER	gtr	C		

Formed in Keokuk in 1966 out of the ashes of garage covers band **The Pagans**. They set out doing covers of Stones, Paul Revere, Standells, Byrds, Yardbirds and Spencer Davis. At 'live' gigs they tried to present an obnoxious and controversial image. After a gig in Burlington (Iowa) a guy called Bill Egan approached the band after the show and asked them to back him on a 45 he was about to cut. They responded saying they'd back him on two songs if he'd agree to pay for them to record two of their own. So the four song session consisted of Egan backed by the band singing Eddie Cochran's 'C'mon Everybody' and 'Kansas City' and the band played 'Blackout Of Gretely', a self-penned Moore-Garrett composition from mid-1966, backed by 'Pain In My Heart'. Bill Egan's recording never saw the light of day but Gonn released 'Blackout' on Bob Mefford's Emir Record label. 2,000 copies were pressed by RCA, about 1,500 sold, the remainder were either given away over the years or lost. Two months later the band returned to the studio to start work on an album. One track, 'Doin' Me In' was earmarked as a follow-up single but never released. Then late in 1966 they went into a basement studio in Quincy, Illinois, to record a tape of cover versions to send to a guy in Florida who they had been told could get them lots of gigs down there. They sent the tape off but never heard anything more about it. Fortunately, though, Craig Moore kept an original of it and many of the songs from it later featured on (1).

Early in 1967 some tensions within the band came to a head and Brent Colvin and Gary Stepp left to be replaced by Larry LaMaster, who'd played earlier with Craig Moore and Gary Gabel in **The Pagans**, and Dave Johnson became their second and last drummer. In September 1967 they returned to Quincy and recorded a Garrett/Moore composition, 'Come With Me (To The Stars)' for their second 45. They used a Kinks cover version for the flip. Quite into the drugs which were part of this era they named their label Merry Jaine Records.

By early 1968 Garrett and La Master had quit and a new line-up, (C), emerged. Gonn was practically at the end of the road, though, although there was a later line-up including Jerry Heath (gtr) and Slink Rand (ld.gtr) which used the name but bore nothing much else in common with the original group. When they finally split, Gerry Gabel formed an 8-piece outfit called **Mother Hooker's Blues Band** and Moore and Johnson teamed up in a blues trio which covered Cream, Hendrix, Mayall and old blues numbers. Gabel and Moore were later reunited in **Ilmo Smokehouse**.

96

The best source for Gonn's music is (1), which also includes extensive liner notes by Craig Moore on which this article is based. It includes their unreleased 45, 'Doin' Me In' - and a quick spin suggests they were probably right not to release it as their follow-up to 'Blackout Of Gretely', which is also on the album, was a much more distinctive fuzz-punker. Also on (1) is 'Come With Me (To The Stars)', a keyboard-led 45 and in many respects a musical progression on their debut effort. Both flip sides (You're Looking Fine' was one of two Ray Davies compositions they covered, the other being 'I Need You') and spirited covers of some of the popular songs of the era:- Ed Cobb's 'Sometimes Good Guys Don't Wear White', Arthur Lee's 'Signed D.C.', Dave Aguilar's 'Don't Need Your Lovin'', Dylan's 'It Ain't Me Babe' and B. Roberts' 'Hey Joe'.

In addition, you'll find 'Blackout Of Gretely' on 'The Chosen Few, Vol.1' (A-Go-Go 1966) and on 'Get Primitive (The Best Of Pebbles)' (Ubik TAKE-1). 'Doin' Me In', their intended never released follow-up 45 has resurfaced on 'Pebbles Box Set' (Ubik Records Boxx 1).

GRAND LARCENY

A late '60s act who covered The Rolling Stones' 'Jumpin' Jack Flash', backed by 'Since I Fell For You' on Galaxy (1003).

GRANDMA'S ROCKERS

Album
1( ) Home Made Apple Pie   (Fredlo 6727) 1967

This is a rare and sought-after item.

THE GREEN GIANTS

A '60s outfit based in Shenandoah whose sole platter was a cover of The Beatles', 'You're Gonna Lose That Girl', backed by 'Pity Me' on Round and Round (4501).

THE GROUP

An obscure punk outfit from eastern Iowa who recorded one psychedelic 45, 'Why Does My Head Go Boom?/5/4 Bathtub' (Freak 9240-01). The label was based in Iowa City and you can hear the 'A' side on 'The Midwest vs. The Rest, Vol.1' (Unlimited Productions UPLP 1001) 1983. There is also a 45 on Warner Brothers by an Iowa band of this name but whether it is the same bunch is anybody's guess. The latter band were likened to Sagittarius.

THE GUYS WHO CAME FROM DOWNSTAIRS

A late '60s outfit from Cedar Rapids whose sole and unsuccessful stab for stardom was 'Growth/Nothing We Can Do' (Disc-Guys 6836) in 1968. 'Growth' resurfaced on 'Hipsville 29 B.C.' (Kramden KRAN-MAR 101) 1983.

BOBBY HANKINS

The Singles
Root Beer/White Lightnin'   (White Lightnin 500) 196?
Walk By Myself/Root Beer   (Cuca   1256) 196?
White Lightnin'/Lonesome Hours   (Cuca   6533) 196?

A '60s country rocker from Oelwein.

HAWKEYES

Played around Iowa City in the late '50s/early '60s. They made vinyl with 'Who Is He/Someone, Someday' (Sky 2636).

THE HAWKS

Albums
1(A) The Hawks   (Columbia 36922) 1981

2( ) 30 Seconds Over Otho   (Columbia 38058) 1982

The Singles
It's All Right, It's OK/It's All Right, It's OK (promo only)   (Columbia 11-02086) 197?
It's All Right, It's Ok/Spend The Evening   (Columbia 11-02086) 197?
Right Away/Need Your Love   (Columbia 11-60500) 197?
Stick Together/Black And White   (Columbia 18-02955) 197?

Personnel			Ex	To
DAVE HEARN	KB	AB	WEST MINST'R	
LARRY ADAMS	dr	AB	WEST MINST'R	
FRANK WIEWEL	bs,voc	AB		
KIRK KAUFMANN	gtr,voc	AB	WEST MINST'R	
DAVE STEEN	gtr,voc	B		

Line-up A recorded demos in the '70s.

Hailed from Otho, evolving out of a '60s punk outfit. '70s demos exist of line-up (A). They later based themselves in Fort Dodge.
Kaufman had also earlier recorded a solo album using the name **Captain Kirk**.

HEAD CANDY

Album
1( ) Starcaster   (Link 61151) 1991

This Cedar Falls band are connected in some way to **The Dangtrippers**. They can also be heard on 'Hollywood Shocks' (Hollywood
) issued in 1991 and more recently on The Plimsouls tribute album, 'This Ain't The Plimsouls' (Zero Hour 1001) issued in 1992.
A quartet.

HEADSTONE

An early '70s rock outfit who cut two 45s:- 'Dancing Shadows/This Time Around' (Magic 8493) and 'She'll Be Gone/You Ain't Goin'
Nowhere' (UA 7015) in 1970.

HERCULES AND BLACK MAGIC

An R & B outfit who played around Des Moines in the late '60s. They released one 45, 'War Pt. I/War Pt. II' (Grants Rec.3124).

THE HERITAGE

Came out of Des Moines in the late '60s/early '70s. They released just one 45, 'Why Shouldn't I (Have A Cry Now)/It's Not Unusual'
(Pip 8921).

HITCHIN' POST

Album
1( ) Zoo Review.   (Triple Crown 3029) 197?

A country-rock band. No other data available.

THE HOLLOWMEN

Albums
1( ) Sinister Flower Gift   (Pravda PR 6528) 1987
2( ) Man Who Would Be King   (Pravda   ) 1988
3(B) Pink Quartz Sun Blasting   (Amoeba   A-005) 1989

Casette
1( ) Poison For Profit   (6-track)   (Hollowmen   ) 1985

Compilation Cuts
Cut on 'Iowa Compilation'   (South East   ) 1987
Cut on 'Uncharted Territories' (Iowa comp) (A)   (South East SER-006) 1988

Personnel			Ex	To
TOM ARMSTRONG	voc,gtr,slg	AB		
JOE PAGE	dr	AB		
MIKE SANGSTER	gtr,voc	AB		
JIM ROTH	bs	A		
ERIC SVENSON	bs	B		

Operating out of Des Moines this outfit formed in 1985 and quickly set about recording a six-song cassette, 'Poison For Profit' in an eight-track studio. This was reputedly full of richly textured jangling guitar work, melodic bass, effective drumming and passionate vocals from Armstrong. Since them they've continued to grow in strength.

WES HOLLY

A late '50s/early '60s rocker from Iowa City who recorded 'Shufflin' Shoes/Truly, I Love You' (Iowana 807).

HORNY GENIUS

Album
1( ) Burn Your Sister   (Community 3   ) 1989

EP
1( ) Man And Beast   (   ) 1988

Personnel incl:	Ex	To
SCOTT SIEGLER		

The band are based in Iowa City and have been around for a number of years. From their first, early 45 they were likened to New York band, Agitpop, a fact that they acknowledge. At times, too, there are hints of Savage Republic. It is melodic guitar slam (eg. 'Cancel My Orders') but slower paced numbers are there too, meandering picture noises. The album was well produced, too, by Butch Vig, recorded at Smart Studios in Madison, Wisconsin. Good band this - try them out. It's like stumbling across strange rituals in the heartland.

HOT JAM

A rock act from Denison in the early '70s. They made vinyl twice with 'Tobacco Road/Stormy Monday' (Sun Dyl 101) and 'I Love To Boogie/I Don't Have To Sing The Blues' (Sun Dyl 102).

HOUSE OF LARGE SIZES

Albums
1(A) One Big Cake   (Toxic Shock TXLP 16) 1988
2(A) Heat Miser   (Toxic Shock   ) 1990
3(A) Bankrupt In Heaven   (Toxic Shock   ) 1991

EP
1( ) House Of Large Sizes   (4-track)   (South East   ) 1987
2( ) Split EP with Tree People   (Toxic Shock   ) 1991
3( ) House Of Large Sizes   (Westworld   ) 1993

Personnel			Ex	To
DAVE DIEBLER	voc,gtr	A		
BARB SCHILF	bs	A		
DAVE BERG	dr	A		

The trio are based in Cedar Falls in eastern Iowa, and pull their audience from a wide pool including punks, metal freaks, thrashers and the colleges. They are a power trio, heavy on guitars, and were formed in late 1986 at the University of Northern Iowa. Initially they aped the then fashionable hardcore styles and opened for the likes of MDC, Pussy Galore and Plan 9. They developed a wider style and offered up a couple of recordings for Iowa compilations before signing with the Tucson, Arizona-based hardcore label, Toxic Shock. (1) was issued in 1988, a strange album sounding like The Minutemen playing REO Speedwagon songs, but an impressive debut. (2) was more relaxed with great guitar and a business-like rhythm section. Lyrically the band are rather oblique - no particular message filters through. Live, they enjoy a dynamic reputation. Diebler is energetic on stage and the band have an almost magical rapport when it comes to the sudden breaks in rhythm and changes of style inherent in their music. 1991 saw a split EP with Tree People and in 1992 they issued a zany version of 'I'm My Own Grandpa'.   At the time of writing they were in the studios working on an album with the provisional title of 'My Ass Kicking Life'.   Hear them at least once.

THE HOUSEROCKERS

A horn rock act from Des Moines whose sole vinyl offering was 'Peace Of Mind/Watch Out Love' (Heavy 101) in 1969.

INNERLIGHT

A late '60s rock outfit who issued 'Temptation/This Girl' (Century no number).

INNER LITE

A different band from Marshalltown (so far as we know), also from the late '60s. They made two 45s:- 'Hold On To Him/Tabula Rush (ssExx 666) and 'All The Way In/If I Only Knew' (ssExx 667). This quintet also featured on the 'Crown Production Sampler'.

THE INSIDE OUT

Album
1( ) Bringing It All Back   (Fredlo 6834) 1968

A rare garage punk album.

INTENT

A hardcore band with a 1991 45 of grinding noise on Redemption Records.

THE IOWA BEEF EXPERIENCE

Album
1( ) Cool Ass Gravy Train   (Vinyl Solution   ) 1988
2( ) Iowa Beef Experience   (Rave   ) 1992
3( ) Pesonalien   (Rave/Pigboy   15) 1993

EP
1( ) Trailer Court   (Noiseville Records) 1990

Personnel	Ex	To
CHRIS RINEHART		

An Iowa rock quartet who also appear on the U.K. compilation put out by the defunct Shigaku Trading Co., 'Beautiful Happiness' (in 1988). They released a 1990 45, 'Guilt And Revenge/Love Muscle' on Pigboy and another on Sympathy For The Record Industry Records. In 1992 they put out 'New South/Octopussy' on Rave and an album for the same label. More followed and the band are now cult favourites in parts of America. At least one member went on to SDT.

IOWA EAR MUSIC

Album
1( ) Iowa Ear Music   (Cornpride   ) 197?

This is a '70s 'new wave' styled album.

J.D.R.

A rock covers band from Primghar who issued 'Ticket To Ride/Six Days On The Road' (IGL 238) during the 1970s.

J. J. AND THE RELATIONS

This outfit hailed from Arnolds Park. They recorded a pop/country 45, 'Garden Of Eden/I Called You On The Telephone' (IGL 245) in the mid-'70s and an EP (Misty/Like A Bird/Harper Valley PTA/Carrie Ann) for River City Records (EP 1).

THE JAGS

An early '60s rock outfit from Le Mars. Their sole vinyl offering was 'Lost Woman/Hey Little Girl' (Soma 1104).

JE RONS

Came out of Cedar Rapids in the late '60s. They released one 45, 'Chains/I'm Going Home' (Studio 4 121776).

JERRY AND THE CASUALS

Late '50s rock 'n' rollers from Spencer. They made vinyl with 'Battle Of The Three Blind Mice' (Big M 1004). The 'A' side was a primitive early rockabilly effort. They also provided the flip side to Big M (1001), a very rare and sought-after disc. The 'A' side was by The Rockin' Tones, who had provided the flip side to Big M (1004).

GARY JOHNSON

A pop artist from Sioux City who issued one 45, 'Silver Wing Blues/Impossible Dream' (IGL 161) in the late '60s.

JOHNSON BROTHERS

Late '60s country-rockers. They released one 45, 'My Woman, My Wife/Joy Into My Heart' (No Label 108412).

RON JORDAN AND THE VOLCANOES

Personnel incl:	Ex	To
RON JORDAN		

Based in Cedar Rapids, they recorded, 'By My Side/Chimay' (Fredlo 6009) in 1960.

JUNCTION

Personnel incl:		Ex	To
TERRY BECKEY	voc,bs	THE DAYBREAKERS	
DENNY MAXWELL	gtr	THE DAYBREAKERS	
RIC STEED	dr		CRUSIN'
ERNIE PENISTON	voc		

RON GRENNE	p
LYNN MURPHY	tpt
JIM AYERS	tb
DAVE HANSEN	sax,fl

This slick Iowa City early '70s band with a strong horn section was essentially a post-**Daybreakers** venture for Beckey and Maxwell. 'Dirty Water: The History Of Eastern Iowa Rock, Vol.2' (Unlimited Productions RRRLP-003) 1986, captures a live performance by the band of Jim Morrison's 'Touch Me' at The Macomber Club, Sioux Falls, South Dakota, circa 1971, which effectively showcases Beckey's considerable vocal talents.

JIMMY KAYE AND THE COACHMEN

Personnel incl:	Ex	To
JIMMY KAYE		

A late '60s outfit from Des Moines who did a good cover of The Shadows Of Knight's 'Gloria' backed by 'Debbie' on Soma (1441) in 1965.

LARRY KEMP AND THE HOBOS

Personnel incl:	Ex	To
LARRY KEMP		

Country-rockers who released 'Hop Scotch/Riders In The Sky' (IGL 104) on the Milford-based label in the late '60s.

KICKINBIRD

Album
1( ) Kickinbird   (IGL 143) 197?

A rock quartet.

THE KIDZ

A minor band who have one cut, 'Jesus Is The Rock' on 'Music For No Man's Land', a compilation on Fly Girl Records (CT 001) issued in September 1981.

THE KINGPINS

Came out of Des Moines with 'Come And See/What Kind Of Love Is This?' (IGL 151) in 1968 and 'For What It's Worth/More Than I Do' (Big G 501), a little later.

DENNY KINTZI

Denny was the former keyboardist with **Dee Jay And The Runaways** who tried his hand at a pop 45, 'Nature's Beat/Cornfield County Blues' (IGL 191) later in the early '70s. Milford-based.

TERRY KLEIN

A singer from Spirit Lake with a cut on the 'Roof Garden Jamboree' compilation (IGL 103) issued in 1967.

THE PETE KLINT QUINTET

The Singles
Walkin' Proud/Shake	(Twin Spin 2057) 1966
Walkin' Proud/Shake	(Mercury 72709) 1967
This Day/Very Last Day	(IGL 127) 1967

| Just Holding On/Hey Diddle Diddle | (Atlantic 2533) 196? |
| Friday Night Band/Blue Eyed Boy | (P.K.Q. 1449) 196? |

| Personnel incl: | _Ex_ | _To_ |
| PETE KLINT | | |

A '60s dance outfit from Mason City whose debut 45 was picked up by Mercury for national distribution the following year.

THE KOATS OF MALE

This rock outfit came out of Spencer with 'Life's Matter/Swinebarn No.9' (IGL 134) in 1967.

JUDY KOENIG

A former member of Iowa band The Dogs who issued a solo 45 on Rave-On Records in 1982.

BONNIE KOLOC

Albums
1	After All This Time	(Ovation 1421) 1971
2	Hold On To Me	(Ovation 1426) 1972
3	Bonnie Koloc	(Ovation 1429) 1973
4	You're Gonna Love Yourself In The Morning	(Ovation 1438) 1974
5	Close Up	(Columbia-Full Moon PC 34184) 1976
6	Wild And Recluse	(Epic PC 35254) 1978
7	With You On My Side	(Flying Fish 437) 1987

The Singles On Ovation
Rainy Day Lady/After All This Time	(Ovation 1033) 197?
Angel From Montgomery/Rainy Day Lady	(Ovation 1035) 197?
Burgundy Wine/We Are Ships	(Ovation 1036) 197?
Mama's Blues/Sunday Morning Movies	(Ovation 1041) 197?
You're Gonna Love Yourself In The Morning/Children's Blues	(Ovation 1049) 197?
Guilty Of Rock And Roll/Roll Me In The Water	(Ovation 1053) 197?

A singer-songwriter from Iowa though she probably operated out of Chicago in the main. She developed her act on the same folk circuit as John Prine and Steve Goodman, both her friends. Her style is poignant and she has a fine voice though as with most such stylists, her success has been confined to the club circuit. Well worth hearing.

LANCE

A rock outfit whose career spanned the late '60s and early '70s. They released two 45s:- 'Working Overtime/Time Goes By' (Sonic 246) and 'Julie/Growing Up' (Riverbend 100).

THE LANCERS

A mid-'60s outfit from Keokuk who made vinyl with 'The Girl I Never Met/Gore' (IT 2306) in 1965.

DON LANGE

Albums
| 1 | Live | (Flying Fish 222) 1981 |
| 2 | Natural Born Heathen | (Flying Fish 270) 1982 |

A singer-songwriter. (1) was recorded at various live performances during 1979. Probably ex-Freeman and Lange.

BORDERLINE

ARE YOU A SMART ASS?

IF YOU CAN SUPPLY MISSING INFO,
CORRECT ERRORS OR MAKE SUGGESTIONS TO
IMPROVE OUR BOOK, WE WANT TO HEAR FROM

YOU!

CONTACT US CARE OF:-

BORDERLINE PRODUCTIONS,
P.O.BOX 93
TELFORD, TF1 1UE
ENGLAND

THE LAW

<u>EP</u>
1(A) The Law   (Fly Girl WAL 0891) 1980

Personnel			Ex	To
CHUCKIE SUICIDE	gtr	A		SCRUFFY THE CAT
TIM P	gtr	A		
BILLY DISEASE	KB	A		
PRINCE MAC PAUL	bs	A		SCRUFFY THE CAT
BOLT UPRIGHT	dr	A		FUN AT THE ZOO

(1), which was released in November 1981, had four cuts, 'King Size Cigarette', 'Hole In My Heart', 'Satellite Rock' and 'Reason For Treason'. The band also had two cuts, 'Fashion Face' and 'Beer Please, Not Politics' on the 'Music From No Man's Land' compilation (Fly Girl CT-001) released in September the following year. Suicide and Mac Paul, using real names Charles Chesterman and MacPaul Stanfield respectively, surfaced in the popular combo **Scruffy The Cat** in Boston in 1986. Similarly, Bolt Upright (Tad Hutchinson) was later with Colorado band, Fun At The Zoo and later still, with Young Fresh Fellows in Seattle.

LAZY DAY BAND

<u>Album</u>
1( ) Straight Atcha   (Magic 6031) 196?

Based in Sioux City this band later became **Bonesteel**.

THE LEATHER SOUL

Late '60s rockers from Quad Cities whose sole vinyl offering was 'How Does It Feel/Take Me Back' (Wald 6948) in 1969.

TERRY LEWSADER

A pop/folk singer from Estherville. His unsuccessful stab for stardom was 'Me And Paul/I Don't Know' (IGL 235) in the early '70s.

THE LIBRARY

An eight piece horn rock band from Mason City who followed their debut release, 'Temptation/Groovin' Is Easy' (Exclusive 1) in 1968 with 'Get Back Evil Woman/What's The World Coming To' (A.L.C. 202) shortly after. 'Temptation' was a highly-rated horn rock disc.

ANITA LOCKMAN AND THE CHAPERONES

Personnel incl:	Ex	To
ANITA LOCKMAN		

Country-rockers from Adel who released 'Mockingbird Hill/Auctioneer Song' (IGL 177) in the early '70s. An earlier release had been 'Nashville Sax/Bye Bye Love' (Taurus 3479).

LOCUST

<u>Album</u>
1   Plague   (Annuit Coeptis Records AC 1004) 1976

Personnel			Ex	To
KEITH BROWN	gtr	A	NOTORIOUS NOBLEMEN	
DEAN DAVIS	dr	A		
COURT HAWLEY	bs	A		IMPALER
RANDY ROSEBERRY	KB	A		

A '70s outfit who also released two 45s:- 'Hold On To America/You Should Have Just Cried' (Magic 45003) and 'I Must Be In Love/The Show Is Over' (Magic 45008).

LONDON FOG

Came from somewhere in Iowa. 'The Midwest vs The Rest, Vol.1' (Unlimited Productions UPLP 1001) 1983 features their 'Mr. Baldi' which was originally released on Coulee (118), which was a La Crosse, Wisconsin label. This is a superior piece of keyboard dominated psychedelia which works itself up into quite a frenetic climax. You'll also find it on the 'Son Of Gathering Of The Tribe' (BF 20183) compilation.

LOST SOULS

A new-wave band who have a cut on the 'Music From No Man's Land' compilation album (Fly Girl CT 001) issued in September 1981.

LUXURY

Album
1(A) Luxury   (Angry Young Records   ) 1980

EP
1(A) Luxury   (5 tracks)   (Angry Young Records EP 1) 1981

Personnel		Ex	To
RICK SWAN	gtr,voc		
KERRY SWAN	gtr,KB		
JEFF SHOTWELL	ld.gtr		
BRYN OHME	bs		
DOUG TAYLOR	dr		

Mainstream rockers from Des Moines who formed in 1977. There are some doubts about the existence of the album (although they certainly started one), but in addition to the EP the band certainly recorded two 45s, 'Stupidist Thing/What Kind Of Question Is That' (AYR 1277) in 1978, and 'Green Hearts/One In A Million' (AYR 2479) in 1979. None of these cuts was on the EP though 'Green Hearts' can be heard on the compilation, 'Declaration of Independents' (Ambition Records AMB-1) issued in 1980. The 45s were produced by Rick Swan. The band were excellent live, opening shows for the likes of Head East and headlining minor Mid-Western tours themselves.

LYNN ALLEN

Albums
1( ) Lynn Allen   (   ) 1987
2(A) Look At Me, I'm The King   (   ) 1988
3( ) Panorama Park   (Barnburner) 1989

Personnel			Ex	To
BILL REFFER ?	voc,gtr	A		
BARRY VESSELS	bs	A		
MARK WATSON	gtr	A		
TOMMY GUILD	dr	A		
CURT BEARDEN				
TIM COMPTON	gtr			PRETTY BOY
RON FRAESE				PRETTY BOY
BILLY PIEFFER ?			PILOT	

A heavy metal band from Davenport in Iowa though they broke through in Minnesota and are now building a signifcant reputation nationally with hard work and good albums. The band were orignally a quintet but replaced their keyboardist with tapes for live gigs.

THE MAD HATTERS

Emerged from Des Moines with a cover version of 'Route 66' backed by 'Her Love' (IGL 117) circa 1966/67. They also had one track, 'I Still Love You' on the 'Roof Garden Jamboree' (IGL 103) 1967.

THE MAD LADS

Recorded 'Runaway/Everything Is Blue' (IGL 136) for the Milford based label in 1967 but may have come from out of state.

MARK V

A '60s band from Ames whose sole release was 'And I'm Glad/I'm A Dog' (Sound City 10759).

JERRY MARTIN AND THE SOUNDS

Personnel incl:	Ex	To
JERRY MARTIN		

The Singles

Janet/Lovely One	(Fredlo 590)	1969
Lovers Promise/Young Boys Love	(R 507)	196?
Sweet Heart/Deep In My Heart	(R 510)	196?
Hold My Hand/ ?	(R)	196?

This band started out in Albia in the late '50s. The Fredlo release is now very sought-after by collectors.

MEGAN McDONOUGH

Albums

1	In The Megan Manner	(Wooden Nickel 1004)	1971
2	Megan Music	(Wooden Nickel 1007)	1972
3	Keepsake	(Wooden Nickel BWL1-0145)	1973
4	Sketches	(Wooden Nickel 0499)	1974
5	Day By Day	(Singing Flower)	19??
6	American Girl	(Singing Flower)	19??

A solo artist from Des Moines, who recorded in Chicago. She also recorded two 45s, 'Blue Eyed Soul/Don't Jump To Conclusions' (Mercury 72904) in 1969 and 'No Return/Broken Guitar' (Wooden Nickel 0112) in 1971. There were probably others. (5) and (6) were cassette only releases issued much later. She also recorded bits for 'Buy Me, Bring Me, Take Me, Don't Mess My Hair', an album by Bitchin' Babes, an occasional group including Patty Larkin, Christine Lavan and Sally Fingerett.

MELONCOLONY

A hard rock quintet of Deep Purple imitators who released one 45, 'Speed King/The Wizard' (IGL 186) in the early '70s.

MEMORY LANE

A '70s rock band from Eagle Grove who released a version of 'Yellow River' backed by 'Teenager In Love' on Galaxy (506).

MERCURY

This rock outfit's sole release was 'Crying Over Yesterday/Down To The Bone' (Magic 8492) in the early '70s.

THE MERRY PRANKSTERS

Personnel		Ex	To
ERIC HEINTZ	ld.gtr,voc		

ROBERT HURST	voc,gtr	
TOM SCHIPPER	dr	IMMACULATE MARY
STAN BOYD	bs	

Standard rock fare from Iowa City. They have a cut on 'Another Iowa Compilation' (South East SER 006) issued in 1988.

MIDKNIGHTS

Originally from Broken Pump where these 12-15 year olds won a 'Battle Of The Bands' at their junior high school they went on to city-wide championships and later did a regional tour during which they were signed in 1965 or 1966 by Style Records of Chattanooga, Tennessee. This explains how one side of their 45, 'Pain' (Style 2001) found its way onto 'Highs In The Mid-Sixties, Vol.8: The South' (AIP 100014) 1984. It's a pretty standard teen-rocker.

MIDNIGHT SAM

Personnel incl:	Ex	To
MIKE CUSSACK		

A hippie quartet from Laurens whose four track EP, 'Heartbreak Survivor/Moonglow/My Imagination/You Ain't Leaving Me' (Green Mountain 12165), contained lots of good guitar work. It was released in the early '70s.

MILK AND HONEY

A pop outfit from Sioux City whose sole stab for stardom was 'Have A Nice Day/Whitebird' (Magic 541) in the early '70s. There was a 45 on UA also which is almost certainly the same band.

MIRAGE

Album
1( ) Out Of Luck, Out Of Money   (Stallion Records 7735) 197?

A country rock act from Storm Lake.

MOEBIUS AND ROEDELIUS

Album
1   Apropos Cluster   (Curious Music   ) 1991

A strange duo from Dubuque who had earlier materials in 1991.

MONTY'S MC'S

These popsters came out of Iowa Falls with 'Little John/Woman Without A Man' (IGL 201) in the early '70s.

THE MORNING TYMES

This Osage garage band's 45, 'Every Day/On Top' (MAAD 522768), was released on a Minnesota label in 1968.

MOTHER HOOKER'S BLUES BAND

Personnel incl:		Ex	To
GERRY GABEL	KB	GONN	ILMO SMOKEHOUSE

A Koekuk-based post-Gonn 8-piece blues outfit formed in the late '60s by Gabel, who later reunited with fellow Gonn member, Craig Moore, in Ilmo Smokehouse.

MOVEABLE FEAST

Personnel		Ex	To
JOHN ROBINSON	ld.gtr		
DOUG HANSEN	voc,gtr		
RICHARD PEREZ	bs		
DENNIS GUNN	dr		

A quartet who have failed to break out of the state to any extent. They can be heard on both South East records albums, 'Iowa Compilation' and 'Another Iowa Compilation' (South East SER-006) issued in 1987 and 1988 respectively.

THE NEW SENDERS

This rock outfit came out of Pocahontas and their sole stab for stardom in the mid-'70s was 'Going To The Hop Tonight/Long Tall Texan' (Sonic 250).

THE NIGHTMARES

Issued one 45, 'Nightmare/Greyhound' (Fredlo 6007) in 1960.

THE NOTEABLES

Late '60s horn-rockers whose sole platter was 'Get Ready/Funky Frog' (Sound City 001).

THE NOTORIOUS NOBLEMEN

Personnel incl:		Ex	To
KEITH BROWN	gtr		LOCUST

This quartet came from Albert City with 'Things Aren't The Same/Night Rider' (IGL 130) in 1967. You'll find the 'A' side on the compilation 'Monsters Of The Midwest, Vol.2'. It's rather melancholic in a raucous way and comes with a surf-styled guitar break. They also released a second 45, 'Yellow Canary/If I Needed Someone' (Bedell 80405), in the same year.

THE ONES

Album
1(A) Tomorrow's Heroes Are Today's Jerks   (Rock 'n' Roll Records LP-0001) 1981

Personnel incl:			Ex	To
PAUL THOMAS	bs	A	CRUSIN'	
RIC STEED	dr	A	CRUSIN'	
BRUCE PETERS	voc	A	CRUSIN'	

This was an offshot of Crusin' following the departure of Max Allan Collins. Based in Iowa City.

OZONE RANGERS

Rock artists from the Milford area whose sole bid for stardom appears to have been 'Truck Drivin' Man/Sweet Lovin' One' (Cracker Jack IGL 216) in the early '70s.

THE PAGANS

Personnel		Ex	To
LARRY LaMASTER	gtr	THE GALLOWS	GONN
CRAIG MOORE	bs	THE GALLOWS	GONN
BILLY	dr		
GERRY GABEL	KB	THE GALLOWS	GONN

GARY COUPER	dr	THE GALLOWS

A short-lived 1965 project from Keokuk which fell apart when Larry left to get on with his life and Billy quit to go to college. They never progressed beyond being a covers band and did not make it onto vinyl.

JERRY PAGE

A rock artist from Spencer who released one 45, 'Be What You Want/Shelly's Winter Love' (Sonic 209) in the early '70s.

THE PAGES

This late '60s horn rock band from Oelwein made vinyl with 'Sugar On The Road/High School' (UA 54300).

JACK PARIS AND THE RHYTHM PLAYBOYS

Personnel incl:	Ex	To
JACK PARIS		

Mid-'60s rockers from Ottumeva who released '13 Steps/Still In Doubt' (2 J Records 6502) in 1965.

THE JAN PARK BAND

Album
1(A) The Jan Park Band   (Columbia JC 35484) 1978

Personnel			Ex	To
JAN PARK	voc	A		
JOHN BARTLE	gtr	A		DVC
BILL BARBER	KB	A		
DICK HEDLUND	bs	A		
GORDY KNUDTSON	dr	A		STEVE MILLER BAND

A quintet fronted by a girl vocalist who also released two 45s:- 'Runnin' After Love(Making It Easy This Time)/No More, Baby' (Columbia 10942) and 'Stranger/Cool Your Hot Head Down' (Columbia 11003), both circa 1978.

PATTI AND THE NITE-LITES

This band were based in Clinton, where they played during the mid to late '60s. Their sole recording was 'A Thousand Stars/Walkin' The Dog' (Nite 7139).

PELICAN PEACE BAND

A rock outfit from S.W. Iowa in the late '60s/early '70s. They recorded one 45, 'Take It Off/Glory Road' (Heads Up 101).

THE PETITES

Based in Des Moines in the early '60s their sole vinyl offering was 'Marguerite/Blessed Are They' (Spinning 6003).

PHAFNER

Album
1(A) Overdrive   (Dragon no number) 1971

NB. Recently reissued on Rockadelic (1990).

Personnel			Ex	To
STEVE 'GUS' GUSTAFSON	dr	A		

DALE SHULTZ	gtr,voc	A	
TOMMY SHULTZ	bs	A	
GREG "SMITTY" SMITH	voc,harp	A	
STEVE "SPIDER" SMITH	ld.gtr	A	NOTORIOUS NOBLEMEN

Taking their name from a fire-breathing dragon of the Shakespearean stage, this mob came together in Marshalltown in 1969. Their album was recorded in a basement studio two years later and just 50 copies were pressed making it inevitably horrendously rare. In 1972 they recorded some further songs for a second album, which was to have been called 'Meathook' but never saw the light of day because they went their separate ways before it was finished. Two of these previously unreleased tracks - 'Breakdown' and 'Cat Black Claw' - eventually found their way onto the recent Rockadelic reissue. 'Cat Black Claw' is by far the better of the two - a great wall of sound guitar. The album overall is fine garage guitar rock presented in a variety of styles - fast and frenetic, slow and bluesy. The finest moment is arguably the opening track, 'Plea From The Soul', which comes with lots of mouth harp and fuzz guitar. The reissue is worth getting hold of. They also released one 45, 'Overdrive/Plea From The Soul' (Dragon 1001).

PILOT

Personnel incl:	Ex	To
BILLY PIEFFER		LYNN ALLEN
JESSE JOHNSON		MELIAH RAGE

A heavy metal outfit probably operating in the early '80s.

PLASTIC MUSHROOM

A late '60s outfit, as their name suggests, from Des Moines, whose only platter was 'Baby I See/Whistle Stop Review' (ssExx 668).

CURT POWELL

Powell was the lead guitarist with the Spirit Lake - based Dee Jay And The Runaways. In late 1967 he released a solo 45, 'This Is The Last Time/Impossible To Find' (Sonic 138).

PRAIRIE

Album
1( ) Prairie   (RCA   ) 197?

Evolved out of the mid-'70s Sioux City outfit, The Velaires. They also released a 45, 'Give Me A Ride/Satisfied' (RCA 0505).

PRIMGHAR H.S. CHOIR

This pop outfit took their name from their hometown of Primghar. They released one 45, 'The World Is Yours/Celebrate' (Sonic 247).

THE PRINCEMEN

A Des Moines garage band whose sole vinyl epitaph remains, 'Love Is A Beautiful Thing/Don't You Even Care' (IGL 137) circa 1967.

PRINCETONS

This band were students at Iowa State University in Ames during the mid-'60s. Their self-released 45, 'Georgiana/Killer Joe' (Princeton 1465) was later picked up and issued on Colpix (793).

THE PROPHETS

From somewhere in Iowa, they recorded a haunting garage ballad, 'Yes I Know' (Twin-Spin ?) which can also be heard on 'Pebbles Vol.22' (AIP 10037) 1987.

THE PROPHETS

This Des Moines outfit may be the same as the previous one - we aren't sure. Their 45, 'I Still Love You/Baby' (Shell 1005) is a highly-rated mid-'60s punker.

PUNISHMENT CLUB

Personnel			Ex	To
TODD BARTLETT	voc,gtr	A		
MATT HORNADAY	bs,voc	A		
DAVE PARSONS	dr,voc	A		

A quirky pop band from Iowa City. They can be heard on the 'Another Iowa Compilation' album (South East SER-006) issued in 1988.

THE PURPLE PRISM

As their name suggests a late '60s band who were based in Estherville. They issued one 45, 'Purple Jam/Hold On' (Fulltone no number).

R AND R'S BAND

Based in Sioux City in the late '60s/early '70s they covered 'Tobacco Road' backed by 'Get Off That Stuff' on Cliche Records (666).

BILLY RAT AND THE FINKS

Personnel incl:		Ex	To
WALLY 'THE ZOMBIE' SHOOP	gtr	WALLY SHOOP AND THE ZOMBIES	

Came out of Spirit Lake with 'Little Queenie/All American Boy' (IGL 122) in 1967. You'll also find 'Little Queenie' on 'The Midwest vs the Rest, Vol.1'. The guitar on this Chuck Berry number was provided by Wally 'The Zombie' Shoop, who'd had an earlier release on the Soma label as Wally Shoop and The Zombies.

THE RAVONS

Hailed from Mason City with 'Hey Little Girl/Can't Leave Your Baby' (Bangar 0621) in 1965.

THE REBS

Album
1( ) 1968 A.D. Break Through   (Fredlo 6830) 1968

A very rare late '60s album. Just 200 copies were pressed. The album mostly consists of inferior cover versions of many of the era's hits. The vocalist comes over best handling ballads, so the finest moment is their cover of The Classics IV hit, 'Spooky'. Particularly bad is their version of Eddie Cochran's 'Summertime Blues'.

RED SKY

Personnel incl:		Ex	To
CRAIG ERIKSON	ld.gtr		
JERRY LOY	dr		

A "White Metal"/Christian rock band from Cedar Rapids who have circulated a seven track demo, 'Time Is Running Out'. Pretty fine stuff it is too - not too heavy on the religious push and with crisp organised guitars. Erikson has been likened to Hendrix (who hasn't?). And lyrics?

> 'It's a crazy world just look around
> And see the morals crumble down.

```
            The people in the public eye
            They wreck their lives and God knows why.
            They're been mislead, they're broken down
            And Babylon is right down-town
            There's corner girls with AIDS for sale
            And crack that rains like deadly hail.  etc. etc.
```

A sort of God-rock 'Eve Of Destruction'!! As far as we know they never recorded an album but the demo is worth seeking out.

RENEGADE

Early '70s rockers from Estherville whose sole 45, 'Rescue Me/Don't Stop - Let's Rock' (Magic 4429), came in a picture sleeve.

THE RESTRICTIONS

Emerged from Sioux City with 'She's Gone Away/Down On The Corner' (IGL 147) in 1968.

RICH MOUNTAIN TOWER

Albums
1(A) Rich Mountain Tower		(Ovation 1412) 1971
2( ) Two		(Ovation) 1972
3(B) Can't You Feel It		(Ovation 1709) 1976

Personnel			Ex	To
DAVID CARR	ld.gtr	AB		
SANDY GARRETT	bs	A		
DANA PAUL	KB,gtr	AB		
BOB TUCCILLO	dr	AB		
LAMONT OUSLEY	perc,voc	A		
SCOTT McCLURE	bs	B		
MICHAEL FOGERTY	voc	B		

A country-rock quintet formed in Knoxville, in the late '60s. They also recorded a 45, 'Thank You Maggie/Uncle Bobwhite' (Ovation 1014) in the early '70s.

RIVER

Played around Ames in the late '60s/early '70s. Their sole release was 'Hurry Up Baby/Chancetaker' (Mohari 175).

THE ROCKERS

Hailed from Sioux City with 'Runaway/There's A Pain' (IGL 102) in 1965.

THE ROCKIN TONES

These late '50s rockers from Spirit Lake supplied the 'A' side, 'What's The Score?' to Big M 1001, a very rare disc now sought-after by collectors. The flip was by Jerry And The Casuals.

ROG AND THE ESCORTS

Personnel incl:		Ex	To
ROG BOOTH	voc,dr		
ZELDA	o		
DICK			

This was a clean-cut outfit who hailed from Ely (south of Cedar Rapids) and sported matching blazers, brillcream and had a female organist called Zelda who was married to Dick, another band member. They first came together as early as 1959 and were known for many years as The Do's And The Don'ts. They cut a number of records and 'Dirty Water: The History Of Eastern Iowa Rock, Vol.2' (Unlimited Productions RRRLP-003) 1986 features their slick, catchy pop number, 'I Wonder' (originally issued on the Zorch label circa 1966).

THE ROGUES

Personnel incl:			Ex	To
DENNY FRY	voc,bs			DEPOT RAINS
NICK RADCLIFFE	dr			DEPOT RAINS

One of Muscatine's earliest and, for a short while, most popular garage bands. They didn't make it on to vinyl.

THE RONDELLS

A pop/rock outfit from N.E. Iowa who recorded one 45, 'Rondell Rock/Phone Keeps Ringing' (IGL 249) in the mid-'70s.

THE ROUSERS

Album
1( ) In Concert   (Fredlo 6520) 1965

Early to mid-'60s rockers from Cedar Rapids.

ROX

Personnel			Ex	To
PAUL THOMAS	bs	AB	THE DAYBREAKERS	CRUSIN'
BRUCE PETERS	voc	AB	THE DAYBREAKERS	CRUSIN'
MAX ALLAN COLLINS	voc,KB	AB	THE DAYBREAKERS	
LARRY BARRETT	voc	B	UNCLE AND THE ANTEATERS	

The core of The Daybreakers became Rox in 1969, with Larry Barrett joining in 1970. Most of the demo recording in this era was left to Paul Thomas and songwriter, Bruce Peters. Peters played most of the instruments on, as well as writing, 'We'll Find A Way', which resurfaced on 'The History Of Eastern Iowa Rock, Vol.2' (Unlimited Productions RRRLP-003) 1986. 'Vol 1' (RRRLP-0002) 1986, of the same series also features four cuts by Rox. Incidentally, Peters re-recorded 'We'll Find A Way', coupling it with 'Little Girl' in 1975 and it was released by PMP Records to radio stations getting some West Coast airplay but no wider release. Rox finally folded in 1971 but Thomas and Peters were both later involved in Crusin', (another post-Daybreakers project).

THE ROYAL FLAIRS

Album
1   Rare Recordings   (Unlimited Productions UPLP 1007) 1988

The Singles
   Suicide/One Pink Box   (Marina 503) 1966
* Feelings/Gone-Away   (Marina 506) 1966
+ Hat On Tie/ ?   (Marina ?) 196?

* as The Unlimited.   + as Bobby and Dave.

Personnel incl:			Ex	To
BOB EVERHART	voc	A		THE UNLIMITED
BRAD STARR	ld.gtr	A		
DAVE KRIVOLAVEK	gtr	A		THE UNLIMITED

This outfit began life playing as a back-up band for singer, Dick Hodge, in the Omaha-Council Bluffs area of Iowa in 1961. In 1962 they became the 'house' band at the Milrose Ballroom, a club just outside of Omaha. Their repertoire at this time included a number of surf instrumentals, including 'Sniper' which was written in 1963 after the assassination of President Kennedy. Featuring gun shots at the beginning, it built into a piercing instrumental tribute to the incident. Another of their popular early songs was 'Surf Sight', written after some of the band had been water skiing on Lake Manawa in Council Bluffs. It was a fast and energetic surf number. Brad Starr, the lead guitarist, eventually quit the group to go college and, sadly, was killed in a water skiing accident on Lake Manawa.

Over the next few years both their music and their line-up underwent considerable changes and in 1965 they headed for Chicago in search of fame and fortune. In early 1965 they recorded an untitled surf instrumental which was used on the flip side to 'Suicide', which was recorded and released in Chicago in 1966. 'Suicide' contained some cool harmonica playing and a frantic guitar break. It has since resurfaced on 'Back From The Grave, Vol.3' (Crypt LP-003) 198? and 'Midwest vs Canada' compilations and is now regarded as a garage classic. The flip was a rather sick number coming as it did with sound effects of nails being driven in and dirt being thrown on a grave. It was appropriately titled, 'One Pine Box', although the pressing plant botched the title calling it 'One Pink Box'!

They now recorded as The Unlimited and their next 45 was 'Feelings' in 1966 and you can find the 'A' side on the 'Midwest vs The Rest' compilation. When it failed to give them a hit they changed their name again to Bobby and Dave for a final 45, 'Hat On Tie'. The 'A' side was a folk-rocker and the flip apparently a funky soul number with a sax solo. The Council Bluffs-based Unlimited Productions' album contains their three 45s and eight other half decent cover versions of the day as well as an interview with group leader, Bob Everhart.

ROZE

Personnel			Ex	To
RANDY VAN HOSEN	bs	A		
TERRY CHUMBLEY	gtr	A		
KEVIN MORRISSEY	dr	A		
JIM THARP	gtr,voc	A		

A quartet from Des Moines who issued a couple of interesting 45s at the beginning of the '80s: 'Whippin' Junior Into Shape/All The Day' (Vain HR 001) in 1980, and 'The Happy Nightcrawler/Dead Men Get No Tails' issued in July 1981 on Angry Young Records (AYR-3999).

RURAL

Album
1( ) One By One   (Mole Records MR 2) 197?

A late '60s/early '70s rock quintet who later concentrated on country rock. They came from Ames and also recorded two 45s:- 'In The Morning/Country Boy' (Front Porch 837) in 1972, and 'Ripe Tomoato Blues/Clear Blue Western Sky' (Mole Records no number) in 1974.

THE JANE RUSSELL ENSEMBLE

A pop outfit from Fort Dodge who actually released an album and two 45s for EGL. We have no details.

SALT RIVER

Personnel incl:	Ex	To
TOMMY TUCKER	FEDERAL RESERVE	

Hailing from Des Moines, this band evolved out of Tommy Tucker and The Esquires and The Federal Reserve. They issued one 45, 'Messenger/I Need A Friend' (Cantaloupe no number) in 1968. The flip side was by a different band.

SASS

Came from Ames in the late '60s/early '70s and cut one 45, 'Take Me/Cold In Winter' (Sound City 976).

THE SCAVENGERS

A quartet from Sutherland who recorded 'It's Over/But If You're Happy' (IGL 106) in 1965.

DAVE SCHERER AND THE CASTELS

Personnel incl:	Ex	To
DAVE SCHERER		

A late '60s outfit from Cedar Rapids whose only bid for stardom was 'Sloopy Can Penguin/Everybody's Doin' It' (Loki 1002).

MIMI SCHNEIDER

Album
1( ) Catasterpiece   (Indelible   ) 1992

A singer/songwriter from Council Bluffs.

GREG SCOTT AND THE EMBERS

Personnel incl:	Ex	To
GREG (MUMBLES) SCOTT	MUMBLES SCOTT AND THE ESQUIRES	

The Singles
When I Say GoodBye/Old Man River   (Soma   1162) 196?
Cheryl/When I Say GoodBye   (De Loss 101) 1967
Tree In The Meadow/Movin' Twistin' Around   (Riviera 4911) 196?

This was Scott's second mid-'60s outfit, also based in Spirit Lake. They are best known for 'When I Say GoodBye', which many regard as one of Iowa's best rockers.

MUMBLES SCOTT AND THE ESQUIRES

Personnel incl:	Ex	To
GREG SCOTT		GREG SCOTT AND THE EMBERS

This Spirit Lake combo was actually Greg Scott with his group The Embers. Their awful cover of Jimmy Reed's 'Baby, What You Want Me To Do?' originally backed by 'Searchin'' and released on Applause (5-1005) has resurfaced on the 'Monsters Of The Midwest, Vol.4' and 'Bod Did It!' compilations. Scott and The Embers released several 45s on minor labels during the 1960s.

THE SCREAMERS

Members of this late '50s/early '60s rock quartet were later involved in The Flairs and The Velaires. Under this name just one 45 was released, 'I Dig/What Did I Do Wrong' (Kay Bank 1519).

SDT

Albums
1( ) Parody   (Smudged   ) 1988
2( ) Sonic Disruption Theory   (Smudged   ) 1989

EP
1( ) SDT   (3-track)   (Paradox   ) 1987

Formed in Iowa but now based in San Francisco. The name was an abbreviation of Sonic Disruption Theory and after (2) they changed the name again to Sonic Disruption. The early EP was issued on Suburban Death Trip and featured a blend of hard-rock with snarling punk vocals. Tight arrangements and strong material are a feature. One member had been in Iowa Beef Experience and at least one moved to Skunkweed.

THE SEALS

Hailed from Keokuk with one 45, 'Hold Me/Got To Make That Girl Mine' (Emir 1612) in the 1960s.

THE SECOND HALF

Emerged from Des Moines with 'Knight In Armor/Forever In Your Mind' (IGL 131) in 1967.

THE SENDERS

Came out of Pocahontas with a cover of The Standells' hit, 'Sometimes Good Guys Don't Wear White' on IGL (149) in 1968. You'll find this on 'Monsters Of The Midwest, Vol.3'. It's not a bad rendition of this Ed Cobb composition. The flip side to the original release was 'She Told Me'. The band reformed in the late '80s playing '60s hits on the dance circuit.

JOHN SENN AND THE FORTUNES

Album
1( ) John Senn and The Fortunes   (IGL 125) 197?

Personnel incl:		Ex	To
JOHN SENN	voc	DEE JAY AND THE RUNAWAYS	See SENN MEN

John Senn was Jay of Dee Jay and The Runaways and this was a later venture by this artist from Spirit Lake.

THE SENN MEN

Spirit Lake was their home and they recorded one track, 'Lucille' for the 'Roof Garden Jamboree' (IGL 103) 1967, which was a various artists compilation. It fetches big bucks these days. This is, of course, another John Senn project.

THE SENSATIONAL SOUL COMPANY

A showband from Estherville in northern Iowa who released 'Our Day Will Come/Who Can I Turn To' (Sonic 180) in the late '60s. They also recorded five tracks on a demo EP for Audio Disc for the Happening 69 TV Show.

THE SEVEN SONS

The Singles
Baby Please Come Back/On The Run	(VTI	20671) 1965
Don't You Dare Say No/House Of The Rising Sun	(IGL	110) 1966
Don't You Dare Say No/House Of The Rising Sun	(Soma	1462) 1966
Product Of Time/Ride Winchester Ride	(Stanal	7308) 1967
And You Would Know/The Loving Vine	(Dynar FM	121568) 1968

This six-piece from Sioux City were all college students at Morningside College. Musically they veered towards horn rock.

THE SHA-DELS

This '60s rock outfit hailed from Sioux City. Their sole vinyl offering was, 'Hand Jive/Suddenly' (IGL 101).

THE SHADES

A late '60s outfit from Webster City who recorded their sole 45, 'When You Said Goodbye/Ballot Bachs' (Princeton 7012) in Chicago.

SHADRACK CHAMELEON

Album
1(A)   Shadrack Chameleon   (IGL SLP-132) 1971

Personnel			Ex	To
STEVE FOX	gtr,bs,voc	A		
DAN DODGER	dr	A		
(JON PORTER	o	A)		
(RANDY BERKA	gtr,voc	A)		
(ARTIE STRUTZENBERG	dr	A)		
(JOHN BRANSGARD	gtr	A)		

An early '70s progressive rock outfit from Humboldt. In addition to (1), they released a non-LP 45, 'It Was Me/I Wonder Why' (Sonic 202) in the same era. (1) is laid back guitar dominated folk with occasional psychedelic influences. Steve Fox and Randy Berka earlier issued a 45 for Sonic.

THE SHEFFIELDS

A seven-piece horn rock band from Des Moines who released just one 45, 'This Road/Right On' (ssExx 672).

SHELL GAME

A band whose only claim to fame to date is being included on 'An Iowa Compilation' issued in 1987 by South East Records.

SHENANDOAH

A country act who took their name from their home town in Iowa. They issued one 45, 'New Car Guaranteed/I Just Came Home' (IGL 236).

THE SHYMEN

Hailed from Algona with 'Lonely Times/Leave No Trace' (Sonic 157) in late 1968.

THE SHY STRANGERS

Album
1( )   Indian Name   (Pravda PR 2616) 1986

Personnel incl:		Ex	To
DOUG ROBERTSON	gtr,hca,voc		

The band, a trio, appear on 'An Iowa Compilation' on South East Records. The album dates from 1987. A fine debut too, strong guitar driven rock with a hint of Creedance Clearwater Revival in the air. 'Cries In Whispers' and 'Fall Rain' are recommended listening. Tom Tatman produced.

SILVER LAUGHTER

Album
1( )   Handle With Care   (Fan Fare 4060) 197?

The Singles
Grey Cloudy Skies/Take My Money   (Fan Fare 4062) 197?
Angela/No One Can Do It   (Fan Fare 4064) 197?
Lover/Rock And Roll Games   (Fan Fare 4072) 197?
Sing Me Your Love Songs/Hand In Hand   (Fan Fare 4074) 197?
Don't Feel Bad/Turn It Down   (Fan Fare 4076) 197?

A '70s rock outfit from Des Moines.

SLOUGH BOYS

From Cedar Rapids, they recorded a folk 45, 'Surfin' On Cedar Lake/Fried Chicken Baby' (No Label S-01/02), in 1965.

SMITH BROTHERS

This mob released 'Linda-Lu/Heartbreak and Misery' (Fredlo 6045) in 1960. It's reputed to be a real rocker.

SONIC DISRUPTION

EP
1( ) Full Metal Basket   (South East   ) 1989

Formed in Iowa City as Sonic Disruption Theory (later shortened to SDT), the band moved for a time to San Francisco. They returned sooner rather than later, renamed themselves yet again and issued (1).

SOTOS BROTHERS

Made vinyl in 1961 with 'Miserlou/Little Lila' (Fredlo 6106).

SOUND HEMISPHERE

A late '60s/early '70s horn rock band from Sioux City. Their sole 45 was 'Jam/Jones Boys' (American 7514).

THE SOULUATION

A soul/rock eight-piece from Mason City whose sole vinyl platter was 'Try A Little Tenderness/Love's Where You Find It' (IGL 166) in 1969.

THE SPARTANS

Another horn rock band, this time from Des Moines, they covered The Kinks' 'Tired Of Waiting' backed by 'Why Do People Run From The Rain?' in the late '60s. They were a seven piece.

THE SPECTACLE

Yet more horn rockers, this time from Le Mars. The 12-piece released two 45s:- 'Going Back To Miami/Exodus' (Fish 2353) and 'It's Not Unusual/Ain't Too Proud To Beg' (Spectacular 61968) in 1968.

SPITFIRE

Emerged from Estherville with a rock 45, 'Ride Captain Ride/Vehicle' (Sonic 221), in the early '70s.

STACK

Played during the late '60s/early '70s. They released one 45, 'Evil Woman/Nights On Broadway' (Daddy 813) and also played on one side of a promotional 45, which featured a band called Catch from Belmond on the flip.

STICKDOG

Albums
1( ) Suburban Death Trip   (Smudged   ) 1986
2( ) Stickdog   (Smudged   ) 1987
3( ) Human   (Alternative Tentacles 64) 1988

EPs

1( )	Stiff Legged Sheep	(Smudged	) 1986
2( )	Beef Experience	(Smudged	) 1986

Cassette

1( )	Live	(Smudged	) 1986

Formed in Iowa City but now based in San Francisco. The early work formed logical building blocks for the second album. Someone once called their style abattoir music. Like a horror comic come to life on cuts such as 'Cure' and 'Sin'. They are not unlike The Swans in places. (3) features more shouting, screaming and musical bludgeoning, painful to both the ears and intelligence. Hints of Sonic Youth's intensity and more guitar hate feedback. You will love or hate this band depending on how you feel about mindless youthful angst.

STICKS AND STONES

An early '70s rock outfit from Estherville whose sole platter was 'African Lady/The Flowers And The Rain' (Sonic 208). The 'A' side was written by Neil Ridley.

THE STOMPERS

Garage rockers out of Mount Vernon with two 45s in the mid-'60s:- 'I Know/Hey Baby' (Studio City SC 1028) in 1965 and 'I Still Love You/You're Gone' (Stomp 5477) around the same time. 'I Know' has since resurfaced on 'Root 66, Vol.1' (Paraquat TP LP 84). They were a quartet.

DENNY STOREY

Denny was the Dee of Dee Jay and The Runaways. Later based in Dickens he embarked on a solo career recording 'Kind Of A Hush/Someone Told My Story In A Song', a rock/pop 45, in the early '70s.

STONE AWAKENING

Personnel			Ex	To
AARON CURTIS	dr	A		
JEFF EASTMAN	voc	A		
JASON KERNS	bs	A		
GREY WEDEKING	gtr	A		

A mainstream pop band from Cedar Falls. (A) appear on 'Another Iowa Compilation' (South East SER-006) issued in 1988.

THE SUNDAY SOCIAL

A late '60s rock act from Des Moines. Their two discs were:- 'Vancover City/Soul Sacriface' (ssExx 114), and 'Too Heavy To Carry/Soul Break' (R-Jay 5566).

SUNDOWN

A '70s country-rock act from Sioux City which involved former members of The Velaires. Their sole vinyl offering was 'Huff and Puff/Old Man Down The Street' (UA 2750).

SWEET POISON

An early '70s rock outfit who recorded 'Glidin' Flyin'/Night Shadows' (IGL 242) in Milford, Iowa.

THE TAPE BEATLES

Cassettes

1( )	A Subtle Buoyancy of Pulse	(	) 1988

2( ) Music With Sound		(Plagiarism	) 1991

Personnel	Ex	To
LLOYD DUNN		
JOHN HECK		
RALPH JOHNSON		
PAUL NEFF		

A curious quartet from Iowa City. They have a couple of cuts on the 'Another Iowa Compilation' album (South East SER-006).

TARZAN AND THE GRAPES

They issued one 45, 'You'd Better Come Home/ ? ' on the Purple label circa 1964.

IVAN TAYLOR AND THE BLUESTRINGS

Personnel incl:	Ex	To
IVAN TAYLOR		

This country outfit from Jefferson released 'I'll Live For You/If You Want To Be My Woman' (IGL 178) and 'Brand New Life/Just Pickin'' (Bucketlid 114) in the early '70s.

TERRY TEEN

The Singles
Orchids Mean Goodbye/Just Wait 'Till I Get You Along	(Warwick	637)	196?
+ You Call Everybody Darling/San Antonio	(Gaslight	778)	196?
Pussy Galore/Rockin' Chair	(Jet	112)	196?
* High Priest Of Camp/Gotta Get A Mustang	(Jet	116)	196?
The Hearse/Kiss and Tease	(Gemini	207)	196?
x Curse Of The Hearse/Pussy Galore	(Weaks no number)		196?
x Fun To Be With You/Sand Castles	(Weaks no number)		196?

+ as Tab Malone: * as Terry and The Trip-Outs: x as Terry Teene.

This early '60s rocker from Eagle Grove had quite a phenomenal output.

THE TEMPOS

Early '60s rockers from Cedar Rapids whose only release was 'Twistin' The Blues/Only One' (Fredlo 6062) 1962.

THINKING FELLERS UNION 282

Albums
1( ) Tangle	(Thwart	) 1990
2( ) Lovelyville - Live 6.7.91 at Czar Bar, Chicago	(Matador OLE 031) 1991	
3( ) Mother Of All Saints	(Matador	) 1992

EP
1( ) The Natural Finger	(Ajax	010) 1988

Cassette
1( ) Wormed By Leonard	(Local	282) 1989

Other Recordings
Cut on 'Not All That Terrifics Harons'	(Ajax-Nuf Sed	) 1992
Cut on 'Mesomorph Enduros'	(Big Cat	) 1992

Cut on 'Soluble Fish'   (Homestead   ) 1993

Personnel		Ex	To
JAY PAGET	dr	WORLD OF POOH	
BRIAN HAGEMAN	gtr,va	also BROWN SUPPER	
MARK DAVIS	bs		

This combo are Iowa transplants to San Francisco. They have a solid reputation and have achieved cult status in Europe too. There is a 45 on Ajax-Nuf Sed.

DALE THOMAS

Hello, Lonesome/Too Young To Love   (Dot   16343) 196?
Pity Please/The Silent Sea   (Wahoo 1103) 196?
Fool's Gold/Once In The Morning   (Wahoo 64767) 196?
Brella Girl/Maybe Tomorrow   (Wahoo 2191) 196?

A six-piece band not a solo artist out of Forrest City whose career seems to have spanned the 1960s.

THOSE GUYS

Recorded two 45s for IGL in 1967:- 'You're Going To Leave Me/Sinner Man' (IGL 128) and 'Love Is A Beautiful Thing/It's Been A Long Time A Comin' (IGL 129). The label was based in Milford (Iowa) but the band may have come from out of state.

TIME LTD.

A '70s outfit from Des Moines whose sole release was 'Taking Time/Live, Learn, Love' (Front Porch 837).

THE TORKAYS

Mid-'60s rockers from Spirit Lake who made vinyl with 'Linda, I'm Worried So/You Don't Know About Love' (Coulee 112) in 1965.

TRINITY

Personnel incl:		Ex	To
CRAIG MOORE	bs	GONN	ILMO SMOKEHOUSE
DAVE JOHNSON	dr	GONN	

A Keokuk-based post-Gonn, late '60s blues project for Craig Moore who later reunited with his fellow Gonn member, Gerry Gabel in Ilmo Smokehouse.

TRUTH

Album
1   Truth   (People PLP 5002) 1970

Personnel	Ex	To
M. DEGREVE		
BOB DORAN		
J. KERR		
T. JACKOBSON		
D. SMITH		

Originally from Cedar Rapids, the album blended acoustic and orchestrated folk-rock with Jefferson Airplane-style three-part harmonies. It is now a minor collector's item. There was also a 45, 'Around And Around/Straight Eight Pontiac' (Driving Wheel 7302), which appeared in a picture sleeve in the early '70s. The 45 may not have been by the same band. It's also been reported that a band called Truth teamed up with guitarist Bill Janey to become Truth And Janey.

TRUTH AND JANEY

Albums
1( ) No Rest For The Wicked	(Montross MR 376)	1975
3( ) Just A Little Bit Of Magic	(Bee Bee Records)	1977
2( ) Live 4-8-76	(Rock and Bach Records)	1986

NB. (1) was released in 1975. (3) was recorded in 1976 but not released until 1988.

Personnel incl:		Ex	To
BILLY JANEY	gtr		
STEVEN BOCK			

A rock trio from Ottumwa who covered 'Under My Thumb' backed by 'Midnight Horsemen' (Sound Comm. 81472) in 1972. The band came about from a merger of Billy Janey with the band **Truth**. Janey is a wild guitarist. They started out as psychedelic in the late '60s and (1) fetches high prices now. It is full of driving guitar work, which on tracks like 'Remember' is stunning.

TOMMY TUCKER AND THE ESQUIRES

The Singles
Peace Of Mind/How Did I Know?	(IGL 108)	1966
Don't Tell Me Lies/What Would You Do?	(IGL 121)	1967

Came out of Des Moines. Their 'Don't Tell Me Lies', a pounding three chord raver and something of a garage classic can also be heard on 'Monsters Of The Midwest, Vol.2'.

BRAD TUTTLE

Came out of Spirit Lake with a 45, 'Okoboji Summers/Singin' In The Backseat' (H-R 5050) in the early '70s.

TYDE

A very obscure late '60s outfit who released one 45, 'Psychedelic Pill/Lost' (Fredlo 6901) in 1969. You'll also find 'Psychedelic Pill' on 'Hipsville, Vol.3' (Kramden KRAN-MAR 103) 1986.

UNCLE AND THE ANTEATERS

Personnel incl:		Ex	To
LARRY BARRETT	voc,gtr	THE COUNTDOWNS	THE XL'S
GARY HORRELL	bs		

Out of Coralville and previously known as **The Countdowns**, the name change is said to have come about at the suggestion of a drunk at a frat party! They made at least two recordings on various local labels:- 'Kathy Ran Around/I Can't Go On' (Hunt 605) 1966 and 'I Wanna Be Happy/Lover Boy' (National 19241) in 1967. 'Dirty Water: The History of Eastern Iowa Rock, Vol.2' (Unlimited Productions RRRLP-003) 1986 features three of their songs:- 'Kathy Ran Around' has a great hook, a vintage Farfisa organ solo and captures Barrett's vocals at their best; 'Lover Boy' featured some nice layered harmonies by Barrett and 'Let's Be Happy' (from late 1967), a much slicker attempt at Turtles-style rock. Larry Barrett's father was a popular jazz musician and Midwest deejay. Larry was later in Rox (a post **Daybreakers** project).

THE UNIQUES

This rock quintet came from Mallard and released one 45, 'Baby Don't Cry/Little Angel' (Bangar 00609) in the 1960s.

UNLIMITED

Personnel incl:		Ex	To
BOB EVERHART	voc	THE ROYAL FLARES	
DAVE KRIVOLAVEK	gtr	THE ROYAL FLARES	

BOBBY WILLIAMS

This is actually **The Royal Flares** with Bobby Williams who were originally from Council Bluffs but also spent time in Omaha, Nebraska before going to Chicago in search of fame and fortune. One 45, 'Feelings/Gone Away' (Marina 506) 1966 was recorded under this name. You can check out the 'A' side on 'The Midwest vs. The Rest, Vol.1' (Unlimited Productions UPLP 1001) 1983. It's pretty good too, coming with a thunderous beat augmented by screaming vocals, pulsating organ and slashing guitar. All recorded in two takes. Everhart and Krivolavek recorded a further 45 for Marina as **Bobby and Dave**.

THE UNTOUCHABLES

Personnel incl:		Ex	To
DICK DOUGLAS	gtr,voc	AL AND THE UNTOUCHABLES	ENOCH SMOKEY
AL HUNTZINGER	dr	AL AND THE UNTOUCHABLES	
TOMMY HANKINS	KB		
RON BRESLER	dr		

This rock quartet began as The Orphans in Cedar Rapids but relocated to Iowa City when drummer/promoter, Al Huntzinger's original outfit, **Al And The Untouchables** broke up, leaving Huntzinger with contracts to fulfill. Essentially a loud guitar band, Douglas' remarkable playing on 'Come On Baby' can now be heard on the 'Dirty Water: The History of Eastern Iowa Rock, Vol.2' (Unlimited Productions RRRLP-003) 1986 compilation. In all, two 45s were released:- 'Church Key/Danny Boy' (Hunt 450) and 'Come On Baby/Stick Around' (Hunt 1410).

UPSON DOWNS

Albums
1( ) Upson Downs   (Sonic   141) 197?
2( ) Upson Downs II   (Sonic 33157) 197?

This pop/rock covers outfit came out of Spirit Lake. They also released one 45, 'Take Good Care Of My Baby/Here, There and Everywhere' (Sonic 220) in the early '70s.

ADELE VARNER

A pop artist from Cedar Rapids who released two 45s on Milford-based labels in the early '70s:- 'Wastin' His Time/Proud To Be A Mother' (Sonic 210) and later the same songs with the sides reversed on IGL (213).

THE VELAIRES

The Singles
Roll Over Beethoven/Brazil   (Jamie   1198) 196?
Roll Over Beethoven/Frankie and Johnny   (Jamie   1198) 196?
Dream/Sticks And Stones   (Jamie   1203) 196?
Ubangi Stomp/It's Almost Tomorrow   (Jamie   1211) 196?
Summertime Blues/Will I   (Palms   730) 196?
Yes, I Loved You/Fantasy   (Mercury 72924) 196?
Shaggy Dog/What Am I Livin' For   (Brent   2072) 196?
I Found A Love/It's Over   (Ramco   1983) 196?

This Sioux City rock outfit recorded a string of guitar driven rockers throughout the 1960s and later evolved into **Prairie**. The Mercury release was recorded at the IGL studios. They were originally known as **The Flairs** and some members were later involved in **Sundown**.

VOODOO GEARSHIFT

Albums
1( ) Voodoo Gearshift   (Link   ) 1989
2( ) Glue Goat   (C/Z   052) 1992

EP
1( ) China Wall   (12")   (   ) 1990

This band features members of **The Hollowmen** and **The Dangtrippers**.   There is also a 45 on Red Decibel issued in 1992.

VULCAN

Album
1( ) Meet Your Ghost   (Star   13) 1978

A heavy rock band who offer distorted sludge metal.   A pretty rare item!

BURT WARD AND THE KIDDIES

A band who were featured with two cuts, 'Come On, Get Outta Here' and 'The Riddler Laughs' on the 'Music For No-Man's Land' compilation (Fly Girl CT-001) in 1981.

THE WEBB

Horn-rockers from Sioux City.   Their sole platter was 'Summertime/You Don't Know Like I Know' (Classic 1789) in the late '60s.

WESTMINST'R

The Singles
Bright Lights, Windy City/Carnival   (Razzberry 2975) 196?
Sister Jane/I Want You   (Magic 45001) 196?
My Life/Mr. Fingers   (Magic KK 7432) 196?

Personnel incl:		Ex	To
DAVE HEARN	KB		HAWKS
LARRY ADAMS	dr		HAWKS
DAVE COTTRELL	bs		
KIRK KAUFMAN	gtr,voc		HAWKS

This first class punk outfit spend time in Omaha, Nebraska before moving on to Fort Dodge in Iowa.   All three 'A' sides, which are worth seeking out, have resurfaced on recent compilations:-
> 'Bright Lights, Windy City' on 'Glimpses, Vol.2' (Wellington no No.)
> 'Sister Jane' on the cassette compilation 'Monsters Of The Midwest, Vol.1'
> and   'My Life' on 'Glimpses, Vol.1' (Wellington 201085).

Basing themselves in Otho the core of the band evolved into **The Hawks** during the '70s.   Prior to this Kaufman recorded a solo LP using the name Captain Kirk.

THE WEATHERMEN

Evolved rapidly into Full Fathom Five after a six-track demo cassette.

THE WESTONES WITH BOB CREAGER

Personnel incl:	Ex	To
BOB CREAGER		

The Singles
Hidden Treasure/Poor Loser   (Wes Tone 1002) 197?
How Wrong I've Been/Do You Really Love Me?   (Wes Tone 1004) 197?
Company Time/Back Again To Try   (IGL   144) 197?

A '70s country rock outfit.

WE THE PEOPLE

Unconnected to the better known Florida band, this outfit (also from the late '60s) were based in Iowa and issued just one 45, 'Point Panic' (DJ DRS 251). The 'A' side came with vocals, the flip was an instrumental version of the same song.

WE WHO ARE

A very short-lived group from Waterloo who disbanded within a year when their equipment was destroyed by a flood. They did record one 45, however, 'Last Trip/Remember When' (Love 6739) during 1967. You can also check out the 'A' side on 'The Midwest vs Canada, Vol.2' (Unlimited Productions UPLP 1002) 1984 and this keyboard-dominated psychedelic rocker which comes with a striking intro is worth a listen.

WHISTLE STOP

Hailed from Des Moines in the late '60s with 'Boogie Music/Honky Tonk Downstairs' (Spunk 2223).

WIKKED GYPSY

Personnel		Ex	To
STEFAN M'loy	voc		
ASHLEE	gtr		
JUSLIN SHAW	bs		
P.J.	dr		

A metal quartet formed in 1988 in Des Moines, though they have since relocated to Hollywood. The band have issued two demo tapes.

THE WILD CHERRIES

Personnel incl:		Ex	To
DAVE SANDLER			

A late '60s/early '70s outfit also from Des Moines. They cut two 45s:- 'You Know What Cha Want/Baby I See' (Kapp 2113) 19?? and 'Wigwaum/Whistle Stop Revue' (Kapp 2137) 19?? The first was written, arranged and produced by Dave Sandler.

THE WILD PROPHETS

This '60s rock act came from Ames. 'Can't Stop Loving You/Do I Have To Say?' (Kustom 169), was their sole vinyl offering.

THE WITCHING HOUR

One 45 emerged from this Des Moines-based outfit which included half of The Hollowmen.

XENOGLOSSIA

A hardcore band.from North Liberty. The band have a demo cassette in circulation. The music is deathcore and there are some nice ideas. Wierd vocals, springy bass and some odd titles.

THE XL'S

Personnel			Ex	To
JOE McCLEAN	bs,voc,tpt	A		FIRE AND ICE
BOB GUY	o,voc,tb	A		
LES THEDE	dr	A		FIRE AND ICE
MIKE HEINRICH	gtr	A		
GARY MARTIN	sax,perc	A		

Originally hailing from Wilton Junction in 1963 as a high school dance band-style outfit called The Swinging Shepherds they later became the XL's. They recorded just one 45, 'Silver Wings/I Need A Ride' (MMC 015) in 1968. 'Dirty Water: The History of Eastern Iowa Rock, Vol.2 (Unlimited Productions RRRLP-003) 1986, features two of their songs:- 'I Need A Ride', a catchy Bob Guy number which they recorded for the Omaha-based CBC label which went bankrupt before they could get the record into the stores and 'Summer Love In The Sand', a song about teenage sex on the beach. The demo for this rather commercial pop song, with Joe McClean playing some appealing lead trumpet, was surprisingly turned down by quite a few record companies. The group then entered it for the national Vox battle of the bands, which it won against stiff competition from hundreds of others. They were duly flown to Hollywood where they appeared miming their song in the MGM Hank Williams Jr. film, 'A Time to Sing'.

The band often made use of fill-in guitarists like Jim Grothusen and Craig Ziegenhorn (who played bass on 'Summer Love In The Sand') when McClean and guy added a horn section and Larry Barrett (previously of **The Countdowns** and **Uncle And The Anteaters**) was a later member. Gary Martin was primarily The XL's business manager. When Guy and Heinrich were drafted McClean and Thede changed their name to **Fire And Ice**.

THE YETTI BLUES BAND

From somewhere in Iowa, they had 'Born In Chicago' included on the 1967 Various Artists compilation, 'Roof Garden Jamboree' (IGL 103).

The following artists were also based in Iowa, but had no recording output that we know of:-

Name	Comment	Time Frame
BRILLO AND THE FIREBIRDS	From Keokuk	1960s
DEPUTY DAWG BAND	Rock band	1983
ENCOUNTER	Hardcore punk	1991
THE OUTCASTS	Keokuk-based	1960s
THE PLAYBOYS	A Keokuk band	1960s
THE TWILIGHTS	From Keokuk	1960s
THE WILDCATS	Keokuk-based	1960s

M I S S O U R I

Nicknamed the "Show Me State", Missouri covers 69,686 square miles in the heart of America. Its nickname dates back to 1899 when Missouri Congressman, William Duncan Vandiver said, "I come from a country that raises corn, cotton, cockleburrs, and Democrats. I'm from Missouri and you've got to show me." Missouri became the 24th state to secure statehood on 10th August 1821. The state flower is the hawthorne.

The State Capital, Jefferson City, is relatively small. It's built on top of a bluff overlooking the Missouri river. It contains famous Thomas Hart Benton murals and museums which display firearms, Civil War memorabilia and an Indian burial site.

Eastern Missouri is dominated by St. Louis, an old French town whose skyline is pierced by a 630-foot Gateway Arch, which offers marvellous views from its observation tower and represents the gateway to the West for the wagon trains of the 1800s. A city of museums, parks and sprawling suburbs, it grew great on water-borne commerce. Kansas City is the metropolis of the Western part of the State and is famous for its boulevards, parks and fountains. It is a grain and livestock centre and visitors can enjoy an excellent view of the city from the top of the Liberty Memorial. It also contains plenty of museums and art galleries and is host to part of the University of Missouri. Other significant centres of population are Springfield, in the South of the State, which changed hands several times in the Civil War; Columbia, in the heart of the State, where another part of the University of Missouri is based; Independence, the birthplace of President Harry S. Truman, which naturally contains much memorabilia about his career and Joplin, in the South-West of the State near the border with Kansas and Oklahoma, which is known for its lead and zinc mines and for vacationers, is the gateway to the Ozark lakes in the South of the State.

Today, Missouri still raises corn, cotton, wine and tobacco, but it is now equally known for its lead and iron mines. In terms of leisure activities the State boasts a great "huntin', shootin' and fishin'" industry plus parks, museums, etc. For lovers of water sports there is the vast artificial lake at Old Bagnell formed when the Union Electric Company dammed the Osage River. The lake attracts over three million tourists a year. The State also boasts more natural caves than any other state in America. Over 45,000 have been recorded and more are discovered annually. Some of them were used as refuges by the likes of Jesse and Frank James and The Dalton Gang when the big railroad companies were pressuring poor whites to give up land to make way for the rail-lines.

Now read on and find out about its rock artists.

KANSAS CITY
● ● INDEPENDENCE

● COLUMBIA

ST.
LOUIS ●

MISSOURI

●JOPLIN   ●SPRINGFIELD

M I S S O U R I

3-D MONSTER

Albums
1	3-D Monster	(Sawtooth	) 1990
2(A)	Grind Time	(Sawtooth	) 1991

EP
1	Thrash Metal Baby	(Fear Factory	) 1989

Cassette
1	Brand Name (14 tracks)	(Fear Factory	) 1989

Personnel			Ex	To
TERRY JONES	voc,bs	A		
JOE DOMINGOS	gtr	A		
BRAD MARTIN	dr	A		

A busy hardcore band formed in Belleville. They may now be based in Wood River, Illinois.

3 MERRY WIDOWS

Album
1( )	Which Dreamed It	(TVT	) 1991

A St. Louis-based rock band.

TONY ALL

Album
1	New Girl, Old Story	(Cruz	) 1993

A member of Los Angeles punk band. All (once The Adolescents) who moved to Brookfield.

ANACRUSIS

Albums
1( )	Suffering Hour	(Axis-Metal Blade 4)	1988
2(A)	Reason	(Active ATV 90)	1989
3(B)	Manic Impressions	(Metal Blade 26616)	1991
4(C)	Screams And Whispers	(Metal Blade	) 1993

Personnel			Ex	To
KEN NARDI	voc,gtr	ABC		
KEVIN HEIDBREDER.	gtr	ABC		
JOHN EMERY	bs	ABC		
MIKE OWENS	dr	A		
CHAD SMITH	dr	B	RED HOT CHILI PEPPERS	
PAUL MILES	dr	C	BEDLAM	

Formed in 1984 in St. Charles as a 'covers' band playing the hits of the day, Anacrusis moved rapidly to St. Louis and began again as a metal band. No easy task in a state not famous for clubs catering for the metal scene. Emery and Heidbreder are the only survivors from those early beginnings with (A) having been together since 1986 when Ken joined from another local band. They completed a 9-track demo ('Annihilation') in 1987, a rather clumsy affair not unlike Slayer in style. Tracks included 'Reign of Terror' and 'Frigid Bitch'. Two other cuts, 'Annihilation Complete' and 'Imprisoned' appeared on the Metal Forces compilation

130

'Scream Your Brains Out'. A second demo was issued in 1988 which showed great improvement - total thrash intermixed with slow passages. Good lyrics and new influences (Metal Church/Metallica) were now evident. (1) emerged in July 1988 and cost only $1,200 in the studio. It resulted though in them being firmly tagged a thrash band. Lyrically it covered world events with Ken sounding somewhat squeaky at times. The album features some cuts from the demos (including 'Frigid Bitch') and newer material like 'Fighting Evil' and 'A World To Gain'. The album suffered most from poor production, the result of only <u>five</u> hours studio time. Given the budget, a remarkable debut. (2) was a vast improvement even so. A more personal album (according to the band themselves). Production (by Ken Nardi with some help from the boys) was much better showing greater maturity and reflecting far more studio time and a better budget.

THE AQUINOS

<u>Albums</u>
1( )	The Aquinos	(Ingram-Tieken	) 1967
2( )	More Adventures With The Aquinos	(St. Thomas	) 1968

This '60s outfit came from Hannibal.

ARLIS

A quintet from Kansas City with two cuts, 'Good Friends' and 'No Way Baby' on the compilation album, 'Just Another Pop Album' on Titan (TP-8001) issued in 1980. A 45 also appeared, 'I Wanna Be/No Way Baby' (Titan 1422).

BAKERS PINK

<u>Album</u>
1( )	Bakers Pink	(Columbia 48799) 1993

A new face for some old friends who previously operated as The Front. Kansas City-based.

THE BASE APES

<u>Cassette</u>
1	Basement Masquerade	(	) 1990

<u>EP</u>
1	Orgy of Hatred	(Utjsen	) 1989

A hardcore band based in Waynesville. Prior to the above they released a demo cassette called 'Screw Glam'.

BEDLAM

Personnel		Ex	To
BOB KNARR	voc		
JOE MOLITOR	gtr		
JOHN VAN COUTREN	bs		
PAUL MILES	dr		ANACRUSIS

The personnel listed produced a four-track demo in late 1987. They were based in St. Louis. The demo was a disappointing affair including the wooden 'Scarface Lives' and the confused and somewhat directionless 'The Rupture'. In addition, the demo is poorly produced.

THE BENT

Personnel		Ex	To
ROB	gtr	ULTRAMAN	
RICK	gtr,voc	ULTRAMAN	
MARK DENISZUK	dr	ULTRAMAN	

A St. Louis-based band formed from the fragments of the defunct Ultraman in the Summer of 1992.

CHUCK BERRY

Chuck was originally from Missouri but we covered him in our earlier Chicago Volume because that's where he was based.

THE BLAZERS

The Singles
Hula Hop Party/Vive la Campagne	(Golden Crest 552)	196?
Beaver Patrol/Shore Break	(Acree 101)	1963
Bangalore/Sound Of Mecca	(Acree 102)	1963
Grasshopper/A Little Bit Of Slop	(Mundo 864)	1964
I Don't Need You/ ? '	(Brass 306)	1966

This early '60s outfit from Kansas City, Missouri can be heard playing 'I Don't Need You' on 'Monsters Of The Midwest, Vol.1' and you'll find their version of 'Beaver Patrol' on 'Garage Punk Unknowns, Vol.6' (Stone Age SA 666).

BLIND IDIOT GOD

Albums
1(A)	Blind Idiots God	(SST 104)	1987
2(A)	Undertow	(Enemy 010)	1988
3(A)	Cyclotron	(Avant)	1993

Personnel			Ex	To
TED EPSTEIN	dr	A		
ANDY HAWKINS	gtr	A		
GABRIEL KATZ	bs	A		

St. Louis band believed to have migrated to Brooklyn, New York City. They can be heard on the SST compilation 'No Age' (SST 102) issued in 1987, and have been likened to Blue Cheer, Hendrix, and the Velvet Underground. Loud acidic music with a nod in the direction of Bob Marley.

BLOOD BATH

Album
1	Hero	( )	1990

Personnel		Ex	To
KARL		of WISHFUL THINKING	
JAIME		of LAST BREATH	
PAUL		of LAST BREATH	
BRIAN	voc		

A hardcore band based in Springfield, South-East Missouri.

MIKE BREWER

Album
1	Beauty Lies	(Warner-Full Moon 23815)	1983

Brewer, born in Oklahoma City, came to prominence as part of the Brewer & Shipley duo in the late '60s and early '70s. Although frequently thought of as a San Francisco based act, they were based near Kansas City, Missouri, where they owned a large farm. (1) was produced by singer/songwriter, Dan Fogelberg, and is similar in style to the albums by the duo.

BREWER AND SHIPLEY

Albums

1(A)	Down In LA	(A & M SP 4154)	1969
2(A)	Weeds	(Kama Sutra BS 2016)	1969
3(A)	Tarkio Road	(Kama Sutra BS 2024)	1970
4(A)	Shake Off The Demon	(Kama Sutra BS 2039)	1971
5(A)	Rural Space	(Kama Sutra BS 2058)	1972
6(A)	Brewer And Shipley *	(Capitol ST-11261)	1974
7(A)	Welcome To Riddle Bridge	(Capitol ST-11402)	1975
8(A)	Best Of Brewer And Shipley	(Kama Sutra BS 2613)	1977
9(A)	Not Far From Free	(Mercury 9100 044)	1978

NB * This album is also known as ST-11261, the label prefix and number.

The Singles (on Kama Sutra)

		Peak Position
People Love Each Other/Witchi-Tai-To	(Kama Sutra 512) 1969	-
One Toke Over The Line/Oh Mommy	(Kama Sutra 516) 1970	10
Tarkio Road/Seems Like A Long Time	(Kama Sutra 524) 1970	55
Shake Off The Demon/Indian Summer	(Kama Sutra 539) 1972	98
Natural Child/Yankee Lady	(Kama Sutra 547) 1972	-
Black Sky/Fly Fly Fly	(Kama Sutra 567) 1972	-

Personnel

Personnel		Ex	To
MIKE BREWER	gtr,voc,KB	BREWER AND BREWER	Solo
TOM SHIPLEY	gtr,voc,bs		

This soft rock duo formed when Mike Brewer, who was born in Oklahoma City in 1944, and Tom Shipley, who entered the world in 1942 at Mineral Ridge, Ohio, met whilst playing as soloists on the folk circuit during 1968. They were initially based in LA, which is where (1) was recorded. It is this album which contains the original version of 'Keeper Of The Keys' picked up by so many '60s bands, most notably H.P. Lovecraft for their second LP. The album has never been released in the UK. Later they moved to San Francisco to record (2) supported by the likes of Richard Greene (vln), Mike Bloomfield (gtr) and Nicky Hopkins (p). Recorded after they had signed to Kama Sutra, it was produced by Nick Gravenites. However, it was (3) that took them into the US Album Charts peaking at No.34 and a 45 from it, 'One Toke Over The Line' peaked at No.10 in the Spring of 1971. They enjoyed a minor hit with the title cut from (3) which climbed to No.55 in the summer of 1971 and the title cut to (4) crept into the No.98 spot early in 1972. That was their last 45 hit, although (4), (5) and (6) made Nos. 164, 174 and 185 respectively in the Album Charts. Although often considered a Californian band, they lived just outside Kansas City, Missouri, (Jesse James country) where they owned a large farm. In 1974 they signed to Capitol. However, neither (6) or (7) or (9) for Mercury sustained their earlier commercial success though the material retained the melody and quality which had propelled them briefly into the spotlight. Mike Brewer later cut an album detailed his solo entry.

CAFÉ DES MOINES

A band who issued one 45 on CDM Records in 1990.

RICHIE CALLISON

Personnel		Ex	To
RICHIE CALLISON	gtr,voc		
RON BREM	gtr,bs		
TOM KNOWLE	dr		

A heavy trio based in St. Louis who had studio time in the Spring of 1983 which resulted in an album. No details available.

CELEBRATED RENAISSANCE BAND

They recorded just one 45, 'Vibration 2.2/Heavy Is The Sundown' (Lion 1001) 1969, which was issued in a picture sleeve.

ARE YOU A SMART ASS?

IF YOU CAN SUPPLY MISSING INFO,
CORRECT ERRORS OR MAKE SUGGESTIONS TO
IMPROVE OUR BOOK, WE WANT TO HEAR FROM

YOU!

CONTACT US CARE OF:-

BORDERLINE PRODUCTIONS,
P.O.BOX 93
TELFORD, TF1 1UE
ENGLAND

GARY CHARLSON

Album
1   Under Covers   (10" mini LP)   (Bomp BLP 4018) 1981

EP
1   Real Live Gary   (Titan TP 8100) 1981

Other Recordings
Burning In You   on 'Waves - An Anthology'   (Bomp   4008) 1980 *
Goodbye Goodtimes   )
Brown Eyes   )   on 'Just Another Pop Album'   (Titan TP 8001) 1980
Shark   )
Not The Way It Seems   )
Real Life Saver/Not The Way It Seems   (Titan   8914)
Shark/Brown Eyes   (Titan   1420)

* also on 'Experiments In Destiny'   (Bomp   4016/2) 1980

A pleasant popster from Kansas City who looked for a brief time in 1980/81 as though he might just break into the big time.
Needless to say he did not.

CHESMANN SQUARE

Personnel			Ex	To
GARY HODGESON	ld.gtr	AB		BECKIES/SHOOTING STAR
RON HODGESON		AB		MISSOURI
STEVE HODGESON		AB		
DAVE HUFFINGS		A		
JIM McALLISTER		B		BECKIES

Hailed from Kansas City with one 45, 'Circles (Instant Party)/Try' (Lion 1002) 1969, which came in a picture sleeve. The 'A' side
was a Pete Townsend song. You can check out the 'A' side on the cassette compilation, 'Monsters Of The Midwest, Vol.1'. Originally
known as The Chesmann in 1964 they tried to perfect a Beatles-based look and sound and had a large local following. They eventually
split in 1973. Gary Hodgeson and Jim McAllister later re-emerged in Michael Browne's post-Stories venture, The Beckies, alongside
Scott Trusty.

RANDALL CHOWNING BAND

Album
1(A) Hearts On Fire   (A & M SP 4715) 1978

Personnel			Ex	To
RANDALL CHOWNING	gtr.voc	A	OZARK MOUNTAIN DAREDEVILS	
KEN SHEPHERD	gtr	A		
LARRY VAN FLEET	bs	A		
JASON LAMASTER	gtr	A		
STAN SCHWARTZ	sax	A		
LLOYD HICKS	dr	A		SKELETONS

A solo outing from former Ozark's lead guitarist, based in Missouri. It's a pleasant album with some fine guitar work and good
production. They also recorded a 45, 'Gettin' Higher/So Close To The Feeling' (A & M 2104) in 1978.

THE CLANN

Personnel			Ex	To
ROSS DICKERSON	ld.gtr,voc	ABC	JAGUARS	

DAVE DISTER	gtr,voc	ABC	
BILL STONE	bs,voc	ABC	
JEFF GORMAN	dr	A	
TERRY KOLLMANN	dr	B	
TERRY DIONISIO	dr	C	VANDALS

A Colombia band who issued two 45s:- 'Stubborn Kind Of Fellow/I Found Somebody' (Gar 103) in 1966, and 'Tall Towers/Hey Baby' (Gar 109) in 1967.

THE CLASSMEN

Hailed from Kansas City, they cut one 45, 'Julie/Any Old Time' (Pearce 5806) 1967. 'Julie' got a further airing on the compilation 'Monsters Of The Midwest, Vol.1'. Other 45s were:- 'His Girl/Michaelangelo' (Pearce   ) and 'Graduation Goodbye/ ? ', label unknown. The band were still working in the '80s!!

THE COACHMEN

A very obscure '60s outfit from Independence who have a previously unreleased cut called 'Too Many Reasons' from a Damon Recording studio acetate included on 'Monsters Of The Midwest, Vol.2'. It's a pretty routine garage punker.

COLE AND THE EMBERS

A St. Louis band whose sole 45 was 'Hey Girl/Love Won't Hurt You' (Star Trek 1220) 1967. 'Hey Girl' later resurfaced on 'Pebbles, Vol.13'. Basically it's an atypical punker (droaning farfisa organ backing) with a hint of the progressivism and a brief organ solo midway through.

THE COLLECTION

This '60s outfit's sole and unsuccessful bid for stardom was the 45, '...Good Times Are Over/A Little Game ...' (J.E.K. 6801) in 1968.

COLOR ENTERTAINMENT

Cassette
1	Color Entertainment	(Fresh Sounds) 1982	
2	4 cuts on 'Fresh Sounds From Middle America'	(Fresh Sounds 101/102) 1982	

Personnel		Ex	To
FRED SKELLENGER	gtr	DUCHAMP	
KATHI INUKA			

A new wave duo from Kansas City. The tracks on (2) are:- 'Instrumental', 'Come On', 'Plants' and 'Fruit Of The Womb'.

CONQUEST

Personnel		Ex	To
DERRICK BRUMLEY ·	gtr		
TONY PRIVITOR	voc		
TONY RESVITO	bs		
TIM FLEETWOOD	dr		

A metal quartet from St. Louis who issued a four-track demo in late 1988 and shared management with Anacrusis. A straight ahead metal band, strongly influenced by the British style of arena metal. The best cuts on the demo are 'Fight For Metal', a sort of band anthem, and the very strong 'No Second Chance'. None of this has helped them so far, however, as they remain, as far as we know, unsigned.

COUNT ZEE

A new band from Waynesville who have a coloured flexi-disc, 'Idylife' out.

THE CRAPPY BOYS

A hardcore band from Columbia who evolved into Like A Horse and later still into 3 Legged Dog.

C.R.I.

Cassettes
1	Crud	(	) 1989
2	C.R.I.	(	) 1990

A hardcore punk band from Grover.

CULTURE SHOCK

A hardcore band from St. Louis containing the prolific Freddie Beatoff who has been in a number of hardcore projects including White Pride, Homosexual Satan, White Suburban Youth, Dred Finks and most notably The Strangulated Beatoffs.

DAVID AND THE BOYS NEXT DOOR

Came out of Springfield with 'Land O'Love/If I Was King' (Skipper 828R-1240) in 1965. You can check out the 'A' side on the 1985 compilation 'The Garage Zone, Vol.1' (Moxie MLP 17).

DEAR JOHN

A St. Louis-based new wave band who issued one 45, 'I Don't Want Her To Know/Frustrated Conversation' on A.K.A. Records in 1981.

DOG PEOPLE

Personnel incl:		Ex	To
JOHN MARSHALL	dr	THE LIMIT	ROYAL NONESUCH
TOMMY WHITLOCK	dr	JIM WUNDERLE	

No data available though they operated around 1987-1988.

THE DRAPES

An early outing for Webb Wilder. Based in Hattiesburg. There was an EP issued in 1984.

DRED FINKS

One of a string of bands, mostly hardcore, featuring Freddie Beatoff. All were Missouri-based.

DRUNKS WITH GUNS

Album
1( )	Second Verses	(Orphanage	) 1990

EPs
1( )	Drunks With Guns	(ACR	009)	1986
2( )	After Human Industrial Fetishism	(Dental	)	1987
3( )	Drunks With Guns	(Chopper	)	1988
4( )	Punched In The Head	(	)	198?
5( )	Drug Problem	(Orphanage	)	1990

6( )   Theme   (Orphanage   ) 199?

Personnel incl:		Ex	To
MIKE DOSKOCIL			
STAN SEITRICK	gtr		STRANGULATED BEATOFFS
MIKE DE LEON	gtr	TITANS	
FRED BROHACKER			

A hardcore band with a hot reputation among those who enjoy such stuff. Based in St. Louis. The album includes the third and fourth EPs. The band have been likened to The Stooges at their best. Fine praise indeed. They disbanded in 1991 but were back together the following year with a 45 on the Bag Of Hammers label.

DUCHAMP

Personnel			Ex	To
B. MINK	bs	A		
J. SCANLAN	syn,gtr	A		
T. SCANLAN	dr	A		
B. SCANLAN	gtr,voc	A		
FRED SKELLENGER	gtr	A		COLOR ENTERTAINMENT

A 'new-wave' style band who issued three 45s:- 'Elect/Pipeline' (Champ D-1065) in 1980; 'Intimacy/Energy' the same year on Champ (D-1055) and 'Rain/What You Say' (Grimplimusic D-1050).

DUCK DUCK SOUP

Cassette
1   People House   (   ) 1989

A hardcore trio who began life as **Unjust Cause**. There is also a 45.

EARWACKS

Album
1( ) Distances   (   ) 197?

A St. Louis-based band. There is also reputed to be a five-track EP although that could be (1).

THE ESQUIRES

Unconnected with the better known Texan band featured in an earlier volume, this outfit was from Springfield. They issued at least two 45s:- 'Settle Down/Down The Track' on Scratch (1235), a local label, and 'She's My Woman/Misfortune' (Dot 16954) in 1966. You can check this last one out on 'Monsters Of The Midwest, Vol.2'. There's some effective organ backing and quite appealing vocals but it suffers from rather lame guitar work.

EXPOSURE

A St. Louis-based garage band who cut one 45, 'St. Louis Sun/ ? ' on the Cyril label in the mid-'60s.

THE FAB FOUR

The Singles		
Now You Cry/Got To Get Her Back	(Brass 311)	1964
Now You Cry/Got To Get Her Back	(Coral 62479)	1964
Welcome Me Home/Oop Shoobee Doop	(Melic 4114)	196?
Happy/Who Could Be	(Brass 314)	1966
I'm Always Doing Something Wrong/Young Blood.	(Brass 316)	1966

River Days/Got A Feeling In My Body   (Pearce 5842) 196?

Originally known as The Fabulous Four they later changed their name to Kansas City, which is where they were from. 'Happy' and 'I'm Always Doing Something Wrong' both later resurfaced on the cassette compilation, 'Monsters Of The Midwest, Vol.1'.

FAIRCHILD

A blues-rock outfit from St. Louis. They signed to Gold Mountain in 1984 though we know of no output. In 1991 they circulated a three-track demo.

THE FELONS

Personnel		Ex	To
JIMMIE TRIMBLE	gtr		
RON FERNANDEZ	dr		
PETE SIKICH	bs		
JEFF SCHNEIDER	KB		
MARC CONDELLIRE	voc		
SPIKE DOWNEY	gtr		

A St. Louis-based band who issued a 45, 'Big Shot/Change Your Style' (label unknown) in 1980, and had two cuts ('Love and Skank' and 'Dancing School') on the compilation album 'Test Patterns' (Hi Test HIT 5981) in 1981.

ELLEN FOLEY

Albums
1	Night Out	(Cleveland Int. JE 36052) 1979
2	Spirit of St. Louis	(Cleveland Int. JE 36984) 1981
3	Another Breath	(Cleveland Int. JE 38459) 1983

The Singles
What's A Matter Baby/Hideaway	(Epic	50770) 1979
Sad Song/Don't Let Go	(Epic	50839) 198?

Foley, from St. Louis, trained initially as an opera singer but ended up as a contributor to various shows put on by National Lampoon, which also included at that time, one Meatloaf. As a result of this association she regularly worked with him on stage (including his 'Bat Out Of Hell' album and tour) and this in turn led to her solo career based in New York. (1), which borrowed heavily from Meatloaf's approach to rock music, was produced by Ian Hunter and Mick Ranson, and spawned one minor hit, 'What's A Matter Baby' which peaked at 92 in December 1979. (2), a much more contrived and "arty" piece of work, was produced by her then boyfriend Mick Jones (of The Clash) and half the songs were penned by him or his bandmates. (3) was an unsuccessful blend of the first two and sank without trace. In 1989 she reappeared as a member of Pandora's Box, an all girl group who recorded for Virgin. In 1993 she was once again involved with Meatloaf on his 'Bat Out Of Hell' sequel.

FOOLS FACE

Albums
1(A)	Here To Observe	(Talk	) 1979
2(A)	Tell America	(Talk	D-2036) 1981
3( )	Public Places	(Talk	) 1983

Cassette
1( )	The Red Tape	(	) 1984

Personnel			Ex	To
DALE McCOY	KB	A		
TOMMY DWYER	dr	A		
JIMMY FRINK	gtr	. A	JIM WUNDERLE	

| JIM WIRT | bs | A | JIM WUNDERLE | SECRET LIFE |
| BRIAN COFFMAN | gtr | A | | SECRET LIFE |

Fools Face enjoyed considerable success in Springfield during the late '70s and early '80s. They were formed by members of Jim Wunderle's band in 1978. After (3), the band decided to move to Los Angeles, tempted by the big-time. They issued a cassette but broke up shortly after arriving in LA. Musically they had much to offer - a talent for sharp pop hooks and a bar band brashness - hints of Cheap Trick. If you can only find one of the above, let us hope it is (2) with its style and zest best heard on the Sci-Fi influenced 'L5' and the awesome 'American Guilt'.

THE FRONT

Albums
1(A) The Front   (Columbia 45260) 1989
2( ) 30,000 Feet Of Separation   (Columbia   ) 1992

Personnel			Ex	To
MICHAEL ANTHONY FRANANO	voc	A		
BOBBY FRANANO	KB	A		
MIKE GREENE	gtr	A		
RANDY JORDAN	bs	A		
SHANE	dr	A		

A Kansas City sleaze band formed in 1987 by experienced local musicians who were likened by early critic to 'old style' Alice Cooper and the Doors. Their earliest vinyl foray was a four-track independently issued EP. They were picked up by (Scott) McGhee Entertainment who manage the likes of Skid Row, Bon Jovi and Motley Crue. They travelled to New York to tout their demos around the major labels to no avail initially. Then a deal was offered by Warner/Sire but the band held out for a better offer (bold move!) and received one they couldn't refuse from Columbia in 1989. The metal press were delighted and the band received a great deal of pre-LP publicity. (1) was produced by Andy Wallace who had previously worked with The Cult and The Godfathers. It was released in November 1989. A pleasing mix of rock styles with a blues theme running throughout, it opens with 'Fire', a rebel yell anthem. The rest of the material including 'Sunshine Girl', 'Pain' and the driving 'Ritual', is just as good and the critics drooled and fell over themselves competing for superlatives. One cut, 'Violent World' features a narration by respected actor Walter Matthau. The keyboards call to mind Ray Manzarek. All good stuff if a little self-conscious and contrived at times. MTV loved them and the album sold respectably if unspectacularly. They also had a cassette 45, 'Fire/Sister Moon' (Columbia 73222 38T), put out during 1980. They toured America with the likes of Enuff Z'Enuff and Bonham and, once again, were well reviewed. So far they had failed to meet expectations of them so they changed names to Bakers Pink and issued an album under that name.

FYDLSTYX

Cassette
1   Dew-Dah   (   ) 1990

A kind of folk-ethnic-rock ensemble. Curious stuff indeed from St. Louis.

GERMBOX

EP
1( ) Groaning Bridge   (Aural Rape   ) 1991

A hardcore band operating in Kansas City in 1990 who produced at least one private cassette before (1). The EP features muscular thrash similar to Scratch Acid or Repulse Kava. Rather fragmented which makes it a bit difficult to come to terms with.

GRANMAX

Albums
1(A) A Ninth Alive   (Panama PRS 1001) 1977
2(B) Kiss Heaven Goodbye   (Panama PRS 1023) 1978

Personnel		Ex	To
TIM CcCORKLE	bs,voc	ABC	
LEWIS McCORKLE	dr	ABC	
STEVE MEYERS	ld.gtr,voc	ABC	
NICK CHRISTOPHER	voc	B	
ARIK JENSEN	gtr	C	
GRANT GORACY	voc	C	

Formed as a hard rock trio in St. Louis, (although we have also seen them credited as being from Omaha) in the mid-'70s. They rapidly produced (1), a striking record visually, many being pressed on white vinyl with a black label. Sadly the music, though very competent, was hardly imaginative. Nevertheless (2) followed and like its predecessor, vanished without trace. The band worked regularly and, somewhere along the line moved to Hollywood, hoping to cash in on the boom in metal music. They managed to have a cut included on 'Son of Pure Rock', a Rhino-Rampage Records collection (RI-70083) in 1988 and are currently hawking demos around trying to attract label attention. Time will tell, but we have some doubts. Sad thing is, if they were to make it big they would be hailed as overnight sensations!

GREG GUIDRY

Album
1   Over The Line   (Badland/Columbia PC 37735) 1982

A singer/songwriter from St. Louis. Playing his own keyboards, he scored heavily with a cut fron (1), 'Goin' Down' (Columbia 02691) in the Spring of '82, reaching 17 on the Top 100. A follow up 45, 'Into My Love' (Columbia 02984) failed to make it further than 92 in the Summer of the same year.

THE GUISE

Personnel incl:		Ex	To
WALTER SCOTT	voc	BOB KUBAN AND INMEN	Solo/own band
MIKE KRENSKI	bs	BOB KUBAN AND INMEN	JAKE JONES
GREG HOELTZEL	KB	BOB KUBAN AND INMEN	

Formed in St. Louis in July 1966, after the demise of **Bob Kuban and The Inmen**, this outfit issued three 45s in all:- 'Long Haired Music/When You're Sorry' (Musicland USA 20011) 1966; 'Half A Man/Champy McGee' (Musicland USA 20015) 1967, and 'Mornin' Mornin'/Waitin' Round The Corner' (Atco 6686) 1968.

HAPPY RETURN

A garage band from St. Louis whose sole vinyl offering was 'Longed For/ ? ' issued on the Stack label in the mid-'60s.

HEAD EAST

Albums
1(A)	Flat As A Pancake	(A & M SP 4537) 1975
2(A)	Get Y'Self Up	(A & M SP 4579) 1976
3(A)	III Gettin' Lucky	(A & M SP 4624) 1977
4(A)	Head East	(A & M SP 4680) 1978
5(A)	Head East - Live (dbl.)	(A & M SP 6007) 1979
6( )	Radio Sampler Interview Album	(A & M) 1979
7(B)	A Different Kind Of Crazy	(A & M SP 4795) 1979
8(B)	U.S. 1	(A & M SP 4826) 1980
9( )	Promo - Live (8 cuts)	(A & M) 198?
10(C)	Onwards And Upwards	(Allegiance 432) 1982
11(D)	Choice Of Weapons	(Dark Heat 2001) 1989

NB. (1) originally issued on Pyramid.

The Singles				Peak Position
Never Been Any Reason/One Against The Other		(A & M 1718)	1975	-
Brother Jacob/Ay By Night/Love Me Tonight		(A & M 1784)	1976	68
Fly By Night Lady/Separate Ways		(A & M 1872)	1976	-
Pictures/Since You Been Gone		(A & M 2026)	1978	54
Got To Be Real/Morning		(A & M 2208)	1979	103
I Surrender/ ?		(A & M 2278)	1980	-

Personnel		Ex	To
MIKE SOMMERVILLE	ld.gtr,voc	A	
ROGER BOYD	KB,voc	ABCD	
STEVE HUSTON	dr.voc	ABC	
DAN BIRNEY	bs,gtr,voc	A	
JOHN SCHLITT +	voc	A C	JOHNNY
MARK BOATMAN	bs	B	
DAN ODUM	perc,voc	BC	
TONY GATES/GROSS	gtr,voc	BCD	
ROBBIE ROBINSON	bs	C	
DONNIE DOBBINS	dr	D	
KURT HANSEN	bs,voc	D	

+ Schlitt returned for 1982 album but left again for PETRA.

This rock quintet was based in St. Louis although they formed whilst at University of Illinois in Champaign, Illinois, and are therefore often quoted as being from that State. They achieved some commercial success with (1), (2), (3), (4), (5), (7) and (8), peaking at Nos. 126, 161, 136, 78, 65, 96 and 137 respectively in the US Album Charts. Vocalist, John Schlitt, a committed Christian, had left the band after (5) in 1979 to join Johnny but returned for (10) in 1982. He left again shortly after, this time for Petra, another Christian metal outfit. The band reformed in 1989, this time in Corpus Christi, Texas, and recorded (11).

THE HERDSMEN

This '60s band recorded 'Fed Up/House Of The Rising Sun' (Rap 110).

HOMOSEXUAL SATAN

Another of a string of Missouri-based hardcore bands featuring Freddie Beatoff. Others were White Pride, White Suburban Youth, Culture Shock, Dred Finks, and The Strangulated Beatoffs.

THE HOOTERVILLE TROLLEY

Issued at least one 45, 'No Silver Bird/ ? ' (Lynnette 551) during the 1960s. 'No Silver Bird' can be heard on the 'Magic Carpet Ride' (TVAA 001) 1986 and 'Beyond The Calico Wall' (Voxx VXS 200.051) 1990 compilations. A rather trippy, if poorly recorded number with swirling sound effects. It was produced by Tom Bee of Xit/Lincoln St. Exit fame and we have also seen them quoted as a New Mexico band.

HOT WATER

A mid-'60s garage band who put out one 45, 'Reaction/ ? ' on the Norman label.

THE HOUNDS

This was a later version of Pavlov's Dog who were based in St. Louis. Their third privately pressed album was entitled the St. Louis Hounds.

IDIOTS DELIGHT

<u>EP</u>
1( ) Idiots Delight (5-track)   (   ) 1990

Kansas City-based rockers.

INFESTED

<u>Cassette</u>
1   Infestation Of The Population   (Head First   ) 1989

A hardcore band based in St. Louis.

INQUIRES

A garage band whose sole stab for stardom was 'Never Meant To Be/ ? ' on the Diamond label in the mid-'60s.

THE INTRUDERS

This sixpiece operated around the St. Louis area and issued 'I'll Go On/ ? ' (Marlo 1545) in the mid-'60s plus a second 45 which appeared in a picture sleeve on the Marlo subsidiary label, Cinema. You'll find 'I'll Go On' on 'Monsters Of The Midwest, Vol.4' It features some catchy echoed guitar work.

INVIXIOUS

<u>Personnel incl:</u>	<u>Ex</u>	<u>To</u>
LUTHER		TUFF NUTZ

A hardcore band.

JAKE JONES

<u>Albums</u>
1( ) Jake Jones		(Kapp KS 3648)	1971
2(A) Different Roads		(Kapp KS 3657)	1972
3( ) Advance Chess		(Green Bottle)	1973

<u>The Singles on Kapp:</u>
Mirrored Door/Feather Bed	(Kapp 2138)	1971
Breathe Deep/Trippin' Down A Country Road	(Kapp 2143)	1971
I'll See You Though/No Concern	(Kapp 2154)	1971

<u>Personnel</u>			<u>Ex</u>	<u>To</u>
MIKE KRENSKI	bs	A	THE GUISE	
CHUCK SABATINO	fl,rec	A		
JOEY MARSHALL	gtr,psg	A		
PHIL JOST	KB,sax,syn,gtr	A		
JIM BILDERBECK	dr	A		TOUCH

A St. Louis-connected band. Krenski had, prior to the Guise, been with Bob Kuban and The In-men.

JEKYLL AND HYDES

A garage band whose sole vinyl offering was 'High Heeled Sneakers/To Forgive' (GAR 107) in the mid-'60s.

THE JETSONS

A short-lived hardcore band from Kirkwood. Bass player, Ed Smith, was murdered while travelling inter-state on a bus. He was replaced by Tim Molloy. The band did produce a cassette.

JOHNNY

Personnel incl:		Ex	To
JOHN SCHLITT	voc	HEAD EAST	ASCENSION

A quintet fronted by the former Head East vocalist who has been involved primarily with Christian rock bands.

KINGOFTHEHILL

Album
1( ) Kingofthehill   (SBK   95827) 1991

Personnel incl:			Ex	To
JIMMY GRIFFIN	gtr	A		
FRANKIE GRIFFIN	voc	A		
VITO BONO	dr	A		
GEORGE POTSOS	bs	A		

A heavy metal four-piece based in St. Louis. They made a name for themselves on the club circuit in town before recording (1). This led to some East Coast touring with Steelheart and Lynch Mob including some headlining gigs. A 45 taken from (1), 'If I Say Yes' (SBK 07358) reached No.63 on the US Top 100.

KING'S ENGLISH

Snotty-voiced garage punkers from Kansas City. 'Monsters Of The Midwest, Vol.4' includes their 'Doctor Hunger', which was previously unissued and taken from an acetate ('Doctor Hunger/She Lied To Me' (Mid Western no number) in 1968). Very raw and poorly recorded it does feature pretty frantic guitar work.

KRAZY KATS

Personnel incl:	Ex	To
LEE DRESSER		Solo

Formed in 1957, this bunch soldiered on until 1965 before calling it a day in the face of the British onslaught in that year. The band were based in Moberley, though Dresser had been born in Washington D.C. After the band dissolved, he went to work in LA (1968) and gigged around the clubs, doing the occasional T.V. show. In 1975 he recorded material for the film 'The Wilderness Family' which led to a contract with Capitol and a couple of minor country hits in 1978. In 1983 he had two more minor country chart appearances for Air International Records.

BOB KUBAN AND THE IN-MEN

Albums
1(B) Look Out For The Cheater   (Musicland USA SLP 3500) 1966
2( ) The Bob Kuban Explosion   (Musicland USA SLP 3501) 1966
3( ) Get Ready For Some Rock And Roll   (Bob Kuban no cat. no.) 19??

NB. (2) credited to Bob Kuban.

The Singles		Peak Position
* I Don't Want To Know/Dance With Me	(Norman 553) 1965	-
* Jerkin' Time/Turn On Your Love Light	(Norman 558) 1965	-
The Cheater/Try Me Baby	(Musicland USA 20,001) 1965	12

The Teaser/All I Want	(Musicland USA 20,006) 1966	70
Drive My Car/The Pretzel	(Musicland USA 20,007) 1966	93
Harlem Shuffle/Theme From Virginia Wolf	(Musicland USA 20,013) 1966	-
You Better Run, You Better Hide/The Batman Theme	(Musicland USA 20,017) 1967	-

* credited to the Bob Kuban Band.

Personnel			Ex	To
BOB KUBAN	dr	AB		Solo
GREG HOELTZEL	KB	AB	PACEMAKERS	THE GUISE
MIKE KRENSKI	bs	AB	PACEMAKERS	THE GUISE
KEN SMITH	ld.gtr	AB		
WALTER SCOTT (Sir)	voc	B	PACEMAKERS	THE GUISE
PAT HIXON	hns	AB		
HARRY SIMON	hns	AB		
SKIP WEISSER	hns	AB		WAYNE COCHRAN AND C.C. RIDERS

Bob Kuban formed this band in 1963 in St. Louis whilst he was teaching at DuBorg High School there. Its' horn section gave it rather a soulful sound and they used to gig in his spare time and during the summers. He recruited Walter Scott as lead vocalist after seeing him play with The Pacemakers. Kuban's band were originally known as simply The Bob Kuban Band, becoming Bob Kuban and The In-men in late 1965. Their first break came when record producer Mel Friedman got to hear 'Jerkin' Time' through Norman Weinstrohr, the owner of Norman Records, who had released it. The song had been written by Mike Krenski, a St. Louis University student who played bass in the band, and Greg Hoeltzel, the organist, back in 1964, whilst Hoeltzel was attending Washington University (in St. Louis). Friedman asked Kuban if the band were interested in recording something for national release and they duly spent six to eight months working on 'The Cheater', which was released in October 1965, with Walter Scott on lead vocals. By January 1966 it had become the No.1 song in St. Louis. The access to a national label (Musicland USA) helped make it a nationwide hit. It reached the No.12 slot. (1), released in April 1966, was also quite successful commercially, peaking at No.129 in the US Album Charts that Spring. This pop/rock album now attracts some interest from collectors.

By now the band were quite popular and billing themselves as Bob Kuban and The In-men, featuring Walter Scott. Whilst on a West Coast tour they performed in 'Where The Action Is', 'American Bandstand' and a TV soap opera, 'Never Too Much'. When they returned to St. Louis, with everything seemingly rosy, disaster struck. Kuban's father died suddenly of a heart attack and Krenski and Hoeltzel left to form an English-style band, The Guise, taking Scott with them to perform on vocals. Kuban didn't want to go in this direction so the group split temporarily in late July 1966, having enjoyed two further minor hits with 'The Teaser' and 'Drive My Car'. The Guise proved to be a short term project, though, and by 1968 the band was back together again performing as 'Bob Kuban and The In-men, featuring Walter Scott', but Scott soon went to Chicago to form his own band, The Cheaters, and later embarked on a solo career. Kuban, meanwhile, renamed his band The Bob Kuban Band, although it later changed its name to Bob Kuban Brass, who became a very popular local St. Louis live band and also issued (3). Scott was later murdered - his solo entry gives the details.

KYKS

A central Missouri '60s combo whose name is pronounced 'Kicks'. Influenced by Kansas' Blue Things they cut one 45, 'Where Are You?/When Love Comes...' (RAF Productions 1001) which was recorded by Lou Renau at the Fairyland Studio in 1966 and came with a wild picture sleeve of the band in a field, surrounded by their Vox Super Beatles, with superimposed blue psychedelic lettering. They actually recorded enough material for an album, which was scrapped, but you'll find 'Where Are You?' on 'Monsters Of The Midwest, Vol.2'. It contains nothing to distinguish it from the mass of garage bands.

LARRY LEE

Album
1   Marooned   (Columbia PC 37692) 1982

Lee is the former drummer with Missouri-based Ozark Mountain Daredevils. He was rumoured to have been recording a solo LP as early as 1977 for A & M, the Ozark's label, but we know of no output until (1) some five years later.

THE LEOPARDS

Albums
1(A) Kansas City Slickers   (Moon-Voxx   ) 1985
2(A) Magic Still Exists   (Voxx   200.048) 1986

Personnel			Ex	To
DENNIS PASH	voc	A		
ROSS INDEN	bs	A		VIVA SATURN
JAMES BORDY	gtr,voc	A		
DENNIS BOUCH	dr	A		

A quartet of sleazy rockers from Kansas City who headed for LA as their reputation grew but fell apart shortly after (2).

LIKE A HORSE

Personnel incl:	Ex	To
NORLEY HAWKINS		
KEVIN COLLINS		

A hardcore band from Columbia who seem to have had some difficulty settling on a name. They began as The Crappy Boys and eventually changed again into 3 Legged Dog.

BOBBY LLOYD AND THE WINDFALL PROFITS

Personnel incl:		Ex	To
BOBBY LLOYD	gtr,voc		SKELETONS

An early version of The Skeletons one of Springfield's finest bands. A 45 appeared on Borrowed ('I Need Some Gas Money/Crazy Country Hop').

MAMA'S PRIDE

Albums
1(A) Mama's Pride   (Atlantic SD 36-122) 1975
2(B) Uptown And Lowdown   (Atco   SD 36-146) 1977

The Singles
Blue Mist/Missouri Skyline   (Atco 7040) 1975
She's A Stranger To Me Now/ ?   (Atco 7081) 1977

Personnel			Ex	To
PAT LISTON	voc,gtr,o	AB		
DANNY LISTON	voc,gtr	AB		
KEVIN SAUNDERS	dr	AB		
MAX BAKER	ld.gtr	AB		
JOE TUREK	bs	AB		
FRANK GAGLIANO	KB	A		
DICKIE STETTENPOHL	bs	B		
PAUL WILLEL	KB	B		

Hailed from St. Louis. In addition to (1) and (2) they were reputed to have completed a third album for Tapestry in November 1980. It never appears to have been released and was presumably scrapped leading to their disintegration.

MAX LOAD

<u>Cassette</u>
1   Max Load   (198X   ) 1980

A new wave combo from St. Louis. They also issued a 45 on 198X Records. At some stage they moved their home base to Belleville, Illinois.

MEDALLION

<u>Personnel</u>		<u>Ex</u>	<u>To</u>
CARL LAWSON	voc		
BUTCH ROBINSON	gtr		
TOM HIRSH	gtr		
JIM OSMOND	KB		
MARK STRICKLIN	bs		
DAVE GOLDSMITH	dr		

A promising metal band from St. Louis who fell by the wayside. Operated in Missouri in 1983-84.

MIKE AND THE MAJESTICS

<u>Personnel incl:</u>		<u>Ex</u>	<u>To</u>
MIKE McDONALD	voc,KB		JERRY JAY AND SHERATONS

Based in St. Louis in 1964. We know of no recorded output.

MISSOURI

<u>Albums</u>
1(A) Missouri   (Panama   1022) 1977
2(B) Welcome Two Missouri   (Polydor 1-6206) 1979

<u>The Singles (on Polydor)</u>
Movin' On/Can't Stop   (Polydor 14571) 197?
Gotta Be Me/Sunshine Girl   (Polydor 2009) 197?

<u>Personnel</u>			<u>Ex</u>	<u>To</u>
RON WEST	gtr,KB,voc	AB	CHESSMAN SQUARE	
ALAN COHEN	bs	AB		
WEB WATERMAN	gtr	B		
RANDALL PLATT	KB	B		
DAN BILLINGS	dr	B		
LANE TURNER	gtr	A		
BILL LARSON	dr	A		

A mainstream rock combo who offered little out of the ordinary. (1) was aimed at U.S. Radio with a blend of heavy rock and pomp styled music. (2), was a partly remixed version of (1) with some new material. Both flopped miserably and the band split.

MO HAWK

A highly-rated metal band from 1981. They were based in St. Louis but never progressed beyond local compilation status. They were influenced by Jimi Hendrix and demos contained long cuts with airy interludes sandwiched between blistering guitars. They had a cut included on 'Home Brewed Rock And Roll' issued on Star Stream in 1981.

MOONCALF

A Kansas City band who went into the studios in 1991 to begin an album for Big Chief Records. But did it ever come out?

THE MOPEDS

A new wave outfit from St. Louis. They have two cuts on the 'Test Patterns' compilation issued on Hi-Test (HIT-5981) in 1981. The tracks are 'She's A Mongrel' and 'Woe Is Me'. Only five hundred copies of the album were pressed.

THE MORELLS

Albums
1(A)	Shake And Push		(Borrowed BORO 3302)	1982
2( )	Live Concert		(Penthouse/Omni)	1991

Personnel			Ex	To
LOU WHITNEY	bs,voc,gtr	A	See SKELETONS	
D. CLINTON THOMPSON	gtr,voc	A	See SKELETONS	
RON GREMP	dr,voc	A		
MARALIE	KB	A		

A sort of rockabilly bar band from Springfield. Not a great deal on (1) for your average rock fan, though the instrumental 'Big Guitar' is excellent. For those with a feel for 'late fifties black and white movie America' however, this is jammed with thrills and memories. Dust off the blue suede shoes, check the sideboards and let's go!

MORNING STARR

Came out of Kansas City with 'Virgin Lover/If I Didn't Want To See You Anymore' (Lion 1003), which was issued in a picture sleeve in August 1969.

MUDHEAD

EP
1	The Jumbo Sound Of ...	(Mudhead)	1988

A quintet from Kansas City who also appear on the 'Live From Lawrence' compilation issued by Fresh Sounds label in 1988. Their inclusion on that album would suggest that they work both sides of the State-line.

MUSIC TREE

Personnel		Ex	To
LARRY CRAVENS	ld.gtr		PAGE BLUES BAND
JOE McATEE	bs		PAGE BLUES BAND
SIMON CARROLL	dr		SOLAR ECLIPSE

Operated out of Excelsior Springs, North West of Kansas City. We know of no vinyl output.

NO SLACK

Album
1(A)	No Slack	(Mercury SRM1-3749) 1979

Personnel		Ex	To
GREG CALLOWAY	bs,voc		
TOM WHITLOCK	dr,voc		JIM WUNDERLE
TERRY WILSON	ld.gtr,voc		JIM WUNDERLE
JEFF GRINNELL	KB,voc		

Mainstream rock from Springfield. Faded away.

OOZ KICKS

A St. Louis band with two cuts ('I'm So Young' and 'Unknown') on the Test Patterns compilation (Hi Test 5981) issued in 1981.

OVIATT BROTHERS

A mid-'60s garage band who cut one 45, 'How Can I?/ ? ' for the Norman label.

OZARK MOUNTAIN DAREDEVILS

Albums

1(A)	The Ozark Mountain Daredevils	(A & M SP	4411) 1973
2(A)	It Will Shine When It Will Shine	(A & M SP	3654?) 1974
3(A)	Car Over The Lake	(A & M SP	4549) 1975
4(B)	Men From Earth	(A & M SP	4601) 1976
5(C)	Don't Look Down	(A & M SP	4662) 1977
6(C)	It's Alive (dbl)	(A & M SP	6006) 1978
7(D)	The Ozark Mountain Daredevils	(Columbia PC 36375) 1980
8( )	The Lost Cabin Sessions (pre- A & M days)	(Sounds Great 5004) 1985
9( )	Heart Of The Country	(Dixie Frog) 1988

The Singles

			Peak Position
Country Girl/Within Without	(A & M	1477) 1973	-
If You Wanna Get To Heaven/Spaceship Orion	(A & M	1515) 1974	25
Look Away/It Probably Always Will	(A & M	1623) 1974	101
Jackie Blue/Better Days	(A & M	1654) 1975	3
Colorado Song/Thin Ice	(A & M	1709) 1975	-
If I Only Knew/Dreams	(A & M	1772) 1976	65
Keep On Churnin'/Time Warp	(A & M	1808) 1976	-
Dreams/You Made It Right	(A & M	1809) 1976	-
Chicken Train Stomp/Journey To The Centre Of Your Heart	(A & M	1842) 1976	-
Noah (Let It Rain)/Red Plum	(A & M	1880) 1976	-
You Know Like I Know/Arroyo	(A & M	1888) 1977	74
Crazy Lovin'/Stinghead	(A & M	1989) 1977	-
Following (The Way That I Feel)/Snowbound	(A & M	2016) 1977	-
Take You Tonight/Runnin' Out	(Columbia 11247) 1980		67
Oh Darlin'/Sailin' Round The World	(Columbia 11357) 1980		-

Personnel			Ex	To
RANDALL CHOWNING	ld.gtr	A		own band
JOHN DILLON	gtr,f,KB	ABCD		
LARRY LEE	gtr,dr	ABC		See solo also/DEL BEATLES
BUDDY BRAYFIELD	KB	AB		
STEVE CASH	voc,hca	ABCD		
MICHAEL GRANDA	bs	ABCD		
RUNE WALLE	ld.gtr	BCD		
JERRY MILLS	ma	C		
STEVE CANADY	gtr,dr	C		
RUELL CHAPPEL	KB	C		
MIKE BOTTS	dr		LINDA RONSTADT	

This country-rock outfit formed in Springfield in 1972 and were originally known as Buffalo Chips. All except for Cash had played in minor in-state bands, but none had any real musical pedigree. Cash had never played harmonica before. They recorded some demos (which later emerged as (8) in album form) before signing to the A & M label. (1) was generally well received, indeed they were widely regarded as one of the best of the then new breed of country rock bands and frequently compared to The Eagles. This was partly because both bands produced their debut albums in England with Glyn Johns at the helm and partly because of the country-rock music. (1) also gave them their first hit single, 'If You Wanna Get To Heaven' which peaked at No.26 in the US Album Charts. (2) met with equally high acclaim and rather more commercial success, climbing to No.19 in the US Album Charts. This time the bulk of the album was recorded at Randall Chowning's Missouri ranch. It also gave them their only Top Ten hit, 'Jackie Blue', a song with immediate appeal. (3) was also produced at Chowning's ranch, although he left the band immediately afterwards to form his own band more in keeping with his Christian beliefs.

Rune Walle, another fine guitarist, took his place. (3) was perhaps a little less acclaimed than (1) or (2) and commercially it heralded the start of a slow decline only managing No.57 in the US Album Charts. Dave Anderle (who had co-produced (1) and (2) with Glyn Johns) took on sole production responsibility for (3). (4) peaked at No.74 in the US Album Charts and gave them another minor hit single, 'If Only I Knew'. They recruited additional personnel for (5) and (6), a live double, which peaked at Nos. 132 and 176 respectively and signed to Columbia for (7) which peaked at No.170. By now Lee had also left for a solo career and former Ronstadt drummer, Mike Botts, was recruited as a replacement. Although commerical success has long since eluded them the band has continued to gig in various forms.

In their heyday the Ozarks were an agreeable blend of country-rock and gritty rock and roll and they do not deserve to be forgotten.

THE PACEMAKERS

Personnel		Ex	To
WALTER SCOTT	voc		BOB KUBAN AND IN-MEN
GREG HOELTZEL	KB		BOB KUBAN AND IN-MEN
MIKE KRENSKI	bs		BOB KUBAN AND IN-MEN

A St. Louis-based outfit circa 1962 who Scott was playing with when Bob Kuban recruited him into Bob Kuban and The In-men.

THE PAGE BLUES BAND

Personnel		Ex	To
DALE DUNCAN	gtr,voc	MOURNING REIGN	
LARRY CRAVENS	ld.gtr	MUSIC TREE	
JOE McATEE	bs	MUSIC TREE	
SIMON CARROLL	dr	SOLAR ECLIPSE	

Operated in Excelsior Spring during 1969 and did produce a flexi 45. Prior to his spell in Solar Eclipse Simon Carroll had been in Music Tree along with Cravens and McAtee.

PAVLOV'S DOG

Albums
1(A)	Pampered Menial *	(ABC D 866/Columbia 33552)	1975
2(B)	At The Sound Of The Bell	(Columbia 33694)	1976
3( )	Saint Louis Hounds	(Private pressing)	1977

* Reissued by Columbia who bought the master.

Cassette
1( )	Lost In America	( )	1990

EP
1	4-track one-sided demo	(unissued)

The Singles
Julia/Episode	(ABC 12086)	1975
Julia/Episode	(Columbia 10152)	1975

Personnel			Ex	To
SIGFRIED CARVER	v,viola	A		
DAVID SURKAMP	voc,gtr	AB		solo/HI FI
STEVE SCORFINA	ld.gtr	AB	REO SPEEDWAGON	SOMERVILLE-SCORFINA BAND
DAVID HAMILTON	KB	AB		
DOVE RAYBURN	mellatron,fl	AB		with David Surkamp
MIKE SAFFRON	dr	A	CHUCK BERRY	SOMERVILLE-SCORFINA BAND
RICK STOCKTON	bs	AB		
THOMAS NICKESON	gtr,voc	B		
BILL BRUFORD	dr	(B)	of YES fame	

Formed in St. Louis in 1973 with an original line-up which featured former Chuck Berry drummer, Mike Saffron and the excellent former REO Speedwagon guitarist, Mike Scorfina, although it was the eerie soaring vocals of David Surkamp and the brilliant violin/viola playing of Sigfried Carver that gave them their stunningly original sound. They were signed by ABC for a considerable sum and (1) was issued though not widely promoted. By chance, country rock band, Poco, were disillusioned with their deal with the giant Columbia subsidiary, Epic. They were interested in a deal with ABC/MCA who, looking to attain a major name, agreed to swap contracts for Pavlov's Dog for that of Poco. The deal was completed and as a result (1) emerged in a splendid sleeve, on both labels. Sadly, the shuffle meant that neither label directed much effort to promotion and in commercial terms, it bombed. It was, however, a stunning debut comprised entirely of original compositions and maintained a very high quality throughout and did creep up to No.181 in the US Album Charts and the group enjoyed a minor cult following.

Both Saffron and Carver departed prior to (2) with Nickeson coming in on vocals and guitar and British drummer, Bill Bruford (who had been with Yes and King Crimson) filling in as session drummer. (2) was also an excellent album, though materially weaker than, and not necessarily a progression on (1). The band recorded a third album with Phil Spector producing, but we cannot confirm whether that was (3).

When the group disintegrated in 1977 Surkamp went solo and Doug Rayburn went with him. Surkamp was signed by Janus and began an LP. He was later in the Seattle band, Hi Fi, with former Fairport Convention vocalist, Ian Matthews. Despite his considerable talent however, commerical success eluded him.

THE PEDAL JETS

Albums
1( )	Today Today	(Twilight	) 1988
2( )	The Pedal Jets	(Communion	13) 1990

Personnel incl:		Ex	To
MIKE ALLMAYER	voc,gtr		

A quartet reported as being from Kansas City. In fact they mnay well have originated from (and even be based in) Kansas. Certainly between (1) and (2) they appear on 'Fresh Sounds From Middle America Vol.3', one of a series of albums issued by the Kansas-based Fresh Sounds label. As the two cities are a mere hop, skip and a jump away from each other, it's largely academic. The band formed in 1985 as a trio. There was an early 45, 'Hide & Go Seek'

DIANE PFEIFER

Album
1	Diane Pfeifer	(Capitol	12046) 1980

A singer/songwriter from St. Louis. She had previously been in an all girl rock band whilst at college. She enjoyed a string of minor country hits in the early eighties:-

Title	Label/Cat.No.	Year	Peak Position
Free To Be Lonely Again	Capitol 4823	1980	85
Roses Ain't Red	Capitol 4858	1980	59
Wishful Drinkin'	Capitol 4916	1980	83
Play Something We Could Love To	Capitol 5060	1981	35

| Something To Love For Again | Capitol 5116 | 1982 | 85 |
| Let's Get Crazy Again | Capitol 5154 | 1982 | 76 |

PHILOSOPHIC COLLEGE

EP
1(A) Philosophic College   (American Aesthetic Industries   ) 1981

Personnel			Ex	To
TIMOTHY TYME	bs,voc	A		
DAVID GOWLER	gtr,voc	A		
JEFF KERSTING	dr	A		

A St. Louis-based trio. (1) contained four cuts, 'Genius', 'Planned Obsolescence', 'Toxic Poppies', and 'Headline Deadline'.

PLATO AND THE PHILOSOPHERS

Personnel incl:	Ex	To
KEN TEBOW		

This quintet came from Moberly in mid-Missouri. They cut a 45, 'I Don't Mind/c.m. I Love You' at ITCO studios which came out on It (2313) and General American (GAR 104). You'll find it on 'Monsters Of The Midwest, Vol.3'. It's pretty standard mid-'60s garage fayre but the vocals are quite appealing and there are some catchy organ chord progressions. A second 45, '13 O'clock Flight To Psychedelphia/Wishes' (Fairyland 1002), was released in August 1967. The 'A' side, which was penned by Ken Tebow, has resurfaced on 'Monsters Of The Midwest, Vol.2'. If truth be told it doesn't really live up to its title at all but it does contain some quite haunting harmonies which are separated by some arresting double lead guitar breaks. The band also recorded an, as yet, unreleased psychedelic number, 'Doomsday Nowhere City'. Half of the original line-up (including Tebow) still perform today!

PSYCHOPATH

Album
1(A) Making The Transition   (C+C/Major 6243) 1991

Personnel		Ex	To
DOUG McINTOSH	dr		
BEN TROST	bs,voc		
BILL LYNN	gtr,voc		

A new St. Louis trio. They have recorded and distributed a six-track demo, 'The Soul Personification'. It contains trash metal and is a class act which should have attracted considerable label interest. The boys were all eighteen at the time (the fall of 1990) and the demo sold well via the U.S. Mail.

THE RAINMAKERS

Albums
1(A) The Rainmakers   (Mercury 832.214) 1986
2( ) Tornado   (Mercury 832.795) 1987
3( ) The Good News and The Bad News   (Mercury 832.232) 1989

Personnel			Ex	To
RICH RUTH	bs	A		WEBB WILDER
BOB WALKENHORST	voc	A		
PAT TOMEK	dr	A		
STEVE PHILLIPS	ld.gtr	A		

A Missouri-based quartet who have hovered on the brink of bigger things since their debut album in 1986.

THE REACTIONS

Based themselves on the campus of the University of Missouri's Engineering School in the sleepy backwater of Rolly, where they printed a monthly newsletter and organised and promoted local dances. Fuelled by ambition but short on talent they made it onto vinyl with 'In My Grave/Love Is A Funny Thing' (Rock 5810). 'In My Grave' has resurfaced on 'Monsters Of The Midwest, Vol.4'. With some inept if enthusiastic guitar work this one is certainly nothing to shout about.

REKNOWN

Originally from Missouri they travelled up to Chicago to record their sole vinyl platter, 'You And Me/Leave' (General American GAR 108) during the 1960s.

RONDO'S BLUE DELUXE

Album
1( ) 11.59   (   ) 1990

An outfit from St. Louis. No other data available.

ROYAL NONESUCH

Personnel		Ex	To
WALTER PAISLEY *	bs		
BARRI WATTS	voc		
JOHN MARSHALL	dr	DOG PEOPLE	LETTUCE HEADS
JABEZ PETEFISH			
WALT RESSMEYER			
JOEY SKIDMORE *			solo

* possibly the same character!

A new-psych outfit from Springfield formed by ex-members of local bands, The Limit (including Marshall) and The Sparrows, about whom we know nothing. The band recorded two 45s, 'Something Strange/You Need Love' (Get Hip   ) and 'Why Should I Care/Two Can Play At That Game' (Get Hip GH 121) in 1989 and 1990 respectively. The band disintegrated when some members heading to California to join a reformed Tell Tale Hearts in San Diego. The band also appear on some compilation albums.

SATAN'S CHEERLEADERS

Cassettes
1(A) Bark Twice For Freedom				(Unsound	) 1985
2(A) Created In Your Image				(Unsound	) 1986

Personnel incl:			Ex	To
LUX INTERIOR	voc	A	CRAMPS	
TIGER BEAT	dr			
LATHER	gtr			
VIC ST. STEPHEN	gtr			
MARK CHAPMAN	bs		also SATAN'S DISCIPLES	CHILDREN OF GOD

A post-Cramps project for Lux Interior which we believe to have been based in St. Louis (though they have also been quoted as being from Long Beach, California). Three 45s were also issued on Unsound. A fourth appeared on Living Eye Records.

SAVAGE PENGUIN

Personnel incl:	Ex	To
MIKE HERZBERG		

Another hardcore quartet. No data available except that they have issued a cassette.

SCICCOX

A hardcore band comprising ex-members of **Dead Planet** and **The Odd Squad**.

WALTER SCOTT

Albums
1	Great Scott	(Musicland USA 3502)	1967
2	Walter Scott 'Just You Wait'	(White Whale 7131)	1970
3	Walter Scott	(WS 001)	197?

The Singles
My Shadow Is Gone/Watch Out	(Musicland USA 20,009)	1967
It's Been A Long Time/Proud	(Musicland USA 20,104)	1967
Just You Wait/Silly Girl	(Musicland USA 111)	1967
Just You Wait/Silly Girl	(White Whale 259)	1967
Feelin' Something New Inside/Soul Stew Recipe	(Pzazz 026)	1969
Soul Man/Hard To Handle	(Reprise 0937)	1970
The Cheater/The Teaser	(Eric 153)	197?
The Cheater/There'll Always Be A Long Song	(Vanessa 131)	1974

Walter Scott played in a number of St. Louis bands during the '60s including **The Pacemakers**, **Bob Kuban And The In-men** and **The Guise** and he'd had his own **Walter Scott Band** which evolved out of **Walter Scott and The Cheaters**. He also recovered fully from a nervous breakdown in 1968. As a solo artist he became a local live attraction and played regularly at venues such as Myrtle Beach, the Pocanos and the Playboy Club circuit. He also enjoyed a resonably prolific recording career although none of his releases met with much commercial success.

On 27 December 1983 at about 7 p.m. Scott left his home in St. Louis to buy a battery for his 1978 Lincoln. The car was found abandoned the next day covered with snow on the top deck of a parking garage. In the forty months that followed all attempts by friends, relatives, private investigators and the police to find him were in vain. There were rumours that he had fled abroad or was in hiding. Then on 10 April 1987 the sheriff's officers found a body which they believed to be Scott's floating in a 12-foot-deep cistern (water holding tank). The cistern was nearby a house owned by Jim Williams who Scott's second wife, Jo Ann, had married in April 1986 after divorcing Scott in his absence back in August 1984. Forensic tests indicated that the body had been in the cistern for three years. Scott's mother always believed her son had been murdered and piecing together the story the Sheriff's Department deduced that Jim Williams had shot Scott in the back and also beaten to death his first wife, Sharon Williams, who had seemingly died from head injuries back in October 1983 received in an automobile accident. Sharon's body had been exhumed in March 1987 when an autopsy had shown that Sharon died of 'blunt force trauma' not of injuries received in the crash, as previously believed. It transpired that Jim Williams and Jo Ann had been having an affair for about a year before Williams murdered his first wife, Sharon. Jim and Jo Ann were both arrested to stand trial. Ironically the manner of Scott's death and the charging for the crime of his wife and her lover and accomplice is in the title of the song which brought him his fame, 'The Cheater'.

WALTER SCOTT AND THE CHEATERS

Personnel incl:		Ex	To
WALTER SCOTT	voc	THE GUISE	WALTER SCOTT BAND

Scott formed this outfit in 1967 in St. Louis but they relocated to Chicago. They didn't make it onto vinyl.

WALTER SCOTT BAND

Album
1(A)	The Walter Scott Band	(Private pressing) 196?

Personnel			Ex	To
WALTER SCOTT	voc	A	WALTER SCOTT AND THE CHEATERS	
ED ECKERT	ld.gtr,psg	A		
BILL MALOBERTI	KB	A		

| ROB McDONNELL | bs | A |
| GRAVY CANTNER | dr | A |

This was a late '60s venture for Scott.

SCREAMING MEE MEES

Album
1( ) Clutching Hand Monster Mitt   (Dog Face 002) 1978

EP
1( ) Live From The Basement   (Dog Face 001) 1977

Personnel	Ex	To
BRUCE COLE		WORM CAN
JON ASHLINE		WORM CAN

A St. Louis-based duo who returned in the '90s with more stuff on their Dog Face label using the new name of Worm Can.

SCREAMIN' POPEYES

Cassettes
1( ) Ah, Squid   (   ) 1991
2( ) Gas Music From Jupiter   (   ) 1991

This is strange stuff indeed from (and perhaps for) disturbed souls. Curious tape loops, animal sounds, chitenous insect rhetoric, blended with anthemic and hymn-like intrusions. Imagine a Wall of Voodoo set live in the lunatic asylum. There may well be something alien drifting in the air around Branson because (2) offers further evidence of a deranged but cunning mind. This one is similar, ethnic doodling, UFO's and synthesized guitars thrashing together in a closet located somewhere nasty.

SEASON TO RISK

A Kansas City band who can be heard on the 'Kansas City Compilation' album issued by Round-Up Records in mid-1992.

SECRETS*

Album
1( ) Secrets*   (Why-Fi   ) 1982

A power pop quartet from Kansas City who also had an earlier 45, 'It's Your Heart Tonight/Get Your Radio' issued in 1979. The reason for the asterix eludes us. The album was co-produced by Stan Lynch (he of Tom Petty fame) and features oodles of scintillating guitar driven tracks. Fine stuff!

SHOOTING STAR

Albums
1(A) Shooting Star   (Virgin   13133) 1980
2(A) Hang On For Your Life   (Virgin   37404) 1981
3(A) Ill Wishes   (Virgin?   38020) 1982
4(B) Burning   (Virgin?   38683) 1983
5(B) Silent Scream   (Geffen GHS 24056) 1985
6(A/B)Touch Me Tonight   (a 'best of' collection)   (Enigma   73549) 1989
7(C) It's Not Over   (V & R   ) 1991

Personnel		Ex	To
CHARLES WALTZ	voc,v,KB	AB	
VAN McCLAIN	voc,ld.gtr	ABC	

```
GARY WEST    *          voc,dr,KB,gtr    AB
BILL GUFFEY             KB               A
RON VERLIN              bs               ABC
STEVE THOMAS            dr               AB
KEITH MITCHELL          voc                C
DENNIS LAFFOON          KB                 C
ROD LINCOLN             dr                 C
NORMAN DAHLOR           bs
GARY HODGESON *         gtr                        CHESSMAN SQUARE          BECKIES
* Same guy.
```

A high class rock band formed in Kansas City in 1978. They may be more Kansas than Missouri. They quickly caught the attention of Virgin Records who were looking to bolster up their American roster. (1), a collection of crisp incisive tracks produced an initial hit single, 'You've Got What I Need' (Virgin 67005) which reached 76 on the Top 100 in the Spring of 1980. The follow-up, 'Bring It On' (Virgin 67010), later that year flopped. A second hit, 'Hollywood' (Epic 02755) appeared in 1982 and reached 70 but that was the last chart action for the band who soldiered on until 1986 producing quality albums. The band vanished from general view in 1986 though they still may have been working. Enigma put out a compilation of their best work in 1989 which revived interest in the band. In November of that year 'Touch Me Tonight' (Enigma 75054) entered the charts at 88 and subsequently rose to 67. At the time of writing the reactivated band were recording a new album for Enigma.

SINISTER DANE

Album
1( ) Sinister Dane   (   ) 1989

An all-black hardcore punk outfit. (1) is an 8-track mini-album.

THE SKELETONS

```
Albums
1( )  Rockin' Bones                              (Next Big Thing     ) 1987
2( )  In The Flesh                               (Next Big Thing 3302) 1988
3(A)  Warting                                    (Alias         030) 1992

Personnel                                   Ex                     To
D. CLINTON THOMPSON  ?    ld.gtr        A                          MORELLS
BOBBY LLOYD HICKS         voc,gtr,dr    A    RANDALL CHOWNING       STEVE FORBERT
LOU WHITNEY               bs            A                          MORELLS
DONNIE THOMPSON  ?        gtr
KELLY BROWN              KB             A
JOE TERRY               KB             A
```

Formed as The Symptoms in Springfield, this band issued 45s under a number of names including D. Clinton Thompson and Bobby Lloyd and the Windfall Profits. Their singles were probably all originally on Borrowed Records and possibly the albums, too, if they were ever issued in America. Thompson's subsequent band, The Morells, were a very disappointing rockabilly combo. (1) and (2) were re-issued as 'In The Flesh' in the UK by Demon (Fiend 178) in 1991. An American CD of (2) included the earlier 45s. The band never really disbanded and gigged regularly. They signed to Alias in 1992 and released (3).

JOEY SKIDMORE

```
Albums
1    The Word Is Out                             (Mop Top    ) 1987
2    Welcome to Humansville                      (Mop Top    ) 1992
```

Missouri-based artist ex-Royal Nonesuch, a new-psych band with a hot reputation. He has released at least two more albums but we have no details.

SOLAR ECLIPSE

Personnel incl:		Ex	To
SIMON CARROLL		MUSIC TREE	PAGE BLUES BAND

This was a short-lived 1968 band based in Excelsior Springs which occupied Carroll's time between his spells in Music Tree and The Page Blues Band.

THE SOLID GOLD BAND

Personnel			Ex	To
JIM ROWLAND	gtr,voc	A		
JOHN GREEN	bs,voc	A		
MIKE BARTLETT	gtr,voc	A		
TYLER OGLE	KB	A		
BUDDY BURR	dr	A		

Formed in Galena, Kansas as a rock band, this combo migrated just across the border to base themselves in Joplin, Missouri, where they evolved into a country-rock band.

SOMERVILLE-SCORFINA BAND

Personnel			Ex	To
MIKE SOMERVILLE	voc,gtr	A	HEAD EAST	
STEVE SCORFINA	ld.gtr	A	PAVLOV'S DOG	
MIKE SAFFRON	dr	A	PAVOLV'S DOG	
GEOFF BEETER	bs	A		

On paper, an intriguing prospect, even an exciting one. In reality the band based in St. Louis, never progressed beyond the demo stage. They operated around 1984. Scorfina had previously been with those mid-western stalwarts R.E.O. Speedwagon, and Saffron with Chuck Berry.

SOUNDS LTD.

Personnel incl:		Ex	To
PHILIP JACKSON	voc,gtr		

A mob-topped teen combo from St. Joseph fronted by Philip Jackson who was also their songwriter. They cut one 45, 'Slimy Sue/ ? (Peak 108) during the mid-'60s and the 'A' side can be heard on 'Monsters Of The Midwest, Vol.4'. It's a crudely recorded frat-tinged teen entry with nothing to commend it.

Philip Jackson went on to perform with various other Midwestern artists throughout the seventies, including the Jefferson Airplane-influenced White Eyes and the country-rock outfit, White Rock Prairie Band. He also performed as part of a duo with his wife and as a solo folky. We've seen it reported that Jackson was formerly Little Phil of The Nightshadows (although his name was Phil Ross) so we can't confirm this.

SPECTER

Personnel			Ex	To
MIKE CARTER	gtr,voc,KB	A		
RUSS BAKER	gtr	A		
JERRY COX	bs	A		
WALT MORRISON	dr	A		

A St. Louis-based heavy rock band from the early eighties. The line-up detailed recorded some compilation cuts but do not appear to have progressed any further.

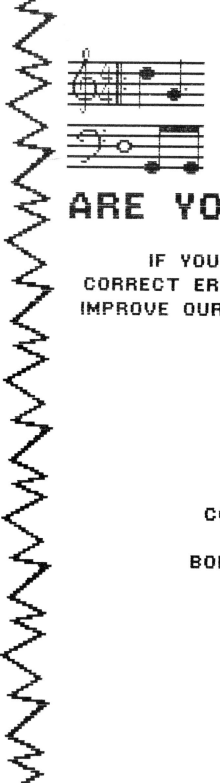

BORDERLINE

ARE YOU A SMART ASS?

IF YOU CAN SUPPLY MISSING INFO,
CORRECT ERRORS OR MAKE SUGGESTIONS TO
IMPROVE OUR BOOK, WE WANT TO HEAR FROM

YOU!

CONTACT US CARE OF:-

BORDERLINE PRODUCTIONS,
P.O.BOX 93
TELFORD, TF1 1UE
ENGLAND

SPLIT IMAGE

Album
1( ) Mirror   (Capitol   ) 1984

A Missouri-based band. No other data held.

STARCASTLE

Albums
1(A) Starcastle   (Epic PE 33914) 1976
2(A) Fountains of Light   (Epic PE 34375) 1977
3(B) Citadel   (Epic PE 34935) 1977
4( ) Real To Reel   (Epic JE 35441) 1978

The Singles
Lady Of The Lake/Nova   (Epic   50226) 1976
Diamond Song (Deep Is The Light)/Silver Winds   (Epic   50348) 1977
Change In Time/Could This Be Love   (Epic   50486) 1977
Song For Alaya/Half A Mind To Leave You   (Epic   50630) 1978

Personnel			Ex	To
STEPHEN HAGLER	gtr,voc	AB		
MATTHEW STEWART	gtr,voc	A		
HERB SCHILDT	KB	AB		DEBBIE'S PROJECT
STEPHEN TASSLER	dr	AB		
GARY STRATER	bs	AB		
TERRY LUTTRELL	voc	A	R.E.O. SPEEDWAGON	
MARK McGEE	gtr			VICIOUS RUMOURS

A mainstream six-piece from St. Louis with a hot live reputation. The band had an early break when WGPU Radio in Champaign, Illinois, picked up a demo cut, 'Lady Of The Lake' and gave it considerable needletime. This and the buzz from their live concerts led to major label interest, and eventually to a deal with Epic in late 1975. Although undoubtedly talented, they failed to translate their live energy to a decent album.

STONED CIRCUS

Issued a 45 on Harmon during the 1960s.

STORYTELLER

Personnel			Ex	To
JEROME STORY	voc	A		
JP	ld.gtr	A		
JOHN DONOVAN	bs	A		
CRAIG CAMPBELL	KB	A		
STEPHEN TELLER	dr	A		

A metal band formed in St. Louis in 1990 but who relocated to LA shortly thereafter. A three track demo was recorded but they seem to have vanished since. Probably long gone.

THE STRANGULATED BEATOFFS

Albums
1( ) White   (Chopper   ) 1990
2( ) Fake Eyeball   (Glitterhouse) 1990
3( ) Red And Black   (Skin Graft   ) 1992

EP
1( ) Meet The Beatoffs   (Chopper   ) 1989

Personnel incl:		Ex	To
STAN SEITRICH	gtr	DRUNKS WITH GUNS	
FREDDIE BEATOFF			

A St. Louis-based band featuring Freddie Beatoff who has been in a string of minor Missouri hardcore bands. There was also an early 45, 'Shake Your Dick', on Fire Fighter. An EP was also released featuring 'Fake Eyeball', 'Face Saucer' and 'Everybody Loves The Circus' but release details are not known.

THE STRIKERS

EP
1( ) The Strikers   (Simplex   ) 1981

A new wave band from St. Louis who first came to note with two cuts ('Kick Around' and 'Knock It Down') on the 'Test Patterns' compilation (Hi-Test HIT-5981) in late 1981. (1) emerged a little later featuring 'Knock It Down' and three new cuts, 'No Reason', 'Original Crown' and 'Running On Ari'.

THE SURF RIDERS

Personnel incl:	Ex	To
GENE CLARK		NEW CHRISTY MINSTRELS

An early outing in Kansas City for Byrd to be, Gene Clark.

DAVID SURKAMP (BAND)

Surkamp was the errie voiced vocalist for St. Louis band **Pavlov's Dog** whose first album ranks as one of the all time classics. When that project tottered to an untimely end Surkamp worked first as a solo artist, completing part of a projected album for Janus Records in 1978 and later, as the David Surkamp Band, recording parts of another album projected for issue on 206 Records in 1983. In addition, he joined Ian Matthews, (ex-Fairport Convention, etc.) in the exciting but ill-fated Hi Fi project in Seattle.

SWIFT KICK

EP
1( ) Swift Kick   (   ) 1983

Personnel		Ex	To
RANDY PHILLIPS	gtr,voc		
MARK HOLLAND	voc		
BOBBY JONES	dr		
PAUL McFARLANE	bs		

A St. Louis-based quartet with two cuts, 'Unpredictable' and 'Blushin' Russian Girl' on 'Test Patterns' (Hi Test HIT-5981) issued in 1981. In addition to those cuts and (1), the band signed to 'Rockin' World Records' in 1984.

THE SYMPTOMS

Album
1( ) Live   (private pressing only) 197?

Personnel			Ex	To
LOU WHITNEY	bs	A	SWINGING MEDALLIONS	SKELETONS
DONNIE THOMPSON	gtr	A		SKELETONS

BOBBY LLOYD	dr	A			SKELETONS
D. CLINTON THOMPSON	gtr		See solo		
JIM WUNDERLE	voc				MARBLES

A trio from Springfield who later became **The Skeletons**. Best remembered for backing Steve Forbert rather than any efforts of their own. There were some demo tapes and a couple of private 45s.

TERROR TO SOCIETY

Cassette
1( ) Terrible To Society   (   ) 1989

Hardcore thrash. (1) contains eighteen tracks.

D. CLINTON THOMPSON

An ace guitarist from Springfield best recalled as guitarist with **The Symptoms** and **The Skeletons**. He has issued 45s on Column One, Borrowed and Hole-In-One. He has one foot planted firmly in '50s rock 'n' roll. If you wanted to sample his work you could do much worse than turning your ears in the direction of his 'Driving Guitars' which can be found on 'Declaration of Independents', a compilation issued by Ambition Records (AMB 1) in 1980. A great track.

THREE LEGGED DOG

Album
1(A) Three Legged Dog   (Bomp BLP 4036) 1990

EPs
1( ) Sniff This   (own label issue   ) 1989
2( ) Three Legged Dog   (own label issue   ) 1989

Cassette
1( ) 14   (   ) 1992

Personnel			Ex	To
TIM AYNARDI	bs	A		
DEVA MAHESWARRAN	dr	A		
BOB CHRISTOPHER	gtr,voc	A		

A hardcore trio from Columbia who have also worked under the names **Like A Horse** and **The Crappy Boys**. They came together in 1987. Prior to (1) there were a couple of demos, and the band can also be heard on 'Baby Through The Windshield', one of those hardcore compilation cassettes from Flush. EP (1) is a three-track affair filled with Minutemen/Black Flag style punk with overlays of their own personalities. They certainly warranted an album outing and it came as no surprise then Greg Shaw picked them up for Bomp.

TRAINED ANIMAL

A new-wave band based in St. Louis in 1980/1981. They have two cuts, 'U.R.A. Girl' and 'When You Dance With Me', on the 'Test Patterns' compilation (Hi-Test HIT-5981).

THE TREND

Albums
1( ) Batman, Live At The Budokan   (Northside   ) 1982
2( ) Is In   (Garden   ) 1983

This quintet favoured a Merseybeat/British Invasion sound but failed to cash in on the L.A. led new-psych wave of the early '80s.

TRUST, OBEY

Cassettes
1( )	Rip Saw	(personal output	) 1990
2( )	Room 101	(	) 1991
3( )	Exit Wound	(	) 1991

Kansas City hardcore, a blend of punk and industrial noises coupled with death-rock undertones. Screaming guitars scoop out your brains with white noise and sinister rhythms and at one point part of a radio broadcast about an execution. Listening to this is like picking up a matchbox you have used before, in a small room (the size is important). You open the matchbox and a full grown elephant emerges instantly to occupy every available cubic foot. Try listening to this in the garden. Preferably in company. The U.S. Fanzine Factsheet 5 described it as mood music for mass murderers.

TRUTH

'Why/Pending' (Circle 953) was this garage band's sole release in the mid-'60s.

IKE TURNER

Albums
1	Ike Turner And The Kings Of Rhythm	(Sue	2004) 195?
2	Ike Turner Rocks The Blues	(Crown	367) 1969
3	Blues Roots	(United Artists	5576) 1972
4	Bad Dreams	(United Artists	) 1973
5	Confined To Soul	(United Artists	OCi) 197?
6	Funky Mule	(DJM DJ5LM	2010) 1975 - UK only
7	I'm Tore Up	(Red Lighting RL 0047) 1978 - UK only	
8	The Edge	(	) 1980

The Singles			Peak Position
My Love/That's All I Need	(Sue	722) 1959	-
+ Love You Baby/Drifting	(Kent	378) 1962	-
Too Hot To Hold/You Got What You Wanted	(Pompeii	66682) 1969	-
Right On/Tacks In My Shoes	(United Artists 50900) 1972		-
Little Miss Clawdy/ ?	(United Artists 50930) 1972		-
Father Alone/Take My Hand Precious Lord	(United Artists 460) 1974		-

+ with Bobby Bland.

Ike Turner was born on 5 November 1931 in Clarksdale, Mississippi. A discography for his solo recordings is given above, but details of his career appear under the Ike And Tina Turner entry. Although, like Tina, he spent much of his time in California and also worked in several other American cities, we've decided to include all three entries in our Missouri section as they first met in St. Louis and also did much of their work there.

IKE AND TINA TURNER

Albums
1(A)	The Sound Of Ike And Tina Turner	(Sue	LP-2001) 1961
2(A)	The Soul Of Ike And Tina Turner	(Kent	519) 1961
3(A)	Dance With Ike And Tina Turner	(Sue	LP-2003) 1962
4(A)	Festival Of Live Performances	(Kent	538) 1962
5(A)	Please Please Please	(Kent	550) 1962
6(A)	Dynamite	(Sue	LP-2004) 1963
7(A)	Don't Play Me Cheap	(Sue	LP-2005) 1963
8(A)	It's Gonna Work Out Fine	(Sue	LP-2007) 1963
9(A)	The Ike And Tina Turner Revue Live	(Kent	5014) 1964

10(A)	Ike And Tina Turner In Person	(Minit	24018)	196?
11(A)	Ike And Tina Turner's Greatest Hits	(Sue	LP-1038)	1965
12(A)	Live/The Ike And Tina Show	(Loma	5904)	1965
13(A)	The Ike And Tina Show Live	(Warners	WS-1579)	1965
14(A)	Ike And Tina Turner And The Raelettes	(Tangerine	15611)	1965
15(A)	Get It, Get It	(Cenco	104)	1965
16(A)	River Deep - Mountain High	(Philles	4011)	1966
17(A)	So Fine	(Pompeii	SD-6000)	1968
18(A)	Cussin', Cryin' And Carryin' On	(Pompeii	SD-6004)	1969
19(A)	Get It Together	(Pompeii	SD-6006)	1969
20(A)	River Deep - Mountain High	(A & M	SP-4178)	1969
21(A)	Ike And Tina Turner's Greatest Hits	(Warners	WS-1810)	1969
22(A)	Her Man, His Woman	(Capitol	ST-571)	1969
23(A)	Fantastic	(Sunset	5265)	1969
24(A)	Outta Season	(Blue Thumb	BTS-5)	1969
25(A)	The Hunter	(Blue Thumb	BTS-11)	1969
26(A)	Come Together	(Liberty	LST-7637)	1970
27(A)	Workin' Together	(Liberty	LST-7650)	1970
28(A)	What You Hear Is What You Get (dbl)	(United Artists	UAS-9953)	1971
29(A)	Nuff Said	(United Artists	UAS-5530)	1971
30(A)	Feel Good	(United Artists	UAS-5598)	1972
31(A)	Let Me Touch Your Mind	(United Artists	UAS-5660)	1973
32(A)	Ike And Tina Turner's Greatest Hits	(United Artists	UAS-5667)	1973
33(A)	The World Of Ike And Tina Turner Live	(United Artists	LA 064)	1973
34(A)	Nutbush City Limits	(United Artists	LA 180)	1973

NB. There have also been numerous posthumous packages but they have been omitted from this list.

The Singles

					Peak Position
x	Box Top/ ?	(Tune Town	501)	1958	-
	A Fool In Love/The Way You Love Me	(Sue	730)	1960	27
	A Fool Too Long/ ?	(Sue	734)	1960	-
	I Idolize You/Letter From Tina	(Sue	735)	1960	2
	I'm Jealous/You're My Baby	(Sue	740)	1961	-
	It's Gonna Work Out Fine/Won't You Forgive Me	(Sue	749)	1961	14
	Poor Fool/You Can't Blame Me	(Sue	753)	1961	38
	Tra La La La La/Puppy Love	(Sue	757)	1962	50
+	Prancing/It's Gonna Work Out Fine	(Sue	760)	1962	-
	You Shoulda Treated Me Right/Sleepless	(Sue	765)	1962	89
	Tina's Dilemma/I Idolize You	(Sue	768)	1962	-
	Mind In A Whirl/The Argument	(Sue	772)	1962	-
	Please Don't Hurt Me/Worried And Hurtin' Inside	(Sue	774)	1962	-
	Don't Play Me Cheap/Wake Up	(Sue	784)	1963	-
	You've Got Too Many Ties That Bind/I'm Gonna Do All I Can (To Do Right By My Man)	(Sonja	45-5000)	1963	-
	I Can't Believe What You Said/My Baby Now	(Kent	402)	1964	95
	Please Please Please/Am I A Fool In Love?	(Kent	409)	1964	-
	Chicken Shack/He's The One	(Kent	418)	1965	-
	Two Is A Couple/Tin Top House	(Sue	135)	1965	-
	The New Breed (Part 1)/(Part 2)	(Sue	138)	1965	-
	Can't Chance A Breakup/Stagger Lee And Billy	(Sue	139)	1965	-
	Dear John/I Made A Promise Up Above	(Sue	146)	1966	-
	I'm Thru With Love/Tell Her I'm Not Home	(Loma	2011)	1966	-
	Somebody Needs You/Just To Be With You	(Loma	2015)	1966	-
	River Deep Mountain High/I'll Keep You Happy	(Philles	131)	1966	88
	Two To Tango/A Man Is A Man	(Philles	134)	1966	-

I Wish My Dreams Would Come True/Flee Flu Fla	(Kent	457) 1966	-
I'll Never Need More Love Than This/The Cash Box Blues Or			
(Opps We Printed The Wrong Story Again)	(Philles	135) 1967	-
I Idolize You/A Love Like Yours	(Philles	136) 1967	-
So Fine/So Blue Over You	(Pompeii	66667) 1968	-
It Sho' Ain't Me/We Need An Understanding	(Pompeii	66675) 1968	-
Shake A Tail Feather/Cussin', Cryin' And Carryin' On	(Pompeii	66700) 1969	-
Cussin', Cryin' And Carryin' On/Betcha Can't Kiss Me	(Pompeii	7003) 1969	-
River Deep, Mountain High/I'll Keep You Happy	(A & M	1118) 1969	-
A Love Like Yours/Save The Last Dance For Me	(A & M	1170) 1969	-
I've Been Loving You Too Long/Grumbling	(Blue Thumb	101) 1969	68
The Hunter/Crazy 'Bout You Baby	(Blue Thumb	102) 1969	93
Bold Soul Sisters/I Know	(Blue Thumb	104) 1969	59
I've Been Loving You Too Long/Crazy 'Bout You Baby	(Blue Thumb	202) 1969	-
I'm Gonna Do All I Can (To Do Right By My Man)/			
You've Got Too Many Ties That Bind	(Minit	32060) 1969	-
I Wish It Would Rain/With A Little Help From My Friends	(Minit	32068) 1969	-
I Wanna Jump/Treating Us Funky	(Minit	32077) 1969	-
Come Together/Honky Tonk Woman	(Minit	32087) 1970	57
Please, Please, Please (Part 1)/(Part 2)	(Kent	4514) 1970	-
I Want To Take You Higher/Contact High	(Liberty	56177) 1970	34
The Way You Love Me/Workin' Together	(Liberty	56207) 1970	-
Proud Mary/Mosquito's Tweeter	(Liberty	56216) 1970	4
Ooh Poh Pah Doo/I Wanna Jump	(United Artists 50782) 1971	60
Doin' It/I'm Yours	(United Artists 50837) 1971	-
Up In Heah/Doo Wah Ditty (Got To Get Ya)	(United Artists 50881) 1972	83
Feel Good/Outrageous	(United Artists 50913) 1972	-
Games People Play/Pick Me Up	(United Artists 50939) 1972	-
Let Me Touch Your Mind/Chopper	(United Artists 50955) 1973	-
Work On Me/ ?	(United Artists 257) 1973	-
Nutbush City Limits/Help Him	(United Artists 298) 1973	22
Get It Out Of Your Mind/Sweet Rhode Island Red	(United Artists 409) 1973	-
Nutbush City Limited/Ooh Poo Pah Doo	(United Artists 524) 1974	-
Sexy Ida (Part 1)/(Part 2)	(United Artists 528) 1974	65
Baby - Get It On/Help Me Make It Through The Night	(United Artists 598) 1975	88

x Ike Turner, Carlson Oliver and Little Ann.
+ Ike and Tina and the Kings Of Rhythm.

Ike and Tina Turner have been described as the hardest working married couple in show business and when one examines their 15-year career together it's easy to understand why this was.

Ike was born on 5 November 1931 in Clarksdale, Mississippi. He began life as a pianist, formed an R & B band in high school, called the Tophatters, and later, at the age of 16, took a job as a DJ and studio musician for WROX, a Clarksville radio station. Through this job he made a number of contacts in the music business and this helped him to put together his own professional band - Ike and the Kings of Rhythm. They were essentially a quintet consisting of Turner (on piano), Raymond Hill and Jackie Brenston (on sax), Willie Kizart (on guitar) and Eugene Fox, which was supplemented by additional drummers or bassists when required. On 3 March 1951 they entered Sam Phillips' Sun recording studio in Memphis, Tennessee and two 45s resulted from the sessions:- 'Rocket 88/Come Back Where You Belong' (Chess 1458) and 'Heartbroken And Worried/I'm Lonesome, Baby' (Chess 1459). It was 'Rocket 88' that attracted attention. With a fine vocal from Jackie Brenston, some fine tenor sax playing and Turner's driving piano, it topped the US R & B Charts that Summer and has been citied by many as 'the first rock 'n' roll record'. After the 45 Brenston split from Turner taking the band with him in search of further glory. Ike moved into production work and session guitarwork for RPM and Modern Records and later for Sam Phillips' own Sun label. During this time he played on sessions with B. B. King and Howlin' Wolf - both of whom he recruited to Modern Records in LA whilst he was a roving R & B talent scout for the label. Until 1955 Turner recorded mostly in Memphis, although he also worked in Chicago and Cincinnati. In 1955 he moved to St. Louis, Missouri and it was there, in an East St. Louis club in 1956, that he met the future Tina Turner (then Annie Mae Bullock).

Annie Mae Bullock had been born in Brownsville, Tennessee on 26 November 1938. She was raised in a nearby township called Nutbush, where her mother sang in the local gospel choir. Her mother was clearly an important influence on her early musical career and she inherited her powerhouse vocal style. When her family moved to St. Louis in 1954 Annie started to hang around the city's blues clubs and eventually caught the eye of Ike Turner, who invited her up on stage to do a song. He was impressed and recorded a 45, 'Boxtop' on which Annie (credited as Little Ann) had a supporting role in 1958. However, Ike and Annie did not marry that year as is often reported. In fact, Annie became romantically attached to saxophonist Raymond Hill, who had earlier played in Ike Turner's Kings Of Rhythm and later teamed up, along with Jackie Brenston, with Ike again in 1956. In 1959 she bore Hill's child and it was not until Ike invited Annie out to join him in California in 1960 that she became romantically attached to him. Prior to this she did, at Ike's suggestion, take the stage name Tina Turner after she stepped in to record 'A Fool In Love' with Ike when the session singer booked in to work with him didn't show up. The single made No.2 in the R & B Charts and No.27 in the national pop charts and Ike and Tina's career together was launched. Three female backing singers, the Ikettes, were incorporated to support Tina around whom the live Ike and Tina Turner Revue show revolved.

The hits began to flow:- 'I Idolize You', 'It's Gonna Work Out Fine' became their first Top 20 hit (although for this one Ike had handed the production over to Mickey Baker and Sylvia Robinson and wasn't even in the studio when the record was made, although his name still appeared first on the label credits!). 'Poor Fool', 'Tra La La La La' and 'You Shoulda Treated Me Right' were all minor hits. They also recorded no less than five albums for Sue, none of which were released in the UK at the time. Also in 1962 Ike and Tina were formally married at a brief civil ceremony in Tijuana, Mexico.

The tide didn't always go the duo's way in these early days. Ike's attempt to set up his own label (Sonja Records) was a dismal failure - it vanished after just one release, so when they finished recording for Sue records they had a series of brief flirtations with several American record labels. They stopped at Innis Records long enough to tape 'So Fine', which was later recorded by the Ikettes, under Ike's supervision. They then signed to the Kent label for whom they achieved some success with singles like 'I Can't Believe What You Say', 'Please Please Please' and 'Chicken Shack' and albums (4), (5) and (9). Later, in 1964, they signed to Loma recording two 45s and a fine live album (12), which was released in the UK by Warner Brothers. This became the next label they signed to recording a further live album (13), a greatest hits collection (21) and a series of singles including 'A Fool For A Fool', 'Finger Poppin'' and 'Merry Christmas Baby'. Then after a further release on Kent and the hit single 'Goodbye So Long' on Modern, they returned to put out four further singles for Sue Records before cutting an album, 'Ike and Tina Turner and The Raelettes' for Ray Charles' Tangerine label and a minor R & B hit, 'Get It, Get It' and album of the same name on Cenco records. Phew! By 1965 they'd been through 10 contracts in the space of just two years. That must be some sort of record!

In the course of this musical chairs around record companies they met Phil Spector, who, impressed with Tina's voice, offered $20,000 to put her in the studios to record 'River Deep, Mountain High'. Spector didn't like Ike's production of her records, so it was a condition of the deal that Ike took no part in the record. It apparently cost Spector another $22,000 to create the 'wall of sound' backing track on the record. Tina recorded the vocal on 7 March and the record was released on Spector's Philles label. It3 flopped in the US peaking at No.88 and this is thought to have been a major factor in Spector's shutdown of Philles and temporary retirement from production work shortly after. However, in the UK it gave them a No.3 hit and a reputation that has survived until this day. Warner Brothers then released an earlier track, 'Tell Her I'm Not Home' in the UK which also made No.48. The Turners were now considered major stars in the UK, yet in their home country they were only popular on the R & B circuit. In September 1966 they embarked on a major UK tour supporting The Rolling Stones, playing a major London date at the Royal Albert Hall and appearing on 'Ready Steady Go'. (16) also made No.27 in the UK Album Charts and a revival of the Martha and the Vandelles 'B' side, 'A Love Like Yours' reached No.16 in the UK.

Back in the States the Turners signed a new deal with Pompeii Records. Three albums (17), (18), and (19) resulted and material from this label later formed the basis of two later UK compilations, 'Souled From The Vaults' on DJM and 'Rock Me Baby' on Bulldog. Then in 1968 the duo signed for Blue Thumb recording two fine blues-oriented albums, (24) and (25). In the UK (24) was issued on Liberty and (25) on Harvest. 'The Hunter' was also issued on both sides of the Atlantic as a single and was a sizeable R & B hit in the States. (24) also made No.91 in the US Album Charts.

The following year saw a new record deal, in time honoured tradition. This time with Minit, who reissued the Sonja single from 1963 and 'In Person', a highly-rated live album recorded at Basin Street West. This peaked at No.142 in the US and a month later their LP 'River Deep Mountain High' was finally issued in the US on A & M and made the 102 slot.

The duo got a big break when they were invited by Mick Jagger to support The Rolling Stones on a major US tour which commenced in November 1969. The tour was a complete sell-out and gave the Turners exposure to mainstream rock audiences. This helped ensure that their next 45, a cover of The Beatles' 'Come Together' was their most successful 45 for years, peaking at No.57 in the US, where the accompanying album climbed to 130 in the Album Charts. Next up was revival of Sly And The Family Stones' 'I Want To Take

You Higher', their first 45 on Liberty, who had taken over Minit, which reached No.34 in the US (outselling the original) and also became an important pinnacle of their live act. On the strength of this success they picked up important live work in Las Vegas casinos and it was partly with cash from this venture that Ike was able to buy his own Bolic Sound recording studio in Inglewood, California.

Now going from strength to strength they opened 1971 with a R & B style cover of Creedence Clearwater Revival's 'Proud Mary'. Peaking at No.4 it gave them their first US Top 10 hit and became their first million-selling single. It was taken from (27), which became their most successful album so far, climbing to No.25 in the US. They also enjoyed another successful European tour, although they failed to produce quite the same chart success in the UK. By June 1971 Liberty had itself been submerged into United Artists records and their revival of Jesse Hill's 'Ooh Poo Pah Doo' on United Artists made No.60 in the US charts. (28) became their first gold LP peaking at No.25. (29) made 108 and (30) 160 but it was really Tina's raw and stompin' 'Nutbush City Limits' which gave their career fresh impetus climbing to No.22 in the US and No.4 in the UK. Surprisingly the accompanying album (34) could only make it to 163 in the US Album Charts in January 1974. In April that year Tina began filming for the role of the Acid Queen in The Who's film, 'Tommy'. This may have encouraged her towards greater independence for after just two further hit singles, 'Sexy Ida' and 'Baby Get It On', she walked out on Ike whilst he was asleep in a Dallas hotel room. Domestically things had been far from calm and Tina later claimed that Ike has regularly beaten her and imprisoned her in their house and that, strengthened by her newly acquired Buddhist faith, she finally decided she could stand it no longer.

As Ike and Tina were on tour at the time the remainder of the tour had to be cancelled and Tina was forced to pay the bills. Part of the money for this came from her income from her role as 'The Acid Queen' in Ken Russell's film of The Who's 'Tommy' and from her debut album, 'The Acid Queen', but she was also forced to do cabaret work in Las Vegas and Lake Tahoe. When the debts had been settled she became a recluse for the next few years, but details of her subsequent career appear in her solo entry.

Ike continued to work as a producer in Los Angeles and released a solo album called 'The Edge' in America and Europe in 1980. However, in December 1982 his studio was destroyed by fire and he had also developed a serious cocaine problem. He later returned to St. Louis, where he and Tina had first met, but his career, such as it was, continued to be ignored by both press and public. He continued to be hampered by his cocaine addiction and in July 1988 was sentenced to a year's imprisonment for the possession and transportation of cocaine. He also started work on an autobiographical album to be released on the Starforce label.

Since the split, perhaps predictably, Tina's career has blossomed whilst Ike's has plummeted. However, the dynamic duo has never been out of the public gaze for long as Tina's phenominal success in recent years has inevitably led to the reissue of much of the duo's earlier material.

TINA TURNER

Albums

1	The Acid Queen	(United Artists	495)	1975
2	Rough	(United Artists	)	1979
3	Love Explosion	(United Artists	)	1979
4	Private Dancer	(Capitol	)	1984
5	Break Every Rule	(Capitol	)	1988
6	Foreign Affair	(Capitol	91873)	1989
7	Simply The Best	(Capitol	97152)	1991
8	What's Love Got To Do With It (OST)	(Virgin	88189)	1993

The Singles

				Peak Position
Rockin' And Rollin'/Whole Lotta Love	(United Artists	724)	1975	-
Delilah's Power/That's My Power	(United Artists	730)	1975	-
Fire Down Below/Viva La Money	(United Artists	1265)	1976	-
Ball Of Confusion/Instrumental (with B.E.F.)	(Virgin	)	1982	-
Let's Stay Together/I Wrote A Letter	(Capitol	5322)	1984	26
Help/Rock 'n' Roll Widow	(Capitol	5330)	1984	-
What's Love Got To Do With It/Rock 'n' Roll Widow	(Capitol	5354)	1984	1
Better Be Good To Me/When I Was Young	(Capitol	5387)	1984	9
Private Dancer/Nutbush City Limits	(Capitol	5433)	1984	7
Show Some Respect/Let's Pretend We're Married	(Capitol	5461)	1985	37

We Don't Need Another Hero(Thunderdome)/We Don't Need Another Hero (instr.)	(Capitol	5491)	1985	2
One Of The Living/One Of The Living (dub)	(Capitol	5518)	1985	15
+ It's Only Love/The Only One (by Bryan Adams)	(A & M	2791)	1985	15
Typical Male/Don't Turn Around	(Capitol	5615)	1986	2
Two People/Havin' A Party	(Capitol	5644)	1986	30
What You Get Is What You See(Part 1)/(Part 2)	(Capitol	5668)	1987	13
Break Every Rule/Take Me To The River	(Capitol	44003)	1987	74
The Best/Undercover Agent For The Blues	(Capitol	44442)	1989	15
Steamy Windows/The Best (edit)	(Capitol	44473)	1989	39
* Look Me In The Heart/Stronger Than The Wind	(Capitol	44510)	1990	-
I Don't Wanna Fight/ ?	(Virgin	12652)	1993	9
Why Must We Wait Until Tonight?/ ?	(Virgin	12683)	1993	97

+ With Bryan Adams.   * cassette single.

Tina Turner was born Annie Mae Bullock in Brownsville, Tennessee on 23 November 1938. Her early years and her career with Ike Turner are documented in the Ike and Tina Turner entry.

When this partnership split in 1976, after Tina had walked out on Ike (they were divorced in July of that year), Tina had already enjoyed some commercial success with (1), which reached No.155 in the US Album Charts. Still half a million in debt from cancelled bookings after she had left Ike in the middle of a tour, she embarked on a low key comeback in 1979 with (2) and (3) and then linked up with an Australian businessman, Roger Davies, who was trying to make it in the US music business, and formed a new band. However, record company interest at this time was minimal. Not until 1982 when she was invited to support The Rolling Stones on tour did her career prospects brighten. She later returned firmly to the limelight in 1982 when the British Electric Foundation (half of the original Human League who later became Heaven 17) used her to sing The Temptations' 'Ball Of Confusion' on their revivals' album, 'Music Of Quality And Distinction'. Although, with its electronic backing, it was hardly the type of music she wanted to sing, she turned in her usual professional performance and 'Ball Of Confusion' was issued as a single with an instrumental flip side. Although it didn't chart it prepared the way for her full-scale comeback which was not far away. A decisive event here was when David Bowie announced to a listening party for his forthcoming LP, 'Let's Dance', that he was going on to see his favourite singer, Tina Turner, at New York's Ritz afterwards. EMI's executives went with him and saw her storming show, ensuring that she stayed with Capitol (an EMI subsidiary) when she was in danger of being dropped from the new recording contract Davies had negotiated earlier in the year.

Her first single on Capitol was a cover version of Al Green's hit, 'Let's Stay Together'. It showcased her now harsher vocal style brilliantly climbing to No.26 in the US and No.6 in the UK, where her profile had been raised by a series of packed shows at The Venue in London and an appearance on 'The Channel 4' TV show The Tube. She began work on an LP, which was recorded over a period of two week sessions in the UK. Her next 45 release was a stately revival of The Beatles' 'Help', which was only a hit in the UK, where it peaked at the No.40 spot. On 27 March 1984 Tina embarked on a UK tour and the following month she opened as a support act on Lionel Richie's 'Can't Slow Down' tour which continued until September. Meanwhile, in July, the first 45 from the 'Private Dancer' LP sessions was released. 'What's Love Got To Do With It', which had been written by Terry Britten and Graham Lyle (previously one half of Gallagher and Lyle), became one of the great Transatlantic records of the Summer. In the US it became her first No.1 hit, topping the charts for three weeks and selling over a million copies. It also won Grammy Awards as Record of the Year, Song of the Year and Best Female Vocal Performance. In the UK it peaked at No.3. Her album (4), climbed to No.3 in the US and No.4 in the UK. It went on to remain in the US Top Ten until May 1985 selling over 10 million copies worldwide. She also signed a deal with Australian director, George Miller, to appear in his third 'Mad Max' movie with Mel Gibson. She went on to enjoy two further hits from (4), 'Better Be Good To Me' peaked at No.5 in the US in November 1984 (and later won a Grammy Award for Best Female Rock Vocal). It reached No.45 in the UK. In March 1985 the title cut from (4) made No.7 in the US, giving her three consecutive Top Ten US hits from the album. Back in December 1984 it had peaked at No.24 in the UK.

January 1985 saw her project herself on the world stage twice in the space of a month. First, she appeared in the 'Rock In Brazil' Festival along with other megastars, then, late in the month she took part in recording USA For Africa's 'We Are The World'. In March 1985 she played the Wembley Arena in London and in the UK her cover of Ann Pebbles', 'I Can't Stand The Rain' peaked at No.57. Her next US hit came in May 1985 with 'Show Some Respect'.

The movie, 'Mad Max: Beyond Thunderdome' was released in June 1985. Tina turned in a superb performance as Aunty Entity and reportedly declined three times an offer to appear in Steven Spielberg's 'The Color Purple'. 'We Don't Need Another Hero (Thunderdome)' from the 'Mad Max: Beyond The Thunderdome' Soundtrack peaked at No.2 in the US and No.3 in the UK that Summer. A second hit from the Soundtrack, 'One Of The Living', climbed to No.15 in the US, but only made the 55 spot in the UK. She followed this with 'It's Only Love', a duet with Bryan Adams, the Canadian rock singer, which made No.29 in the UK in November 1985 and No.15 in the US in January 1986. 1985 had been another extremely successful year for Tina and she crowned it in December when she won the award as Best Actress from the NAACP for her appearance in 'Mad Max: Beyond The Thunderdome'.

The success story continued in 1986 which saw Tina appearing at the Prince's Trust Concert in London, alongside Bryan Adams, Elton John and Eric Clapton, on 20 June. (5) went platinum in the US, where it peaked at No.4 in November, having climbed to No.2 in the UK the previous month. The inevitable 45 hits followed:- 'Typical Male' making No.2 in the US and No.33 in the UK and 'Two People' peaking at No.30 in the US and No.43 in the UK. On 4 March 1987 she started out on her 'Break Every Rule' World Tour, sponsored by Pepsi Cola. It commenced at Munich in West Germany and when it closed just over a year later in Osaka, Japan, on 28 March 1988, she had played 230 dates in 25 countries to an estimated three and a half million fans. She had broken box office records in 13 countries, her 'Break Every Rule' album had made No.1 in nine countries and at the Maracona Arena in Rio, on the South American leg, she had played to 180,000 people - the largest audience ever assembled for a single performer. She was truely a megastar. (6) was less successful, making only 31 in the U.S. but still going gold. (7) was a compilation which peaked at 113 in the U.S. Album Charts. In 1993 a biographical film was issued. She did not (wisely) play herself but she did record the soundtrack (8). The first 45, 'I Don't Wanna Fight' took her back to the Top 10 for the first time in four years and at the time of writing she was working on a new album from Capitol.

TUFF NUTZ

A hardcore band from St. Louis who were active in mid-1989. They include ex-members of Invixious.

THE TWILIGHTERS

Came out of Kirksville with a frantic frat rouser, 'Spell Bound/ ? ' (Red Flame 1005) in the mid-'60s. You can check out the 'A' side on 'Monsters Of The Midwest, Vol.4'.

ULTRAMAN

Albums
1( )	Freezing Inside	(New Red Archives	) 1989
2( )	Non Existence	(New Red Archives	) 1991

EPs
1( )	Ultramain	(	) 1987
2( )	Destroys All Monsters	(Science Patrol	) 1988

Personnel		Ex	To
JON CORCORAN	bs		VOICE OF GOD
TIM JAMISON	KB		
ROB	gtr		BENT
MARK DENISZUK	dr	WHOPPERS TASTE GOOD	BENT
MIKE STORY	gtr	NEVER ALONE	
RICK	gtr,voc		BENT

A storming hardcore quintet from St. Louis who can also be heard on 'Hardcore Breakout USA', a compilation from New Red Archives.

UNCLE TUPELO

Albums
1(A)	No Depression	(Rockville 6050) 1990
2(A)	Still Feel Gone	(Rockville 6070) 1992
3(A)	March 16-20 1992	(Rockville 6090) 1992

EP
1(A)	Sauget Wind	(Rockville 6089) 1992

Personnel				Ex		To
JAY FARRAR	voc,gtr,ba,ma,f	A				
JEFF TWEEDY	bs	A				
MIKE HEIDORN	dr	A				

A country-rock trio originally from St. Louis but now based in Illinois. They sound like an acoustic Neil Young but can rock with the best of them. Well worth a listen. (2) was produced by R.E.M. mainstay, Peter Buck. The band also have a cut on '20 More Explosive Hits...' (Pravda 6342) issued in 1992.

UNDECIDED

Album
1( ) Undecided   (Undecided   ) 1988

Cassettes
1( ) Been Round Out Now   (Sammich   ) 1989
2( ) What's Done Is Done   (   ) 1989

The band were based in Columbia. Youthful hardcore but certainly nothing new on offer.

UNJUST CAUSE

A hardcore outfit who changed their name in late 1989 to Duck Duck Soup.

UNTAMED YOUTH

Albums
1(B) Some Kinda Fun   (Norton   207) 1988
2( ) No More Gassers   (Norton   215) 1990
3(D) Sophisticated International Playboys   (Norton   223) 1992

Other Recordings
Cut on 'Smiles Vibes and Harmony'   (Venus De Milo 004) 1990

Personnel			Ex	To
DEREK DICKERSON	gtr	ABCD	ROCKIN' TAILFINS	
STEVE MACE	bs	ABCD		
JOEL TRUEBLOOD	dr	A D		
CLARK MARTY	dr	BC		
CHRIS FLETCHER	KB	B		
STEVE RAGER	KB	C		
RON SILVA	dr	(C)		

Stripped down rock from Columbia. Most of the line-up changes depicted were as a result of Clark Marty's reluctance to go on the road. For a time, he tackled in-state gigs and Silva handled the tours. The combo later reverted to the original and more obliging Trueblood. Both of the first two albums were produced by ex-Zantees guitarist, Billy Miller, and ex-Dictators keyboard player, Adny Shernoff, who had seen the band during an early visit to New York. Norton was Miller's own label. The band later relocated to San Diego in California. (3) was produced by Skeleton's bassist, Lou Whitney. The band are also featured on the 'Half Rock' 45 box set on Estrus, issued in 1991. A fine band!

VACANT GRAVE

Album
1(A) Life Or Death   (New Renaissance   ) 1990

Personnel		Ex	To
JEFF BURNETT	bs		

DARYN ZACK	gtr,bs	A
JEFF NOYES	dr	A
DEAN GARRETT	gtr	A
RON SCHODROSKI	bs	A

A thrash metal band based in Manchester. They recorded a couple of fairly well-received demos and in late 1988 New Renaissance signed the band which lead to (1).

THE VANDALS

A mid-'60s garage band whose sole release was 'You Lied To Me/Someone Else Like You' (GAR 105). The band featured Terry Dionisio on drums who later played for **The Clann**.

VOICE OF GOD

Cassette
1( ) Blood And Family   (Church Of The Voice   ) 1991

| Personnel incl: | | Ex | To |
| JON CORCORAN | bs,voc | ULTRAMAN | |

A St. Louis hardcore band which failed to click with the masses.

JACK WAGNER

Albums
1	All I Need	(Qwest 25089) 1984
2	Jack Wagner	(Qwest 25214) 1985
3	Lightning Up The Night	(Qwest 25318) 1986
4	Don't Give Up Your Day Job	(Qwest 25562) 1987

Wagner is an actor/singer/songwriter who was born and raised in Washington, Missouri. He is best known in America for playing Frisco Jones in the popular soap, 'General Hospital'. His foray into music was pop rather than rock and produced one massive hit with the title cut from (1) which, as a single (Qwest 29238) reached No.2 for two weeks in early 1985 and spent 22 weeks on the Top 100. He had two lesser hits with 'Lady Of My Heart' (Qwest 29085 which peaked at 76) and 'Too Young' (Qwest 28931 which reached 52 late in 1985).

JIM WEATHERLEY

Weatherley, from Pontotoc, Missouri, based himself in California, originally as a member of Gordian Knot and later as a solo artist. As a result, a resume of his work was included in 'An American Rock History, Part 1 - California: The Golden State'. During the '80s Weatherley has continued his career as a songwriter.

WHITE PRIDE

One of many '80s Missouri hardcore bands featuring Freddie Beatoff. Others include **Homosexual Satan**, **White Suburban Youth**, **Culture Shock**, **Dred Finks**, and **The Strangulated Beatoffs**. One cassette at least was issued under this name - 'There Goes The Neighbourhood'. The unpleasant and unacceptable face of hardcore!!

WHITE SUBURBAN YOUTH

Another Missouri hardcore band featuring Freddie Beatoff. See **White Pride** for details of his other bands.

WILDER

Album
1( ) Violent Passions   (Rocking Horse 53) 1991

Personnel incl:		Ex	To
CARMEN WILDER	voc		

No other data available.

WHOPPERS TASTE GOOD

<u>EPs</u>
1( )	Haunting White Castle	(Wicked Cool	) 1988
2( )	Don't They?	(Scrapdog	) 1989

Personnel incl:		Ex	To
MARK DENISZUK	dr		ULTRAMAN

The band originated in Florissaint near St. Louis, but may be based in Edwardsville in Illinois. They have also gigged using the name WTG.

THE WILD THINGS

Came out of mid-Missouri with a 40-year old organist and made it on to vinyl with 'Tell Me' (Damon 12680) in the mid-'60s. The 45 was recorded in Kansas City. You can hear the 'A' side on 'Monsters Of The Midwest, Vol.3'. It's quite a catchy organ-led garage punker and one of the few releases from Kansas City's Damon Studios that progressed beyond the metal acetate stage.

THE WOLFMEN

A mid-'60s garage band who recorded 'Take A Walk/ ? ' (Archway 100).

WORM CAN

<u>Cassette</u>
1(A)	Worm Can	(Dog Face	) 1990

Personnel	Ex	To
BRUCE CALE		
JON ASHLINE		

A duo operating out of St. Louis. They had previously recorded as **Screaming Mee Mees** in 1977-78 using their own Dog Face Records.

JIM WUNDERLE

<u>EP</u>
1	Jim Wunderle	(Ayatollah PSHA-001) 1981

Personnel		Ex	To
JIM WUNDERLE	voc	MARBLES/SYMPTOMS	
TERRY WILSON	gtr	NO SLACK	
TOMMY WHITLOCK	dr	NO SLACK	DOG PEOPLE
JIMMY FRINK	gtr		FOOLS FACE
JIM WIRT	bs		FOOLS FACE

The former vocalist with Springfield band **The Symptoms**. He can also be heard on 'Declaration Of Independents' (Ambition AMB-1) with a perky rendition of The Seed's 'Pushin' Too Hard' which adds nothing to the original. (1) also contains that cut plus three others - 'The Hunter Gets Captured By The Game' (the old Marvelettes' hit), 'Almost Grown' (previously by Chuck Berry) and 'Somethin' You Got'. In 1976 he was also involved with New York band The Marbles.

J. D. WYATT AND THE THUNDERBOLTS

Personnel incl:	Ex	To
J. D. WYATT		

Recorded 'How Do You Lose A Girl/ ? ' (GAR 106) in the mid-'60s.

THE XTREEMS

Operated out of St. Louis. Their sole mid-'60s 45, 'Substitute/Facts Of Life' (Star Trek 1221), has resurfaced on several compilations. You'll find their cover of the Who's classic, 'Substitute' on 'A Journey To Tyme, Vol.3' (Phantom PRS 1003) and 'The Garage Zone, Vol.2' (Moxie MLP 17), whilst 'Facts Of Life' has resurfaced on 'A Journey To Tyme, Vol.3' 'Relics' (DB DB 102), 'Psychedelic Unknowns, Vol.3' (Calico EP-0003) and 'Mayhem And Psychosis, Vol.3' (Roxy SX-LP-104). The reason for this extensive coverage is its superb Yardbirds-influenced guitar work.

THE YARD APES

Cassette

1(A) The Yard Apes	(6-track)			(Fresh Sounds 101/102) 198?

Personnel			Ex	To
ELSA HODES	voc,perc	A		
CHRIS FOWLER	voc	A		
DEVIN SHELL	voc,perc	A		
RON ACHELPOHL	gtr,bs	A		
BRUCE EDDY	bs,gtr	A		
LISA VADER	syn	A		
STEVE BEAI	dr	A		

A strange outfit who were based in Kansas City. (1) was a compilation album but six of the cuts were by The Yard Apes. The cuts were, 'Playing With Snakes', 'Your Pretty Face', 'Living On Welfare', 'The Long Walk', 'Jungle Rocks', and 'Never You Mind'. In addition there is a 1984 45 on Y-Tel Records which couples 'Neurosis' and 'Ghost Town'. Enough there for a mini LP, people.

THE YOUNG ARISTOCRACY

Personnel incl:	Ex	To
JIM SWEENEY		

A garage band who recorded 'Don't Lie/Look And See' (Acropolis 6721) in 1967. We have also seen them reported as being from Tulsa, Kansas.

THE ZANTI MISFITS

Personnel		Ex	To
KEVIN GRIFFIN	dr		
MARK SHERIDAN	bs		
PETER KREMER	gtr		

A trio from St. Louis. You can hear them doing 'Holier Than Thou' and 'Bachelors Friend' on 'Test Pattersn' (Hi Test HIT 5981).

The following artists were also based in Missouri had no recording output that we know of or that we have much detail of:-

Name	Comment	Time Frame
AMENDMENT ONE	Hardcore from Belleville.	1989
AWARE	Hardcore from Belleville.	1989
AXE MINSTER	Metal outfit from St. Louis.	1990
BE-VISION	St. Louis rock band.	1987
BFD	St. Louis-based hardcore band.	1989
BIG FUN	St. Louis-based band.	1990
BOORAYS	One 45 issued on Faye Records.	1992
BROKEN TOYZ	Metal from St. Louis. Signed to SBK.	1990
DITCH WITCH	One 45 issued on Faye Records.	1992
DREAMS ABOUT GUNS	One 45 issued on Faye Records.	1992
DUYA DUYA	St. Louis-based.	1991
EYES	New Psychedelia from St. Louis.	1990
THE FINN BROTHERS	St. Louis-based.	1990
FX	Heavy metal.	1989
ISOLATION	St. Louis hardcore - demos recorded.	1989
JUSTIFIED VIOLENCE	Hardcore from St. Louis.	1989
THE MEN	St. Louis hardcore.	1989
MURDER CITY PLAYERS	St. Louis rock.	1987
NEGATIVE POSTURE	Hardcore from Belleville.	1989
NERVE GAS	Mainstream rock from St. Louis.	1979/80
THE NUKES	St. Louis hardcore band.	1989
OVER AND EVER	From Alton.	1989
PRIME	Heavy rockers. Compilation cuts exist.	1984
PUBLIC ASSASSINS	A hardcore outfit from Springfield.	1992
ROUND 2	Ex members of Brace.	198?
RUBBERNECK	A hardcore band.	1992
RUGBURN	St. Louis.	1987
STALE FISH	Hardcore from Rolla in the South.	1989
STONED WALLS	Hardcore band from St. Louis.	1989
TOMBOY	All-girl Kansan City band. Studio time in 1983.	1983
UNCONSCIOUS	St. Louis band.	1990
THE URGE	Hardcore.	1989
WISHFUL THINKING	Hardcore.	1990
THE JERRY WOOD BROTHERHOOD	No data.	1974